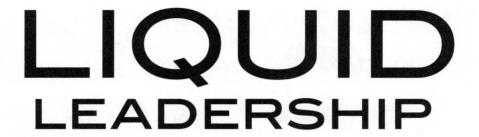

LIQUID
LEADERSHIP

From Woodstock to Wikipedia—

Multigenerational Management Ideas

That Are Changing the Way We Run Things

BRAD SZOLLOSE

GREENLEAF
BOOK GROUP PRESS

Published by Greenleaf Book Group Press
Austin, Texas
www.gbgpress.com

Distributed by Greenleaf Book Group LLC

For ordering information or special discounts for bulk purchases, please contact Greenleaf Book Group LLC at PO Box 91869, Austin, TX 78709, 512.891.6100.

Design and composition by Greenleaf Book Group LLC and Bumpy Design
Cover design by Greenleaf Book Group LLC

Publisher's Cataloging-In-Publication Data
(Prepared by The Donohue Group, Inc.)
Szollose, Brad.
    Liquid leadership : from Woodstock to Wikipedia : multigenerational management ideas that are changing the way we run things / Brad Szollose.—1st ed.
    p. ; cm.
    ISBN: 978-1-60832-055-4
    1. Leadership. 2. Personnel management. 3. Organizational change—Management.
I. Title.
HD57.7 .S96 2010
658.4/092   2010931406

Part of the Tree Neutral® program, which offsets the number of trees consumed in the production and printing of this book by taking proactive steps, such as planting trees in direct proportion to the number of trees used: www.treeneutral.com

TreeNeutral®

Printed in the United States of America on acid-free paper

10 11 12 13 14 15 10 9 8 7 6 5 4 3 2 1

First Edition

Author's Note

All the projects I have developed in my life seem to take on new meaning about halfway through their execution—the scope becomes greater and more alive than the original intention. This book, for instance, started out as a way to help Baby Boomer executives adjust to the overwhelming amount of data they need to absorb in a world that has seemingly ceased to make sense. Yet I soon came to realize that it isn't just Boomers who need help, but individuals from *every* generation. All of us are facing new and unprecedented challenges. Traditional business hierarchies have disappeared. The standard concept of leadership has vaporized. New economic and political realities are reshaping the fundamental laws that help businesses survive.

And so as more and more research came across my desk, a much larger theme emerged, far beyond the scope of my original idea. Each new piece of knowledge was an epiphany, illuminating yet another level of fundamental change. We are truly on the cusp of something never before seen or found in humankind's six thousand years of recorded history. What you hold in your hands is not just a book, but an awakening to the new relationships between generations in the twenty-first-century organization and to the new future of business.

The chasm between generations is blatantly apparent, and yet most ignore it, hoping that Generation Y will calm down, get a mortgage, and have a couple of kids. The secret hope is they will wind up just like us—tired, run-down, and indoctrinated into cubicle life. Unfortunately for Boomers, Gen Y is built for adventure. This is not a fad but a trend, and it's here to stay.

Expecting us to retain the same methodologies from the past is like expecting the United States to retain its agricultural dominance after the Industrial Revolution. We simply can't put the genie back in the bottle.

As comedian Nick Griffin shared on *The Late Show with David Letterman* (July 20, 2007): "As a society we're overstimulated. We have vitamins in our water now, caramel and chocolate in our coffee, and we have cheese in our crust. Cameras in our phones, TVs in our cars, we got BlackBerrys, iPods, TiVo, PSP, *and* GPS—your kids aren't hyper, they're paying attention!"

To stay relevant as a leader in today's new global economy will require us to not cling so tightly to old methodologies and beliefs but instead to adjust to the new, upgrading our knowledge and skills. But at the same time, we need to keep what still works. This type of flexibility will help you catch the next big idea that changes everything.

Liquid Leadership has been designed to help you see which ideas to keep and which to discard in an age when radical disruption seems to be the norm.

Contents

Foreword

It can be extremely intimidating to write a book, and many mere mortals quit before even getting started. In Brad Szollose's incredible new book, *Liquid Leadership*, you, the reader, will quickly discover that his knowledge, wisdom, and insights picked up throughout his own life journey are worth not only noting but, more important, reading and using to improve your own life, career, or business. His brutal honesty is refreshing and inspiring in an age of finger-pointing and a victim mentality that courses through many declining industries that refuse to change and grow.

You will quickly realize that what Brad has dubbed "liquid leadership" is why smart firms and organizations are able to compete and thrive in today's changed and ultra-competitive economy. These firms place high value on people's ideas and talents. This book, if you apply its lessons, serves as both a powerful wake-up call and as a reminder to treat every person you work with, serve, and do business with as a valued human being capable of great ideas. This is especially important for Gen Yers as they enter and attempt to advance their ideas in a battered and fragile economic landscape. I have some great news for you: This is not another boring business book that wastes your valuable time. Brad's wit and ability to engage via powerful stories that jump off the pages will capture your mind and imagination. As someone who's led a successful firm that went public during the go-go 1990s, he has insights that are powerful and directly applicable. Not many people have this on their resume; it takes incredible hustle, persistence, and a unique skill set, which Brad shares up close and from the front line of business battle.

This also isn't another book written by a well-intended academic or management consultant who regurgitates case studies and statistics to cover their ass, since they themselves have never guided a business ship in rough waters or had to meet the payroll. The bookstore's shelves are loaded with those kinds of books, and, frankly, it's a shame. Luckily for you, this book delivers the goods, and it arrives at the perfect time.

Brad speaks from the experience of hiring and managing a very diverse workforce in the city that never sleeps. This eclectic workforce not only changed the way work is defined and conducted, but along the way it also gave him several tips on how the nature of employment in the future will change. Most important, it revealed how leadership needs to look in order to be successfully carried out now and in the future. You can get what we in business call "experience" the slow way, via trial and error, or you can read, absorb, and apply Brad's wisdom to save you time and frustration. A good book such as this does not only that, but also makes you think about both your strengths and what you need to work on to get better. Like a great coach that pushes you, Brad uses these pages to make you better.

As you peruse *Liquid Leadership* with highlighter in hand, you'll discover powerful lessons from not only Brad's company but other firms as well—such as Starbucks, Harley-Davidson, Pixar, and GM, to name a few—and you'll find out why they're important to learn from. Business was a lot easier a few years ago when credit was cheap, consumers were forgiving, and the phone and email brought willing and tolerant buyers ready to spend money. Stop the presses. My, how quickly things have changed! The consumer of today has pulled back and gotten grumpy, and they expect a higher level of service and quality—or else they'll quickly move on and vote with their feet, checkbook, and "word of mouse." In this digital age of massive choice, they'll find someone else who will treat them with respect.

Many of today's so-called leaders are now scratching their heads and wondering why the old leadership playbook isn't working. In many instances their team isn't listening, and it's as plain as day to see they're often just going through the motions until the five o'clock whistle sounds so they can quickly scurry out of the office like newly released suspects on bail. They want to get as far away from the office as possible, to get a leg up on traffic so they can jump online to see how their moonlight gig or exciting part-time business venture is doing.

In conclusion, become like a sponge and soak up *Liquid Leadership* and the many lessons it contains. Brad's wisdom and advice have been gifted to you in the form of this great book you now hold in your hand, and we are all richer for his shared knowledge and wisdom!

—Tony Rubleski, bestselling author of the Mind Capture book series, MindCaptureGroup.com

Whatever Happened to the Future?

Imagine a little boy sitting on the floor of his family's living room, watching television. He is fascinated by a live broadcast—in black and white, of course; the flickering image on the screen is of a man in a space suit, descending a ladder. Anyone alive today knows that image: the first man landing on the moon. It was 1969, and two men were actually standing on another world more than 250,000 miles away. It was the beginning of a new era.

Imagine being that young boy. Everything in his world promised a future where men and women could travel to the farthest corners of the galaxy. This wasn't science fiction or an overactive imagination; all across America, television shows and the media were all telling him, *This is going to happen.* His toys were about the future. Theaters were putting out a barrage of movies to tell him about the future: *The Day The Earth Stood Still, Forbidden Planet, 2001: A Space Odyssey, Omega Man, Planet of the Apes, Soylent Green* (was Charlton Heston busy back then or what?). There were British shows too, like *Dr. Who, Space: 1999,* and *UFO.* Eventually, *THX-1138, Star Trek,* and *Star Wars* would also make it to the big screen.

In the future, the young boy would be able to work in a domed city on the moon, use a flying car or a jet pack to fly to work, and have a business meeting in a floating satellite encircling Earth. His teachers were telling him so. His parents were telling him. Even his scoutmaster was telling him. There was proof—now "astronaut" was a job title, and there he was, driving a jeep on the moon.

This future was going to happen . . . it was real . . . it was just a matter of time.

Well, if you haven't guessed it by now, that little boy was me. And if you were anything like me, by the time you grew into adulthood, a tiny part of you still expected that future they promised—a world where technology would be the support structure, seamlessly integrated into our lives. By the year 2000, technology was going to solve all our problems.

We were also *warned* about the future. If we didn't keep up, we would be feeling a sense of overwhelming anxiety, what Alvin and Heidi Toffler called "future shock."

Well, if you are like me, you are a little disappointed in the future so far. I was supposed to be commanding my own starship by now. So yes, I am a little disappointed. But I can tell you something that might make you a little happier: We are on our way. Yes, I am excited that the technology part is going to keep evolving. But more important, I am excited that for the first time in recorded history, technology may give the human race a chance to put aside our petty differences for a greater purpose and connect globally, a chance to work and play together as brothers and sisters around the world.

Unbeknownst to most of us, certain paradoxes have arisen, and they are what is puzzling the Cusp Baby Boomer. Perhaps I can explain it best like this: There seems to be a new race of beings on planet Earth. They think differently, they act differently, and they want to do things bigger than we could have imagined. These aliens work side by side with us. They are called Generation Y.

As a Cusp Boomer, I managed to stay in touch with this future I had envisioned, by hanging out with the youth while at the same time staying abreast of the latest technological trends, from video games to the Internet to CD-ROMs to laptops and iPhones and iPods. I listened to my nephews as they grew up, and in every company I consult with, I take the Gen Yers out for coffee and pick their brains. These are my techniques for catching the flow of all these new ideas, new trends, and new technologies.

I recently ran into Camille, the daughter of a family friend. My wife and I had watched her grow up and lost touch. Now, at twenty-five, she was excited to see us and catch up, to share with us her new marriage to an incredible guy named Frank, a new farmhouse in Maine, and a new job managing an information-based company for the past two years. When I pressed her about this, she began to explain in detail how she managed more than twenty-five employees in several states, on several continents, and in multiple time zones—all while working from home. She connects via her laptop and videoconferences on Skype. Now, Camille runs a tight ship, but she admits she hasn't been face-to-face with any employees for the past four months. Everything is virtual.

This is the generation prepared for the future.

Whether you want to accept it or not, the younger generations—those born in the past quarter century—deal with a completely different reality from us Boomers and Generation Xers at so many different levels. Gen X is what I like to call the buffer generation—neither completely a Boomer nor part of Generation Y, they have computer and gaming skills yet think like a Baby Boomer. They are trapped between the two worlds but never completely in one category, almost like outside observers between the two generations. They like listening to Pearl Jam but save for retirement.

Although we all work side-by-side, we are not alike. As coworkers, if not managed properly, these groups may sink into total chaos and disharmony and never understand why.

So perhaps we are not living on the moon or flying in a car, but technology *has* changed how we work, how we play, how we romance, and how we pay. Like it or not, we can't put the genie back in the bottle. This is the age of technology, and we all have to keep moving forward. It took barely twenty-five years for the computer to change us completely. It has established brand-new paradigms, impacted our thinking processes, and changed how we live life and conduct business. Computers have changed where, when, and how we work.

Most people today are in touch with more information in one week over the Internet and in our workaday world than our grandparents processed in their entire lifetime. Life is simply speeding up. It took one hundred years for the Industrial Age methodologies and infrastructure to become the global norm, yet the computer—the ubiquitous tool of the Information Age—took only twenty-five years to permeate our world. Not much time to adjust.

Everyone, leaders included, must stay aware of the new ways in which businesses are being run. The average person can partake in global commerce from the comfort of his or her own home. Amazing, isn't it? Instead of resisting, we must embrace and flow with it all. Do you want to be stranded on the shores of the past, or do you want to keep up and stay relevant?

It's easier said than done. So how do you intend to bridge the gap? The best way is to be so flexible that you can take any shape, any direction—so flexible that you can create your own strategic plan. You must adopt a type of fluid, adaptable leadership: *Liquid Leadership*.

This book is based on my experience of being an Information Age entrepreneur. In the following pages we'll look together at what is going on from a managerial standpoint; we'll examine leadership styles from long-established corporations, especially those that have survived for centuries, showing how properly applied leadership skills are the essence of success. I have chosen to review some businesses that have been screened before, primarily because they are innovators and survivors—but we will be exploring their creativity from a new perspective. We will also look at the workforce within these companies: their age range, the integration of technology, their methodologies and results.

Throughout history, whenever human beings lived in a system that allowed freedom of creation and reward within a stable environment, there was an explosion of productivity and abundance. This is proof that centralized control leads to stagnation, while open freedom leads to innovation. Thus we must explore the way we are running things to ensure this sort of productivity. By studying the problems encountered by each of the groups we examine, from the Woodstock generation to the Wikipedia generation, we can gain a clear understanding and provide guidance to those experiencing the multigenerational management shift that is changing the way we run things.

Please keep in mind that technology continues to change and progress. By the time you finish reading this book, lots of concepts may change. My advice? Just be aware of where your business sector is going, how your brand is seen in the Information Age, and what you need to do to remain relevant to your target audience and customer base. Quality is not job one anymore; amazing is. Produce amazing results by getting customers to fall in love with your company—with your products and with everything you do. Anticipate what your customers' needs are before they do . . . and dare to wow us!

The future is now.

The Credo of the Liquid Leader

Empty your mind, be formless, shapeless—like water. Now you put
water into a cup, it becomes the cup; you put water into a bottle, it
becomes the bottle; you put it in a teapot, it becomes the teapot. Now
water can flow or it can crash. Be water, my friend.

—Bruce Lee

It was all the way back in 1997, but I remember the invitation card well. Printed on a bone-white stock, it cordially requested the presence of my wife and me at the State Theater at New York City's Lincoln Center, to attend *Forbes* magazine's eightieth anniversary party. Clearly etched on the invitation was a quote by the science fiction author Arthur C. Clarke: "Any sufficiently advanced technology is indistinguishable from magic."

It was one of my own favorite quotes, but I wondered why it had been included on the invitation. Did it refer to the wave of new technology brought about by the dot-com revolution, or only to the fact that the magician David Copperfield was scheduled to kick off the festivities with a private performance?

I was, at that point in my career, *very* familiar with dot-coms, having cofounded one myself only a few years earlier: K2 Design, Inc. Not only had Douglas Cleek and I created the first full-service interactive agency in the history of advertising, but we'd given the world its first dot-com as well, launching our IPO in 1996 for $7 million. It had taken a lot of ninety-five-hour weeks to sustain a growth rate of 425 percent for five straight years, and by the time of the *Forbes* magazine party, I was feeling tired in every way possible—mentally, emotionally, and physically. Even so, I was ready to be entertained.

Torrential rain had fallen from the Manhattan skies at the exact moment my wife and I had been required to exit our cab, *sans* umbrella, at the front of the New York State Theater (now the David H. Koch Theater), and hustle across the pavement. We arrived in the main hall a little wet— and promptly forgot about it, dazzled as we were by the oversize glass diamonds inlaid into fifty-foot expanses of crushed burgundy- and gold-colored velvet, stretching from floor to ceiling. There's a reason they nick-named this theater the Jewelry Box.

As we took our seats, I noticed members of the Forbes family sitting in the balconies. The lights dimmed. Steve Forbes and many of the people associated with *Forbes* magazine took to the podium and spoke.

Then the real presentation began. A fifteen-minute movie explained to the New York business elite that every hundred years a technological revolution comes along that's so big, it changes our way of life forever. They were talking about the Internet and about the young entrepreneurs who were permanently changing the business landscape. I thought, *So that's why I was invited.*

Of course the movie ended with the same Arthur C. Clarke quote from the invitation, blazing from the screen in gigantic white letters against a burnt sienna background:

Any sufficiently advanced technology
is indistinguishable from magic.

Then the movie screen disappeared, and David Copperfield performed some "real" magic.

After an amazingly intimate performance made up of big-stage illusions mixed with sleight-of-hand card tricks and ending with an indoor snowstorm, we returned to the main lobby. Under dim lights, surrounded by neon-lit palm trees and waiters and waitresses in sci-fi costumes, we watched as a light show and dance music turned the sweeping carpeted staircases and marble-floored lobby into a scene from the future. It seemed as if we had been beamed into the future. Over cocktails and hors d'oeuvres, I met Donald Trump and David Copperfield.

Far away from the festivities, I noticed, Steve Forbes and his wife, Sabina, were enjoying the party—and strangely enough, without facing a long line of well-wishers. I introduced myself and my wife, and we spent twenty minutes chatting with our hosts. It was as if we were old friends.

"I just took my company public," I told him.

"And which one is that?" He appeared to be genuinely curious.

"K2 Design."

"Congratulations. You know, because of guys like you, things will never be the same." That was an understatement. Yet as a longtime entrepreneur, I hadn't seen anything special about what I'd been doing. To me it was just another business venture.

That was the moment I first began to step outside my old paradigm. It wouldn't be long before I realized that the dot-com boom had been the direct result of a different kind of thinking—not just technological advances, but a new type of computer-savvy workforce, with workers who acted more like entrepreneurs than employees. With global opportunities at our fingertips, the business world was undergoing a fundamental change. Something new was on the horizon, but where and how would we get there?

And then an even bigger question: Who would lead us? Historic hierarchies were in the process of being destroyed. *Everyone* would soon be a potential leader—not just the Boomers, but the Gen Xers and Gen Yers whose creativity I'd tapped at K2, and the future generations. We'd be responsible not just for our own careers but also for the futures of our organizations. To make this new era of leadership work, we'd need a primer, a set of basic laws.

That primer—the result of long and hard-thought research, seasoning, and battlefield testing—is what you now hold in your hands. As a speaker and coach, I teach entrepreneurs, executives, and businesses leaders how to manage themselves and their organizations in a time of radical change.

At the center of my teaching is the concept I call "Liquid Leadership." The new leadership requires adaptability, transparency, and strength, all of which are characteristics of water. Instead of resisting change, aren't we better off adopting a flexible attitude, in which anything is possible? Indeed we are, so long as we observe the immutable laws I've identified for a Liquid Leader. There are seven of these laws, as follows.

1st Law: A Liquid Leader Places People First

All I hear about these days is how technology is changing the world and how we will never be the same. I love technology, but I come from a different perspective: The most important changes concern people. Technology is just a tool to get the job done.

Any battlefield general knows that victory depends on the commitment and well-being of the men and women on the front lines. They are the ones facing the gunfire, so they need good food, excellent equipment, and a solid line of communication to perform at their best. The fact is, these troops understand that they're part of a team. Their reliance on one another's skill set is paramount to success, especially in the heat of battle—much more so than on the commanders safely sitting behind the lines.

But they still need to know that someone at the top gives a damn. In this sense, the president of a company is in the same position as a battlefield general. Treat your people badly and you will fail, whether you are a Baby Boomer in the executive office or a Gen Y programmer working out of your apartment. Baby Boomers tend to isolate themselves from younger people and treat them as expendable kids, while Gen Yers tend to undervalue the experience of Boomers and ignore them. Either attitude is a mistake and insulting.

In the new business environment, stereotypes spell doom. Regardless of generational differences, people in large organizations must respect one another *as* people—with different talents, moods, interests, skill sets, strengths, and weaknesses that contribute to an organization's uniqueness. Your brand is only as strong as the talent it retains. Helping your people understand that shifts in organizational responsibilities also create shifts in person-to-person relationships will make change management a little bit easier.

Currently Boomers need to rely heavily on Gen Y because most of the technology, methodologies, and social networks in use today did not exist five years ago. At the same time Gen Y needs to trust Boomers, who rely on strategy and cunning to win the day. Getting both sides to the table is no easy task, and running a meeting will be more like a coaching session—but the payoff will be incredibly rewarding as you begin to see how technology, when used properly, can rock your customers' world.

By placing people first, you create a sense that everyone is working toward something greater and bigger than themselves. Support the rich ideas of your talent pool, and it becomes easier to tap into it. And just as troops support and protect one another on the front line, your people will support and protect one another—as well as you, their leader.

In companies like this, management is connected and knows every inch of their organization's potential.

2nd Law: A Liquid Leader Cultivates an Environment Where It Is Free and Safe to Tell the Truth

Ever work for a company that micromanages everything to death? In these environments a paper trail becomes more important than getting the work done. Our current enthusiasm for technology has created even more potential for micromanagement, via massive amounts of emails and documentation and endless meetings to sort through it all. Yet when this temptation is given into, the result isn't better communication or higher productivity, but the opposite. Management becomes the last to know what is actually happening.

Conversely, in companies that have moved to flatten their hierarchies and create environments where it is safer to point out the truth, you begin to notice that each person takes their role seriously. When responsibility is shifted to the individual—when people are given the freedom and power to manage their time and solve problems—the result is that no one wants to let down even a single member of their team.

An organization like this runs more smoothly and with more trust. The best and the brightest naturally gravitate toward the chance to work with one another. They know courage will be rewarded, not penalized, and innovation will see the light of day. Such environments operate like entrepreneurial start-ups, with each individual engaged in the success of the company. People are encouraged to challenge one another. They operate with confidence and a sense of personal ambition because they have skin in the game.

This approach may fly in the face of every business manual you have ever read, but those manuals are out of date. We are not in easy times. Consider that betting on one direction or a single type of technology can send a company into bankruptcy overnight. All the more reason to put aside your ego, to listen, and to encourage the sharing of knowledge in every area of an organization's operations. Environments such as these do not centralize creativity; they make it a systemic part of what drives their entire organization.

It is your job as a leader to support the development and creation of big ideas, integrating them into your company's mix of products. And that brings us to the next law.

3rd Law: A Liquid Leader Nurtures a Creative Culture

Take a look at the companies that still cling to old methods of controlling information; even when knowledge sharing is integral to their success, they just can't seem to let go. Centralizing and micromanaging your talent stagnates innovative breakthroughs and creates bottlenecks. Waiting for one person to approve hundreds of ideas will not only destroy a company's ability to get profitable products to market, it will also repel the very people who come up with these ideas.

The Information Age is about utilizing technology and people in order to go faster. Eliminating the bottlenecks opens a floodgate of ideas and speeds up the amount of products and services you get to market.

Speed starts with decentralizing decision making while giving your talent the internal structure for their voice to be heard. It's about building a creative environment where ideas can flow.

Creativity, however, is not always pretty. If you have ever worked in a creative environment, you know what I am talking about. Sometimes it's painful, and most of the time it pushes the team to exhaustion. Yet the energy it unleashes is contagious, and at the end of the day, it is also fun. Yes, believe it or not, *fun*.

Intensely intelligent companies such as Microsoft are like futuristic idea farms, with a very self-managed structure, even if it's not obvious to an outsider. Trust me on this one: Starting with MIT graduates and then mixing in the freedom to think outside of the box will get you some amazing ideas. Smart people getting creative? Sounds like fun to me.

If you're following the 2nd Law, you've already enabled an environment in which people can tell the truth without penalty. To that, add the freedom to present even the silliest idea. An environment of safety plus creative freedom is what defines some of the best companies in the world. Many companies are adopting flextime—where an employee is free to choose when and where they work on company projects and personal projects, or when to take time off and make it up later. Self-directed time management seems to work best.

Now, these management ideas may sound silly to a traditional management expert, but people today are doing more complicated and sophisticated problem solving in their work. To get the job done, many companies have encouraged these types of work methods because they've discovered that autonomous work environments inspire engagement from their workforce. Groundbreaking ideas don't always strike when the sun is up. This is how complex high-end work gets done best—when people are given the freedom to work whenever and wherever. As long as they meet their deadlines, what do you care how it gets done?

Whether you like it or not, nine-to-five is over.

Remember, Post-it Notes started as a silly idea. And when you think about it, nearly all the greatest inventions in the world were discovered this same way—by accident. X-rays, Play-Doh, VELCRO, penicillin, and Viagra were all accidents that became industries. Creating an environment that lights the creative fire requires you to be encouraging of such happy accidents. Innovation cannot thrive in environments where anxiety is too high; but in environments where anxiety is low, creativity is high. Fragile thoughts need time to survive and thrive.

Another thing to remember is that creativity is not just for artists. Great ideas come from software developers, executives, IT professionals, administrative assistants, production managers, analysts, and programmers. Your job is to create a supportive environment for *all* of these persons. How many times has your human resources department hired an incredibly talented individual only to have them get lost in your organization? Supporting and integrating new talent into an organization is the hallmark of a cutting-edge company. Get your team members to bring new hires into the fold, and encourage them to contribute.

The primary job for leadership is to see a bigger picture—where new creative ideas can invent dynamic new industries or make the organization an explosive leader in an already existing one.

It's easy to imagine the creative environments inside companies like Pixar, Herman Miller, Four Seasons Hotels, or Adobe Systems—after all, they do "creative" for a living. But how about companies like Genentech, Devon Energy, or Whole Foods Market? It might not be that easy to see how creative *those* companies are, yet creativity is exactly why they lead their markets.

Again, how do you build not just a safe and trusting workplace but also a creative workplace? Look at how NASA was able to build their unmanned Mars probes—now *that* is an intensely creative work environment. Intense people from multiple disciplines can and do create the impossible every day, thanks to strong leadership, best practices, and a deliberately amorphous structure for sharing knowledge. It's not easy, and sometimes it may be downright ugly—but the quality of the work becomes the center of a great work environment. In these environments, each and every member respects one another's contributions—no matter what their background may be—and the results are consistently groundbreaking advances and innovative ideas.

The right chemistry between people cannot be planned, any more than you can predict the success of a TV series such as *Sex and the City*, *Lost*, or *Glee* or books such as the Harry Potter and Twilight series. Runaway ideas that capture our hearts and our imagination need room to take root . . . and for the target audience to fall in love with the idea. Just look at the Chuck Norris Internet phenomenon. Who could have planned that? Even Chuck himself is surprised by it all.

And that is Job One for you: Create an intense culture where raw, exciting, innovative ideas have a chance to incubate. When such an environment is nurtured, it becomes easier for accidental innovation to take place—and to carry through to the bottom line.

4th Law: A Liquid Leader Supports Reinvention of the Organization

When Doug burst into our office at K2 many moons ago, he announced to me that we should become an Internet agency. I stubbornly resisted at first (it was a *very* small market in 1994), but once I said okay, we went from being one of four thousand design firms to one of ten Internet companies in the United States. Overnight we were a leader in a small, but growing, market. Today the Internet is the rule for doing business, not the exception—but don't think for a moment that we've reached a plateau. Change never stands still, and a Liquid Leader must be more willing than ever to move and dodge according to the marketplace.

Technology has given more and more start-ups the ability to compete head-on with larger companies. These start-ups are interested in one thing: disrupting the status quo. Their survival depends on proving themselves to be right. And they take leaps to do so. Many of the top corporations today were started because the original founder didn't like how things were being done. They had a better way, and built a company around it.

The key is to stay open to new ideas and methods, to entrepreneurial startups and their ideas, and to new fads that could become trends. Look high and low for big ideas. Actively support the fact that although you make widgets today, you may be a completely different company doing completely different things within the next five years, and you may be doing these things for companies located on the other side of the globe.

It may seem strange, but the best lessons in managing change come not from twenty-five-year-old newcomers, but from companies that have been around for a while. And when I say "a while," I mean hundreds of years—like Sumitomo, the Japanese *keiretsu*, or "business group," founded circa 1615 as a book and medicine shop in Kyoto by a former Buddhist priest, Masatomo Sumitomo. By adapting copper refinery and advanced smelting techniques, the family began using the spiritual principles of its founder Masatomo and began to grow with each unique idea—integrating it into their mix of product offerings. Today Sumitomo is parent to companies in such industries as electronics, insurance, banking, shipbuilding, automotive, and more. Sumitomo survived one disruptive new technology after another, transitioning amidst great upheaval from one era to the next. It and companies like it around the world endured, emerging stronger than ever despite radical changes that destroyed entire business sectors and left their competitors to the pages of history.

How did they do it? By seamlessly moving into completely new sectors or adding new sectors to their existing mix. They didn't do this because they "had" to. That would have been merely reactive thinking. Sumitomo is proactive and creative, actively seeking out new ideas and emerging markets, because it is part of how they do business—and has been for almost four centuries!

Ironically executives at Sumitomo are still using the Founder's Precepts to guide Masatomo's company to this day. These principles keep them at the cutting edge yet adaptable to change. For them, change is not a problem to overcome but an integral part of their culture.

Organizations that think for the long term pay close attention to the world around them for ideas, technologies, and sectors that can add to the bottom line. They don't get caught up in the idea that they're the leader and that's that. They stay open to possibilities.

To think like this yourself, you must avoid becoming attached to hard beliefs or steadfast rules. Better to stay nimble and quick, to participate in the future by staying flexible about new ideas and methodologies—even those that at first seem disruptive.

Surround yourself with people who keep their eyes open for new markets to explore and new ways to think about those markets. Pay attention to the entrepreneurs. Wherever there are emerging markets, there are new avenues for products and profits and acquisitions. Jumping into the fray of commerce and all its chaos will help you discover a brave new world of ideas—and companies that just might need a parent company to write them a check.

5th Law: A Liquid Leader Leads by Example

On February 26, 2009, every Starbucks nationwide closed for emergency retraining. Why? Because founder Howard Schultz had ordered it. He'd taken a leave of absence, but upon hearing of slipping sales and a rumor that the company's baristas weren't making a decent latte anymore, he not only returned to action but also quickly implemented an emergency retraining program.

And here's the key point: Schultz didn't send out a mandate on a memo pad for someone else to implement. He came out of his sabbatical, got personally involved, then got his managers involved, and finally, in the most dramatic way possible, got every single store involved. That's what Liquid Leadership is about—leading by example. No matter where you fit in an organization, your example is what builds your reputation, your career, and the future of your company.

Leadership in any organization needs to be admired and respected for its success. People secretly sabotage organizations where the leadership isn't admired; through either cynicism or stealing, the mutually disgruntled will find followers within their own work groups. This energy interferes with success. Leading by example sets a more positive tone.

This has always been a touchstone of good leadership, but it's especially true today. Something remarkable took place over the past twenty-five years: People stopped worshipping the companies they work for and began instead to see themselves as value added to the bottom line, partners in success. Today's workforce has amazingly high self-esteem and won't look up to you just because you've "earned" the corner office.

And how do you treat a partner? With respect. You can no longer bark orders from the sidelines, expecting employees to jump and obey. Nor can you stay in total isolation, ignoring their needs. Today's workforce wants their leadership approachable and real.

The only way to engage with your organization is to enroll your people in your vision and then live that vision. In the minds of the people who work for your org, *they are the company.*

Hubris is out; stewardship and integrity are in. And please, don't fake it.

People can smell BS a mile away, and they will run from it. Where cowards blame others for their mistakes, a Liquid Leader is the first to take blame and the last to take credit. Without people to lead, you stand alone.

And do yourself a favor: Mr. Nice Guy doesn't work either. Being respected is what you want to work on. Believe me, I've tried both methods and at the end of the day, people respect those whom they admire.

6th Law: A Liquid Leader Takes Responsibility

Unfortunately, the news today is filled with plenty of examples of business leaders who decided to take the low road, appearing on some financial show and pontificating about how great their company is while secretly dumping the stock. Or my personal pet peeve: when a high profile leader is caught lying and leaves with a multimillion-dollar golden parachute and a book deal. Meanwhile the company employees are ruined and incapable of retiring. As Lee Iacocca says, "Where have all the leaders gone?"

The problem is a small bunch of bad apples making it bad for the group. When you visit companies like Google, W. L. Gore & Associates (makers of GORE-TEX), or Nintendo, you see such great innovation taking place that you begin to realize that the majority of companies out there *are* doing things right.

Even so, integrity can never be taken for granted—and it starts with you. What do you stand for? Today's leader is actually an extension of their brand. Name any top company, and chances are, you can name the CEO or founder as well. The attributes of a great leader can be felt within every inch of an organization: uncompromising, intense, and always on the cutting edge of their market. Taking full responsibility for your actions—with no compromises—is the standard for great leadership. It takes the same amount of energy to be good at something as it does to not be so good. So why not stand for greatness? Setting higher standards is contagious and permeates an organization to its core.

On the negative side, if you're caught in a lie, it hurts morale. And once morale is compromised, cynicism runs amok. Cynicism is a cancer that destroys hope, creativity, and our sense of adventure. And as with cancer, you must detect it early and eradicate it.

THE CREDO OF THE LIQUID LEADER

The key to taking responsibility is to look for your blind spot. This is the area where you may not realize you are weak. Lack of detail, inexperience, and arrogance are all examples of blind spots. The best way to discover a blind spot is to ask your team of trusted advisors and confidants to tell you what your weakness is, and demand the truth—no matter how painful.

By taking responsibility for your actions, you become a person of uncompromising values, incapable of being swayed by a solipsistic ideology or a quick buck. At the same time, you become invincible. When you know your weaknesses and lead with them, there is nothing left for people to sense but your strengths.

It is easy to be a leader when times are good. But when times are tough, these are the moments that make a leader great. Developing working methodologies and profit centers during tough times is what creates an invincible leader. Signs of integrity are written all over a leader who shows up, gets involved, tweaks the business, and stands for reinvention. The news is filled with leaders who say they take full responsibility, yet their actions suggest otherwise. Why not stand for something better? Why not promote a higher standard of excellence where leaders take responsibility for their actions and the actions of their people, and expect the same in return? Wouldn't you follow a leader like that?

7th Law: A Liquid Leader Leaves a Lasting Legacy

If you travel around the world, whether to Sweden or Alaska, Peru or Nigeria, Mexico or Australia, when you look past the modern buildings you will find evidence of ancient civilizations that understood the concept of a legacy. These civilizations considered every action in terms of its impact on the next one hundred generations, and they were serious about this.

Today we have lost this idea of a legacy. Even more so in this new age, we see ourselves and our creations as disposable and transient. The houses built today won't last more than forty years—just in time for you to pay off your mortgage. Our skyscrapers won't last anywhere near as long as the pyramids of Egypt or the Roman Coliseum, and our streets are far from being the Appian Way—they need full repair crews every couple of years. If today's society can be said to have any legacy at all, it's one of planned obsolescence.

Many people claim this is the way it has to be in an advanced society. Really? Tell that to a company like Exxon, which is looking into fuel alternatives like algae; or TESLA Motors and their development of the electric car and battery cells; or Intel, using energy-efficient Celeron processors to control electricity-generating wind turbines along with a multitude of Green products needing artificial intelligence. These companies are looking into alternative technology to build a legacy for the future.

Leaving a lasting legacy is about creating structures that don't require your presence for their success. It's about leaving your company, your world, and your grandchildren's world a better place for having been graced by your presence. I have no time for leaders who think only of now and always want to be the center of attention.

After all, why are you here on Earth? Just to make big money? Or to be of service to others, helping them to acquire the skills they need to align their dreams with a changing planet? To create a place where people feel secure enough to stay and raise their kids, get their first mortgage, and pass on the legacy of doing great work in a great company? What I am proposing may sound bigger than life, but that is what you should expect from yourself and the people you work with—you are changing the world because you believe you can.

In a fast-paced world the idea of delayed gratification seems to have disappeared in favor of quick profits and quick results. But building something great and lasting is about defining a clear vision, planning and effort, persistence over time, and eventual harvest.

A society based on planned obsolescence cannot survive for very long. History is filled with such stories, but many believe that because we have cell phones and e-readers and an interconnected electrical grid system, we could never go backward—yet we could. We can call it the "new economy," but it relies on electricity to function. Many economists agree that when the Roman Empire collapsed and plunged Europe into the Dark Ages, all technological progress came to a halt. It would take more than a thousand years to regain the same momentum. According to author

Richard Maybury, we are actually 1,500 years behind where we could have been technologically.

To explain our world today, we must look at the past and make an educated guess for the future. Yes, old methodologies are changing the way we do things, but we can't abandon everything we've learned over the past six millennia. One thing we know for certain: The Internet has shaken our world to the core. For the first time in human history the planet is connected by a global infrastructure, which is built on the Internet, satellites, machine-to-machine communication, and wireless technology. And it's not just for commerce; it's also for communication, security, socializing, and entertainment. We are no longer mentally isolated by physical borders. If we do it right, the human race is on the cusp of yet another huge leap forward—a global legacy.

As leaders, you have the job of supporting the people who make our companies great—by giving them the tools to win, and by being humble enough to listen to their input and accept their support. Yes, what we do is about the bottom line, but I challenge you to resist quick profits and embrace long-term changes—delay gratification in exchange for something greater than yourself. More than ever, whether you are a Boomer or an eighteen-year-old building your Facebook page, it is your job to create a standard of excellence that catapults us all to another level.

By raising our standards, we raise our expectations. By raising our expectations, we change what we will tolerate. It is time to stop rewarding those who have failed and start rewarding those who do things right. It is time to focus on the real leaders and innovators in every generation.

The world of the future is at our fingertips, and we need to start now. Remember, our thoughts have mass; they have an impact on this world. If you believe it, you can achieve it. Let's change this world together, one visionary idea at a time.

1ST LAW

A Liquid Leader Places People First

"Don't ask what the world needs. Ask what makes you come alive, and go do it. Because what the world needs is people who have come alive."

—Howard Thurman

Why Place People First?

When I was just eighteen years old, I was promoted to a coveted assistant manager position at Hersheypark, the famous amusement park in Hershey, Pennsylvania. I had about twenty-five high school– and college-age employees under my direct supervision, all of whom staffed booths in one of the five games sections of the park.

Staff wore brightly colored uniforms, each of a different style, denoting which division they worked for: games, rides, food prep, or garbage/cleaning crew. Each had their first name displayed on a white tag worn on the left breast pocket. Senior-level employees, on the other hand, wore business casual clothing and color-coded nametags that let everyone know their exact level of authority. Supervisors wore blue tags; managers wore brown tags; and the first rung of management, assistant managers like myself, wore green tags.

There were five major game areas in the park back then, with several hundred employees all told. My little area near the Comet and Sooper-dooperlooper roller coasters may have been small, requiring a rotating staff of only twenty-five, but it covered the length of two football fields. My frustration was that only five of the kids I managed worked hard. I say "kids" laughingly, despite the fact that I was only eighteen years of age myself. The rest were only concerned about showing up for a paycheck. Luckily their laziness led me to learn something incredibly valuable about management that has served me well throughout my career.

Near the end of each day I went from booth to booth collecting the daily proceeds. I gathered mostly quarters and a few stacks of dollar bills from each booth, but it added up. In fact, I collected more than $100,000 in "small change" monthly. Each day, to get the collecting done as quickly as possible, I chose two people whom I considered to be reliable and fast, and who in my view had earned the two-hour luxury of escaping their booths and working with me one-on-one. Naturally, I always picked from among my five hardest-working employees. I am a big fan of rewarding doers.

The work was fast-paced and required coordination. The first employee diligently attended to the collection cart as if working a casino in Vegas. It was my responsibility as assistant manager to physically hop into each booth and make the exchange, using a key to unlock the moneybox and exchange it for a new, empty box I got from the second employee. Everything was numerically coded, and each box had a ticker device to calculate how many quarters it held. I recorded this number on a stat sheet as the empties were replaced. Most of this money exchange took place while twenty people were waiting in line to play the game, so it required speed and stealth.

Once we finished collecting the thirty or so assorted moneyboxes, the three of us pushed the cart—now laden with several hundred pounds of quarters—from the Hollow, the name for our area of the park, to the games division headquarters located in the arcade at the top of the hill.

The summer heat made it hot and sweaty work—especially since a moneybox fully loaded with quarters could weigh anywhere from fifteen to twenty-five pounds. But even so, the employees I picked found it more rewarding than standing in a booth and barking for people to win "fabulous prizes." My helpers also liked it that I would treat them to ice cream sodas once we were done, along with an award of discretionary "bonus hours" I could hand out to anyone at the end of the workweek. This meant an extra $25 in their paycheck for their efforts—and in 1979, that was a lot of money.

Eventually the other, lazier employees noticed what was going on and decided they didn't like it. One beautiful Saturday morning, at our weekly employee meeting, just before the park was due to open, the leader of the disgruntled blurted out, "You play favorites." They all chimed up in unison. "Yeah, you play favorites!" Chatter ensued.

What I said next surprised even me. "You're right," I said. "I *do* play favorites."

They were stunned. They had expected me to deny it, or placate them, or pretend to feel bad and win them over by trying harder to make them happy. Instead, I was honest and direct. "And I will continue to handpick from these five until one of you steps up to the plate and shows me you want it badly enough. I reward those who go the extra mile. You do that, and I will give you the shirt off my back. If you don't, I couldn't care less."

The results of that little speech were astronomical. Within two weeks, these twenty formerly disgruntled employees had entirely new attitudes. It was like the Stepford Wives: They worked harder, complained less, and competed among each other. Foot traffic was the backbone of our sales, and barking was the key . . . and now everyone barked with vim and vigor. The increased booth revenue showed that their efforts were paying off.

Of course, I backed up what I said. Extra effort was rewarded with cash bonus awards and, what they all craved, getting handpicked for collection and an ice cream soda. Within two weeks, everyone was pushing the envelope to see who would get in my good graces.

The main office asked me what I was doing and told me whatever it was, keep it up. How could this possibly have been the same staff of disgruntled workers from two weeks ago?

Set Your Standards

What I had learned was invaluable. In my own naïve and untrained way, I had seen that respect came from the consistent application of the right kind of management style. I maintained my standard of excellence, explained what that standard was, and challenged anyone and everyone to meet it. The results were amazing. And they were continuous and contagious, especially when bonus hours and ice cream sodas were involved. Fair, clear, approachable, and firm seemed to work for me.

Let's fast-forward to today. Our world has shifted dramatically in recent years. Technology has eliminated entire business sectors and uncounted jobs, even while creating new ones. It has disrupted the status quo comfort zone at every level. Yet unlike the Industrial Revolution with its hierarchy, methodologies, machinery, and systems that took a hundred years to spread around the world, the Computer Age has taken a mere twenty-five years to go global. Put simply, life has sped up. There is more information both available and necessary for us to get our jobs done than ever before.

Today's workforce is far more dynamic than those of the generations before, simply because they have to be. Speed, multitasking, and global connectivity are the norm. Just look at the amount of work most employees are required to get done day to day. Or the amount of self-managing and mastery of software required. Or the ability to instantaneously attend a live videoconference with colleagues a continent away. The things that used to take months to coordinate, we now do in a few hours.

And this is just the beginning. To catch the incredible amount of new ideas coming at you at warp speed, you need to speed up your organization's ability to catch these new ideas and get them implemented. By flattening hierarchy, you get everyone involved and aligned to the entire organization's success. It's time to implement a new Information Age standard of excellence.

Some interpret these changes as part of the technological age, yet to do so is to miss the point. It isn't about bandwidth, connectivity, or mass collaboration as much as it is about people. Whether it's using a social network or collaborating on the latest digital project, talent-rich people are the key. Any great general knows a simple fact: To win a war, you have to rely on your people and their abilities. Strategize with the mutual admiration society all you want, but knowing the potential of the people in your organization and utilizing their contributions is vital to leadership in today's disruptive environment. Unfortunately, most of the leadership I work with would rather have a root canal than close the distance between upper management and their frontline people. But how else can you get real answers?

Often, companies bring in so-called change consultants to find any problems and make suggestions as to how the company could operate more efficiently. But why hire an organizational change expert, when all you have to do is walk around your company and actually talk to people on the front lines? Obviously it's hard for upper management to identify core problems, especially when execs show up in a suit and tie. Everyone is very aware of their presence and behaves accordingly. Outside consultants get hired because they can more easily blend in with the rest of the company.

Maintaining the status quo is detrimental these days. If this is happening in your organization, then internal and external forces are somehow keeping things from moving forward. Your job as a leader is to find out what these forces are and deal with them accordingly. You can only do this if you take off your tie and get involved. Destroy resistance, support knowledge and retraining, remove bottlenecks, and give power as quickly as possible to those who need it to make decisions. The idea is to create an environment where even the top leaders are approachable—to employees with new ideas and processes. And that includes the *president and CEO.*

Your job as a leader is to get employees involved at every level of an organization in the success of the company. It sounds like a start-up environment because it is very similar. Full organizational participation and involvement is critical in this day and age for companies (both large and small) to maintain a competitive advantage. Very few companies have innovators at the top. Keeping channels open assures that even tiny ideas make it to the front of the line.

I am not asking management to be more touchy-feely or get sucked into the day-to-day drama. But I am advocating getting more involved with your people, the heart of your organization, to find the potential hidden in the pool of talent right in front of you. Find the doers, the idea implementers, and the creative types—support them and reward them.

Work on your business, but whatever you do to affect the bottom line, remember that it starts with the people you manage and the ideas they carry. If given the chance, that young woman on the front lines can tell you exactly what needs to change in order to make her department run smoothly and more profitably. But are you listening to her voice?

Leaders who are more involved in the day-to-day process can easily see what is creating the status quo environment, which enables them to change it. And when they make changes, they can make them organically, because they are viewed as a trusted ally instead of an intruder. And finally, an involved leader can more easily keep an eye out for those individuals who consistently develop ideas and processes that benefit the bottom line.

The business landscape we are up against is a pool of rapidly-shifting chaos, with one model after another being replaced. Technology is changing the speed and reach of even the smallest company—and threatening the larger established brands. To stay up to date, a consistent stream of new and improved products and services requires an outward commitment from leadership as well as the commitment and support of the individuals throughout your organization. These individuals are the very people who will be discovering the next big thing. After all, it isn't IBM that comes up with the big ideas, but the people who work within its walls.

Becoming a Liquid Leader

On July 26, 1996, I sat at the bar at Harry's at Hanover Square, waiting for the moment to come. My nerves were shot from the excitement, and I didn't feel I could stay in the office any longer. I was about to become a Liquid Leader, one of the first to bridge the gap between Baby Boomers and the younger generations that were changing the complexion of American business forever. Here's how it went down.

For the past hundred years, if a major deal happened, it happened at Harry's. Just three blocks from the New York Stock Exchange, inside an 1851 brownstone, Harry's was well known as *the* place where Wall Street's biggest deals were finalized over drinks, expensive cigars, and a handshake. It was like being at a sports bar, but instead of a Yankees game, the television screens flashed the latest stock exchange quotes with a barrage of financial programming.

My business partners—David Centner, Matthew De Ganon, and Douglas Cleek—stood elbow to elbow with me, staring up at the same screen, waiting for the big play. In the next fifteen minutes, K2 Design, Inc., would be the first Internet company to go public. The executive team would go from business partners to majority shareholders, from founders of an entrepreneurial start-up to C-suite executives. It was exhilarating.

How Did Dungeons & Dragons Geeks Take Over Wall Street?

From 1995 through 2000, Wall Street was flooded with an army of twenty-somethings eager to prove that the Internet was the new frontier for business. The ubiquitous image of the Internet guru with a shaven head, a pierced ear, and a goatee, dressed from head to toe in black, was harshly juxtaposed against the New York Stock Exchange traders dressed in conservative suits and the daily power tie. Two completely different cultures were coming together for the very first time.

Creative types were taking over Wall Street, and I was one of them.

Awkward moments of weirdness were a daily event at the local deli counters as the suits gave Internet-savvy graphic designers the once-over. These vagabond-looking young people standing in line at the Au Bon Pain on Broad Street, with their tattoos and piercings, were the very young people whom the *Wall Street Journal* was following every day.

This was a time when venture capitalists suddenly lost their minds and handed out billions in start-up capital to the first Gen Xer who shouted, "It's the new economy, man; you just don't get it!" The geeks who used to get teased for playing Dungeons & Dragons and being early adopters of everything computerized were now speaking in code like the Oracle at Delphi. And the funny thing was, Wall Street was listening.

Investors threw money at anyone who designed websites, and K2 was the first to do it well. Many of the trends during the first dot-com era made no sense, but as a long-time entrepreneur, I made a decision that made total sense: question everything with the detachment of a seasoned interviewer and the keen eye of a hardened reporter. Since our business models were changing overnight, the best course of action seemed to be to just observe and not judge. "Figure out the model and adapt to it" became my motto.

Sometimes it seemed I was seeing the entire *world* change before me. Everywhere I went in Manhattan there was electricity in the air and something strange taking place—young, savvy, creative types were dabbling in big business, handling their careers with the strategic focus of a hardened battlefield general.

It was becoming apparent that this up-and-coming generation *was* different from mine.

It also explained why the *Wall Street Journal, Barron's,* and the *New York Times* were covering their every move. This new wave of twentysome-things coming out of college didn't seem to want a job; they wanted to start companies and decimate the way their parents worked. They weren't satisfied with forty years in a cubicle and a gold watch at retirement. It was obvious to me that this generation wanted a different experience, and they knew it was there for the taking.

The truth is, this young workforce is just like any other generation that came before them—cocky, resentful, bold, and defiant. The only differ-ence is, Generations X and Y have a skill set that Baby Boomers didn't have, and suddenly that skill is in demand. For the first time in history, youth has money, power, freedom, and media attention. And they exer-cised that power for the first time during the dot-com boom.

HTML programmers were demanding $85,000 a year despite the fact that the code could be taught to a kindergartner. Secretaries wanted stock options before they would even consider an interview. Salespeople wanted to be assured that if they brought in the business, they wouldn't get just commissions but equal partnership. If you didn't give in to their demands, they went to the competition to reveal your supersecret proprietary sys-tem. And there were plenty of companies that would give them all that they asked for and more.

The history of Wall Street was being rewritten as the first wave of tech-nologically immersed Gen X became Internet paper millionaires. To Baby Boomers like myself who had grown up on solid, tried-and-true textbook business ideologies, this made no sense. Why was Wall Street going gaga over a few kids with an Internet company? It was just graphic design in a new medium. Yet despite business plans being scribbled on cocktail nap-kins, and questions about profitability being met with vitriolic cynicism from the techno wunderkinds, venture capitalists were writing big checks.

The old career norm of getting a job after graduating from college, working your way up the ladder over ten to fifteen years, buying a house, getting the corner office, and then retiring was being replaced by a system of young, tech-savvy entrepreneurs starting their own companies imme-diately after college. These Internet entrepreneurs were seen as business rebels—brilliant and uncontrollable—who were shaking up the status quo. But they really were the first generation immersed in everything technological: video games, computers, CD-ROMs, computerized educational toys, and, of course, the Internet. As Boomers sat in shock, venture capitalists gave these kids billions. No one dared say that the emperor wasn't wearing clothes, for fear that maybe, just maybe, the new kids on the block were right. The new economy was still undefined.

The media called them Generation X and Generation Y, and they listened to bands like Nirvana and Pearl Jam leading the grunge movement while comedians like Tom Green and shows like *Jackass* reflected a new generational cynicism.

As Generations X and Y emerged from college into their first jobs, they expected high-speed connectivity, cell phones, good starting salaries, and a laptop. They demanded all this and more at entry level. The assumption was that whatever the company wasn't paying in salary, they could make up for by providing perks. If these new job seekers didn't get these "toys," they quit and ventured out on their own. The explosion of hundreds of new media start-ups in Manhattan from 1995 to 2000 was the direct result of this technologically immersed generation entering the workforce for the very first time—and flipping our world on its ear.

According to John C. Beck and Mitchell Wade, authors of Got Game: How the Gamer Generation Is Reshaping Business Forever, the entire dot-com boom of the mid-90s was due entirely to the first wave of a generation raised on video games, computer technology, and access to the Internet. This is the Dungeons and Dragons crowd, more comfortable with interactivity and video game competitions than sitting around watching TV.

The dot-com boom of the midnineties was the first wave. The Social Network Era called Internet 2.0 was the second wave. And the third wave is upon us now.

Going Undercover

Here's my dirty little secret: I am a Baby Boomer, raised on Saturday-morning cartoons, ABC's Afterschool Specials, the *Apollo* moon missions,

Watergate, and disco. But I looked young enough at the time to pass as a Gen Xer. I used this as camouflage to infiltrate both worlds.

Like a double agent, I learned to bridge the gap between Baby Boomers and this new, terrifying generation. I *had* to do it. And the first thing I had to learn was to accept these "citizens of the Internet" (or "Netizens"). Instead of resisting the changes, I started to view this generation as talent-rich contributors, integral to maintaining K2 Design's cutting-edge status. The amount of knowledge these young people collected was astounding and far greater than any single person could memorize in a year. It's as if their brains were wired completely different from Boomers' brains. They were technology-obsessed vacuum cleaners, comfortably and consistently seeking out the next cool web application.

While the rest of us wanted to go home and get some rest, this new generation was out partying or surfing the Web until the wee hours of the morning.

By staying detached and open to learning, I figured out that to win at business at that time required two things: listening to Gen Y, the very people who were causing the disruption, while also maintaining what worked from the past hundred years of business development.

Today's generation gap is permanent and unlike any gap we've seen before; it is a chasm. We cannot return to the past any more easily than Dorothy Gale could go back to her black-and-white world unchanged. But we can bridge the gap and make it work under a new paradigm, starting with an understanding of how each of us approaches work. The integration of Boomers and Netizens is paramount to our success.

Boomers have been trained in linear thought and methodologies— one thought at a time, with a beginning, middle, and end to the process.

Generation Y, however, has been immersed in technology twenty-four hours a day, seven days a week. It started with Speak & Spell and video games, then computers, CD-ROMs, and the Internet. Gen Ys are parallel thinkers, which means that they process multiple thoughts and ideas at the same time, like a computer: "Hurry up and get it done, and we'll fix the glitches later." Generation X is right in the middle, capable of handling both worlds.

It is not that these newer generations are smarter, merely that they have a skill set that the business world needs right now. Sadly, the majority of Boomers don't have these skills and if they do, gray hair interferes with getting hired. They can imitate Gen Y, but they will never be a match for the younger generations whose training started at childhood.

But Boomers *do* have the ability to see the bigger picture and the ramification of their actions. In other words, Boomers are best at spotting talent and strategizing how best to use it. Why? Because Gen Y hasn't been trained in past methodologies and so may not even see the ramifications of an older model rooted in new technologies. This may result in Gen Yers repeating something that failed in the past.

Unfortunately there is an information gap in most organizations. Seasoned individuals are not passing on their knowledge base, and newer-skilled technocrats aren't really concerned with what they see as the past. Turf protection, absenteeism, vacant meetings, and generational isolationism seem to be a normal part of the business world these days. But the problem is not the people so much as the lack of knowledge sharing—the lack, in organizations where the communication gap is greatest, of systems to pass the knowledge on down (or up) the line.

Somewhere, somehow, someone has to start getting these two sides communicating.

That Friday in July at Harry's, our eyes were glued to the television screen. And suddenly, there it was: the symbol *KTWO* appearing on the streaming ticker tape at the bottom of the screen. We cheered. The bartender poured us a round on the house, we toasted, and that was that. Then the real work began.

Culture Shock

One afternoon as I was preparing for a presentation to the K2 board of advisors later in the evening, a vigorous knock pulled me from my thoughts. Our receptionist, Jennifer Rivers, opened the door and asked, "Do you have time to show some tourists around the office?"

It turned out that a small group of Japanese businessmen wanted to take a tour of our 3,000-square-foot facility. This was back in 1996, and K2's main offices were at 55 Broad Street in the New York Information Technology Center. We were one of fifty new media tech companies but the only one in the building that was publicly traded. So, alas, we attracted the curious.

I had only one hour to spare. As I entered the lobby ten businessmen greeted me, along with the tour guide who served as their interpreter—all from Japan and all very curious about this phenomenon called the "Internet boom." As we shall see, their curiosity was symbolic (and still is) of a much larger divide—not just between East and West, but between comfortably old methodologies smacking into radically new ways of doing business.

I immediately introduced myself and smiled to the group. The tour guide, a woman named Yumi, explained that they wished to see K2. Of course, I agreed. Knowing a little bit about both Japanese and Chinese culture, I bowed and said it would be my honor. Everyone bowed in unison and smiled.

Questions abounded as I began the tour with a description of the processes at K2: the careful balance among programmers, technology, and designers, and the great care taken to assure that an end user's experience was seamless and memorable. Our visitors seemed to be mentally contrasting what appeared to be a loose management style with traditional Japanese management. To them, K2's approach made no sense. Contrasts between East and West are not new, but the dot-com boom made them even more apparent.

Seeing their puzzlement, I attempted to enlighten them. "Everyone here is encouraged to bring fresh ideas to the table, and we do our best to support and reward those ideas. Nothing is considered a dumb idea, and without everyone's input, most projects would be mediocre."

This answer seemed to amaze them. According to Yumi, this was not how business is done in Japan. There must be hierarchy and structure. Communication was one-way in their organizational chart. Some in the group looked confused, and I imagined their blank looks were saying, "How in the hell do these young Americans get any work done?" Where is the taskmaster? They didn't understand that mass collaboration was what made our business most effective. It was like trying to get Boomers to understand the business training a teenager was receiving by playing *World of Warcraft*.

What I failed to mention at the time, and what perhaps could have satisfied their curiosity, is that we always hired smart people at K2 who weren't afraid to speak up. We gave people flexible time to get their work finished while balancing out deadlines. In other words, if it took four hours to get eight hours' worth of work finished, then an employee could work on something else, create a project for the company, or leave early and work from home. Without knowing it we had created at K2 a results-only work environment (ROWE), where our best employees were rewarded for their results rather than the number of hours worked. In these environments, productivity goes up, workers satisfaction goes up, and turnover virtually disappears.

By contrast, whenever a strict cultural paradigm does not allow for input from lower-level employees, executives miss innovations that could have made their companies instant leaders. In such a world, one must earn the "right" to be listened to and lower-rung employees can't possibly have an effective contribution. Without permission, no one shares their insights.

In today's world, self-motivated, peer-to-peer communication speeds up the creation of innovative ideas by giving them the platform to be heard.

This isn't some new-age management philosophy; this has been field-tested all over the world by the best management and behavioral scientists on Earth. Giving smart people autonomy in an organization and the ability to manage their own time creates groundbreaking output.

In our company, project managers pushed every project through in order to meet deadlines, but they were just as responsible for input as they were for receiving a critique. Not seeing an official commander-in-chief must have seemed strange to these visiting hierarchy junkies, but to our project managers, a traditional top-down approach would have seemed like a cattle drive: "I don't care how you get there, just get it to market." Our managers knew that the best way to build dynamic experiences and products for consumers is to give them not just what they want but what they need, and to do so alongside things that are exciting and add value. In order to create such dynamic experiences for a user, the people building the website have the freedom to create one-of-a-kind experiences. Utilitarian doesn't work in Internet development.

I took our tour through the programming department, then into accounting where Seth Bressman our CFO was overseeing payroll, then into the producer's area. Everything at K2 had a tinge of corporate and creative rolled into one: cubicles but fully exposed HVAC and ductwork to give it an industrial air yet retain that loft feeling.

The last stop on the tour was our design department, a five-sided, uneven room with a black Formica wraparound counter with multiple workstations, all Macintosh with twenty-three-inch screens. The only light sources were from the monitors and any light from the sixth-floor terrace outside. The design department was state of the art and the coolest part of our offices, so it was the best place to end our tour.

I opened up the floor to Q&A. A very polished businessman wearing corporate casual, with a camera strapped around his neck and a pair of thick glasses, asked a question. Yumi turned to translate.

"What is your initial market cap?"

"It's $26 million and growing," I responded.

There was a slight delay as Yumi would reinterpret my words into Japanese. I was careful not to use slang or American colloquialisms.

"You appear to be in hyper-growth. Is that true?"

"Yes," I replied. "As a matter of fact we are getting ready to consolidate our other three divisions under one congruous, 13,000-square-foot office across the street at 30 Broad." We were actually two months away from moving our workforce of sixty full-time employees. I wondered how these businessmen from the Land of the Rising Sun could see what we were going through when American investors couldn't. Perhaps they were looking for different things.

Pulling the Lid off the Past

The older Japanese businessmen didn't seem to understand that the greatest innovations in technology and the freshest ideas can come from anyone—young or old—especially when the environment is right. Products that have excited consumers do so because the company that created them built something passionately and creatively to solve a problem or excite the customer. From dishwashing liquid to sports cars to computers, the leaders are always the most creative and the ones that incite an emotional response from their customer. You may not be aware of this, but just about everything you have ever purchased in your life was due to the fact that it was the most creative, coolest thing in your world and it made life better. Period. We don't buy things; we buy experiences. What we think this product or that will give us, whether it's cleaner clothes, faster Internet access, or the most luxurious car our dollar can buy.

Without consistent creativity, there is no innovation.
So why do so many companies ignore creativity as a
line item?

Part of the reason creativity appears to be absent in most companies is that most executives don't really understand it—or how to manage it. The old saying "If it isn't measurable, it isn't manageable" has been flipped. It doesn't look like a real business environment when it appears that people are having fun. And ROWE works only for companies where more complex, conceptual, creative output is their business. Traditional management and reward paradigms work well in companies where there is a narrow band of focus—a simple set of rules, goals, and tasks to follow and a reward for top performers.

But in companies where complex, out-of-the-box thinking is needed to stay consistently in the innovative sweet spot, managers would do well to adopt a results-only environment. With no clearly set work hours, the emphasis is on results—not time at a cubicle. Measuring individual output becomes the standard for measurement in a ROWE-run company. No one cares when you decide to work or where, as long as it comes in on deadline and is impeccable. Not surprisingly these environments have the highest employee satisfaction and the lowest turnover.

But results-only environments are not the best environments for everyone, especially those environments where an actual amount of work is measurable—for example, how many pieces did you assemble during an eight-hour shift? Or how many welds did you accomplish? Certain jobs and departments—accounting, baking, and construction come to mind—just cannot be run openly like this. But we can make these environments better places to work by giving employees the incentive to come forward with money-saving and money-making ideas—ideas that won't interfere with productivity.

Results-only collaborative environments can actually be destructive to people who lack the discipline to self-manage their time or those who are incapable of taking responsibility for their work. People like this should stay in environments where management is hanging over their shoulder, where all they have to do is follow rules and finish a task. For people like this, working alone and taking responsibility for their own time management is not something they can ever get used to. It is too loose for their work ethic. They need (and want) to be managed.

To have consistent breakthroughs, intense creativity, and innovation, however, letting people manage their own time and output is the key to success.

Innovative, groundbreaking ideas that created entire industries came from the icons of business when they were young and didn't follow the old business management manuals of their forefathers. Lucky for us they intuitively created work environments where people were allowed to be driven by results and a larger vision—a vision bigger than themselves. These types of leaders created work environments where they could tap into the dynamism of others. They made sure they didn't listen to what was done in the past but created something brand new. Steve Jobs is such a leader. His team invented the Macintosh back in the eighties yet still maintains a dynamic creative environment to this day. Nicholas Negroponte became known for shaking up the status quo of technology by giving his students an environment in which to play—and he still does so to this day. Ideas can come from any camp as long as the environment supports this. In fact, a dynamic leader encourages disruptive innovation from everywhere, spots it, and takes it to another level, adding the ability to repeat the creative process and thereby nurture continual discovery.

Environments like this become incredibly dynamic—and disruptive—when we stop separating ourselves into Boomers versus Generation Y and instead invent an environment that radically supports multigenerational contribution and engagement: "Let's add the strength of both generations to come up with something completely different."

Countries like Japan are best known for taking existing products from around the world and making them more efficient and smaller. Now the newer emerging economies are shaking things up, even in industrialized, established nations like Japan and Australia. Why?

Future innovations are coming from young college students from all over the world, who are mentally so hungry that they can't help but pull the lid off their computers and game stations, reprogramming software languages while accidentally developing the next killer app. They have no set rules in their heads as to how things should be. The impatience of youth

will be driving the next big-business sectors of the coming quarter century, especially when it comes to technological innovations that can reinvent how and where we work.

Traditionally this is why the majority of life-changing appliances, inventions, and medical breakthroughs have come from the United States. Liberty, and the ability to make money from our creativity, gives us the incentive to break the mold and invent stuff, but more important, to prove ourselves. And now that our system has spread to the rest of the world, there is no telling where the next big ideas will come from.

Never underestimate the driving ambition that the young have in a country like the U.S. that rewards even the little guy for having a brilliant idea. And a greater fact is that almost all of the nation's progress and our movement toward a vastly increased standard of living didn't begin to unfold until after 1776. There is something to be said for a system of liberty, sovereignty, and individualism that supports entrepreneurs with new ideas.

This powerful shift of innovation is now matriculating all over the world. Japan, India, and China are seeing younger and younger entrepreneurs every day. The impatience of youth and the willingness to make their way in the world of business is about to change thousand-year-old paradigms. Today's leadership is about spotting the "Aha!" idea.

Many of you may not want to admit it, but if you don't adapt new management skills, you will be working for a much younger boss. And that future will be very soon. Imagine taking orders from a thirty-five-year-old who rides his skateboard to work and wears $200 Diesel jeans and expects you to chat with him at midnight on Saturday as he's about to go clubbing with his wife. Financial power has shifted to include today's youth.

It's time to collapse that organizational chart and tap into the new ideas of a multigenerational workforce that is just waiting to contribute to a company that appreciates their input.

Micromanaging into the Ground

To manage a company is one thing. To integrate into and influence its culture is another. Respecting the group dynamic goes a long way toward motivating and inspiring a workforce.

I worked for many years in various areas of the design business, from advertising to branding, from corporate events to slide production. It is labor intensive, and to accomplish anything requires designers and creative types with a commando style of getting the work done on each project. But over the years I noticed that the styles of management that worked best seemed to respect the culture, their workforce, the talent, and the environment. Those that did not went out of business.

No one needs to be pushed or prodded to get their work done; college-educated self-starters work just fine without someone standing over their shoulder. Yet I noticed something interesting: When the distance between upper management and the rest of the company was greatest, management took longer to discover internal and external problems. This gap has to shrink for leadership to be successful in the twenty-first century. How can you see the internal workings of your company if you don't get closer?

Here's a case in point: One of the first jobs I had in New York City was at a slide production house. The main product was slides for small corporate presentations (this was *way* before PowerPoint). The new owner, Mr. G (not his real name), had bought the business lock, stock, and barrel. As a former executive with Otis Elevator, he felt it was high time some corporate structure was brought to the design field. Somehow he assumed that the world of production artists and designers was not as structured as the corporate world he came from. (Perhaps the plastic Mr. Potato Head on the twenty-inch monitor convinced him of this.)

Mr. G would walk around the office twice a day like the commander of a ship, wearing his Otis Elevator tie clip to remind us all where he came from and how powerful he used to be. Nevertheless, his twice-daily jaunts were always at the slowest times of production but at the peak time for sales calls. Work would slow down as his Australian accent pierced the office and he forced everyone to listen to his tales from the "real" corporate world. His opinion was forged by what he saw from us when on these walks. To him, we weren't working very hard. And we weren't; we were forced to stop what we were doing and listen to him!

Since he never integrated himself into the company culture, he never found out that every 8:00 AM shift change was filled with mounds of paper work, double tracking, and a check list that only the CIA could have invented, all for the sole purpose of keeping track of billings. Between 8:00 AM and 9:00 AM chaos reigned as messengers arrived to whisk the slides to their destinations. This was before the Macintosh become a household name and desktop publishing became the hot buzzword of the eighties. Back then slides were produced on a Genigraphics computer; run through a programmed slide camera; and processed through an E6 slide-processing machine, a twenty-five-foot-long roller transport automated developing machine, filled and maintained with vat after vat of chemicals. Exposed film was fed manually to a feeder in a separate, attached darkroom. Once processing was finished, the film was cut and mounted into glass and plastic Wess Mounts during the night shift, then rushed to most clients' desks by 9:30 AM.

Where was Mr. G during all this chaos? In his office with the door closed, only fifty feet away from the production station. I guess he was strategizing his big walk. His reality was out of touch with what was really going on. We were busy—busy making corporate America look good.

The second time everything heated up was at around 4:00 PM, when production prepared to pass the day-shift work to the night-shift personnel. Paperwork was meticulously checked and discussed with each designer. Each color had a number that was checked, each typeface was checked, and, of course, we all pored over a set of full-color comps. It was all designed, programmed, photographed, and processed for the following day. Detail was what made this chaos run as smoothly as a well-oiled machine. Nothing could be left to chance. It was intense, high-pressure, deadline-driven work. How someone could see this as playing around is beyond me.

As the year went on, Mr. G added a policy requiring many, many daily memos. But with twelve day-shift employees in a 3,000-square-foot loft space, it was really not necessary to pass a memo to the person sitting next to you. It was like having to pass a note from the commander of a submarine to his navigator before he could actually say the words—a complete waste of time. But that's what Mr. G wanted, and to keep our jobs, we complied.

What Mr. G never understood was that we were making slides for one small meeting after another, when the business of meetings was in fact a multibillion-dollar industry. Companies like Caribiner, MJM, and Weiss Watson were building full-scale meetings, with staging and lighting and giant sets as well as training, breakout rooms, and keynote speakers. The average cost for *one* of these large-scale annual meetings was around $2 million. In comparison, slide production, the physical designing and production of slide film, was a tiny component of the industry.

Mr. G began to wonder why his company was not profitable, and how it was that all these other companies were making so much money. But because he did not respect his staff, no one was willing to help him make the leap from single-slide production to full-scale meetings. And people did *try* to help him for a time . . . but he was always treating his staff like peons—exercising his passive-aggressive behavior whenever the mood struck him. There were plenty on staff who had worked for the big production companies and knew how to handle large-scale meetings. His top salespeople and producers attempted to bring bigger clients through the door, but even when these bigger opportunities came Mr. G's way, he would lose them. Unable to trust his key people and incapable of knowing how to talk with potential clients about a larger engagement, he drove his company into the ground.

People began to show signs of insubordination, simply out of frustration. Many decided to moonlight at bigger production houses. Why bother working with someone when you know they don't appreciate your contribution?

In response, Mr. G began to micromanage his company into the ground even more. In a last-ditch effort to shake things up, he fired his top salespeople. Instead of paying for innovation, he became obsessed with cutting costs and instituting more bureaucracy and fear. To him, the design field was exactly like the elevator business—black and white, up and down, obey my commands or else. He treated creative production like a factory.

Tightening costs seemed logical. But in an industry where the best creative people can command higher fees, cutting your most talented designers becomes a formula for disaster. Furthermore, by demanding memo after memo, Mr. G was actually putting up walls between departments that needed their communication to flow. Imagine that: He was enforcing bottlenecks.

The company went under less than a year after I left. The employees were happy about it. If only Mr. G had integrated his management style into the organization instead of dictating it! He could have easily let his key people take the lead and win the larger pieces of business, but he couldn't see the forest for the trees. He just couldn't let go enough or trust anyone. Everything in his world required that all eyes, accolades, and rewards go to Mr. G.

I moved on and started working for some of the biggest companies in the world, producing their multimillion-dollar meetings while Mr. G couldn't figure out how to get his clients to order more than fifty slides at a time. It didn't take people very long to figure out that Mr. G was not an effective leader, and for leadership to work in any organization, it has to be admired. Since Mr. G was not listening to the marketplace or his key people, he sabotaged himself.

**People don't leave bad companies;
they leave bad management.**

Corporations today need a team builder more than a leader. It's your culture. Learn to understand it. Respect it. Nurture it. And most of all, reward the movers and shakers. Listen to their ideas. Remember, talented people *choose* to give you their best, but only if they feel you are worthy. By giving them the right environment and the acknowledgement, you will retain the people that make your company great. After all, you don't make the products or come up with the ideas that destroy the competition—they do. Your job is to be the best shepherd possible of ideas and implementation.

And here is the saddest part to end my story about Mr. G: Everyone tried to help him every single day. Instead of integrating the new ideas from his staff into his years of experience, he ignored our contribution and expertise. He was so pumped up with his own self-importance that he failed to listen and learn. The industry was changing, and his staff knew it. The industry was giving warning signs, but his arrogance and fear got in the way. He projected his fear onto his staff, then micromanaged us into the ground. Years later he was astounded and confused to hear of my successes. Other people's potential was simply not on his radar. Do me a favor: Don't be like Mr. G. Learn how your products are made. What separates you from the competition? Is it your people? Go to the front lines and help one day; see what production is really like. Instead of creating bottlenecks, get rid of them. And instead of giving in to hubris, listen to the people who are producing your products. I am sure they have a few ideas on how to make things better.

Despite your seasonality and college education, how open to new ideas are you? Be honest. It could make all the difference.

Shaking the Beehive

As the Japanese businessmen wrapped up their visit to our K2 New York City offices, I could feel from them a sort of growing fascination with my youthful appearance. It had been building throughout our tour, though I wasn't completely sure if I was correct in my assumption until their last question: "How old are you?" I was a little embarrassed, because the tone of the question seemed to suggest that my baby face was more than a point of curiosity, it was a point of contention. I had been interviewed for newspapers and appeared on television all over the world—Japan, France, Germany, Finland—and even when asked about it, age had never been a big deal. As a matter of fact, most were impressed. Why was this an issue to the Japanese group? When I explained that I was in my midthirties (at the time), I thought nothing of my answer.

Once Yumi finished translating my answer, a loud murmur went through the crowd. This one thing sent them into some sort of frenzy. Heads were shaking; language was going back and forth faster than I could comprehend. It wasn't anger but shocked amazement.

"What?" I said, more than a little curious. "Why are they so excited?" I was scared for moment. What had I said that seemed to send them into a frenzy?

Yumi explained, "In Japan, no one is allowed to be an executive until they are in their fifties. To them, you are an anomaly."

And there it was—a strict paradigm distinction that seemed to separate East from West. I had heard that many Japanese firms went to Silicon Valley on the West Coast to analyze why the majority of inventions that have revolutionized the entire world came from America, but here I was experiencing that divide on the East Coast in Silicon Alley. A strict bee-hive social structure was running smack-dab into American individualism and entrepreneurship.

Surprisingly, this collision continues today. Watching the head of Toyota, Akio Toyoda, carry the weight of the company on his shoulders is very refreshing and noble in light of today's hubristic C-suites, but now his job is about regaining his customers' trust. That can be done only by working with the entire organization to control quality.

Your talent pool isn't about age anymore or years on the job; it's about consistently creating new ideas and implementing them. While we focus on bandwidth, the latest e-readers, and remote access, remember, it's your people who come up with those ideas. Give them the support, the free-dom, and the guidance to come up with those great ideas every day.

Future Shock

always loved the monthly Movie Fridays at Harding Elementary. The lights would dim to the familiar purring sound of a sixteen-millimeter movie projector. The only problem with Movie Fridays was that we usually saw the same movies over and over. We saw *The Red Balloon*, a French film, five times in one year. But this Friday was very different. My teacher, Ms. Rhodes, fed the film's leader through the projector's grooved pathways, locking each brass sprocket into place. Dieter and Frank, my two best friends, were sitting next to me. As the projector increased its speed and the lights dimmed, the familiar rhythmic pulse began, eventually to become ambient noise to the film's picture and narration. We sat on the edge of our seats hoping it was anything but *Le Balloon Rouge*.

Much to our joy, it was a brand-new film!

The movie started out innocently enough: a couple walking toward the camera, their features shadowed against the trees of a park. Strange jazz music caught our attention as well. The loving couple approaching us was holding hands.

As Orson Wells's narration boomed, onscreen the sunlight revealed to our surprise that the loving couple were robots. Dieter, Frank, and I collectively gasped: "Cool!" Personally, I had no idea that the film I was about to watch would stay in my thoughts for the next thirty years: *Future Shock*.

Based on the book by Alvin Toffler, the film painted a bleak future. Technology would inundate us with its demands, and eventually the world would speed up to such a pace that we would be unable to cope. Humanity would not be ready for the stress and speed that a new world like this would bring.

The world would be divided into two groups: the older generations, untrained and incapable of keeping up with the technological advances taking place, and the younger generations born within the data-immersed, disposable society that technology had brought, who were oblivious and resentful of the older generation and their seemingly slow pace. Sound familiar?

Well, unless you've been in a coma for the past thirty years, you realize that we are indeed living in a science fiction world. Wall Street wunderkinds walk with Borg-like efficiency, talking into their Bluetooth earpiece to an investor three continents away. They are a ubiquitous part of the Canyon—that short, five-block strip of road called Broad Street, starting at the corner of Wall Street and the New York Stock Exchange and heading south toward Water Street and the Staten Island Ferry. It's where concrete-and-steel skyscrapers stand too close together and block out the sun. Hence the nickname "the Canyon." To the uninitiated, these fresh-faced, headset-addicted brokers are talking into thin air like some crazy person. To the initiated, deals are no longer confined to a building; now you can make deals as long as your phone has a decent signal and access to a network.

In a world where wars now have more cameras than a rock concert and you can see your house on Google Earth, logic must be suspended in order to cross the chasm of disruption taking place in businesses everywhere. The business practices that made sense for you over the past century may not apply any longer to your industry or the people with whom you work.

Any street corner, from Manhattan to L.A., reveals a stream of Podsters, grups, bloggers, phonecam paparazzi, Twitter-attis, and caffeine addicts piggybacking onto Wi-Fi networks in trendy cafés and bookstores. Everyone seems to be a "writer" these days. It appears as if no one actually works.

Free open-source websites allow bloggers to post from anywhere, or better yet, allow you and a gaggle of friends to Wiki a big project. On top of all this you're probably starting to wonder if it's time to get a Mac, possibly swayed by an amusing Mac vs. PC commercial or two.

One thing I can say for sure—the corporation as we've known it for the past hundred years is dead.

Many executives I coach are the cream of the crop. They went to the right college, worked their way up the corporate ladder, and followed the rules. They built their businesses with a textbook sense of logic and intelligence. And yet they are still failing. Confused, they beg for an answer to the question, what is really going on?

What they are finding out is that there is no one single way to do business anymore, even within the same sector. A very successful model for one company would guarantee failure at another, and models must work every time to be considered usable. This scares most leaders, because while trying to figure out a new model, their bottom line keeps shrinking.

This search for new methodologies isn't new, but it will require us to awaken to something that has been missing from business for a long time: input from everyone in the organization. For a hundred years, the Industrial Age model of hierarchy—thinkers at the top, employees at the bottom—worked for several reasons. First, workers were trained to do one task at a time. Forget multitasking; there was no room for it if assembly lines were to run efficiently. As nation after nation declared its independence from repressive monarchies, a newly growing global middle class started demanding American-made goods en masse. For the first time in recorded history, commoners could afford stuff. As a society, we went from independent craftsmen to becoming what the Industrial Age of mass production needed: employees. *Output*, not *thinking*, was paramount to profitability. Instead of a handful of products being made each month, machinery was applied to increase output to thousands of products per week.

In other words, pioneering business leaders like Henry Ford felt they needed to dumb their workers down. Just do one task along the line; someone else picks up the next task and the next. An assumption began to grow—that low-level employees were incapable of innovation and needed to just focus on one task to keep the line running smoothly. Strategizing and business analysis were for the executive team to worry about. And hierarchy was created. Ironically, Ford let his best automotive scientists and engineers have the freedom to create—but *separate* from the rest of the company. The top of the organization was where ideas started; the bottom rung was for obedient workers.

Today the technological and cultural pendulum has swung the other way. We have to work with the smartest, most creative people, not the most malleable. The landscape has become so complex, most executives I speak with have no idea how to navigate through the briar patch ahead of them. It isn't so much that economically we are in tough times—boom and bust cycles are a natural part of doing business—it is that *everything* has changed. Technology has given small companies the ability to compete with larger ones. Everyone has easy access to other countries and competitive pricing, while people who were born after 1985 simply have a different paradigm in their heads than Baby Boomers do. This new paradigm shows in the way these young people attack the business world: open and involved in the global marketplace they've been raised within. But most business leaders are not of this new generation; they wait for Gen Yers to change when in fact, they can't. They are products of the Information Age.

As a Boomer you may not like my message, but you will have to admit, it is relevant. Especially in a world where people can make a few million with the right website and the right marketing, while age discrimination is the giant elephant in the room that no one is talking about. It's time to learn what knowledge base and work habits Gen Yers carry, to learn from them and adapt.

Because of all this disruption, businesses today will require constant diligence for new ideas, new perspectives, new strategies, new opportunities, and new approaches to thinking, operating, and winning. One piece of technology can decimate an entire sector. Being attached to business models of the past will cause you to go out of business. Staying flexible to new ideas, new technologies, and even hybrids of the past, present, and future will keep your company alive. Time to act like a commando.

The major reason that this is important is this: A huge chunk of the economy has simply moved to the World Wide Web, unavailable and invisible to the naked eye, unless you turn on your computer. On top of this migration, technology has been consistently applied to the factory floor over the years, resulting in plummeting manufacturing costs. Modular installations at the factory floor are more efficient and have made it cheaper to buy things brand new than to have them repaired. Remember when a TV repairman would come to your house? Today it is more affordable to buy a brand new television than to even consider the simplest repair job.

The phoenix that will be rising from the ashes will be a more flexible, dynamic, and talent-rich organization than the companies of our forefathers—and with it, a new type of leader will be needed as well. Leaders who pay attention to the marketplace rather than dig in their heels and ignore what is happening around them. Leaders who look to the people they have surrounded themselves with—and learn. Leaders who understand that it is not business as usual; a small piece of new technology can aid or destroy a company overnight.

Those who do not adapt will experience what Alvin Toffler warned of—an anxiety so climactic, so terminal, it can feel like slamming into a wall: "Man has a limited biological capacity for change. When this capacity is overwhelmed, the capacity is in future shock."

Many believe they have adult attention deficit disorder when in fact, they are simply overwhelmed.

A Farewell to Kings

The old-fashioned idea that your boss is the smartest person in the room has shifted. The smartest businessperson in the room is most likely your graphic designer. Shocked by that statement? Well, you shouldn't be, because today's graphic designers when working to develop a website need to analyze the end user's needs, habits, and affluence. Their job has shifted to include what a customer's experience should be, how this fits into the chaotic list of choices already swirling in that customer's head, and how to separate your brand from the pack. Then they have to actually build the website based on the accumulated user data: code it, design the graphics, and then test it during an alpha stage to see if it generates revenue and the kind of experience that was planned.

What happened to choosing beautiful typefaces and colors? The answer is, the graphic design business has evolved to include marketing, information architecture, training, and usability studies. And guess what other jobs have evolved as well? Those of your multimedia experts, actuaries, software developers, communications staff, even your administrative assistant.

These professionals have been trained at a higher level than in the past, and they refuse to bow to leadership that wants worship of hierarchy. Nor will they flinch because you command them to do so. Believe it or not, they see themselves as equal to you despite your seasonality and your executive position. ("Seasonality," by the way, is polite Wall Street slang for anyone who has earned his/her wealth through years of experience and has the gray hair to show it.) When executives cling to the old ideology of a corporate organizational chart, this only gives today's younger workforce an incentive to quit. Just give them time.

~~~

**The idea of the CEO as messiah has shifted.
Leadership today is about sharing ideas and
responsibility.**

There has been a backlash against the idea that a CEO is superhuman. The recurring boom and bust cycles have created an air of distrust, especially when it is the people on the front lines who make the products, who make the company profitable, who give the CEO his/her salary.

The entire office hierarchy has indeed shifted at the same time. Baby Boomers to a great extent based their entire careers on learning and developing their own methods and then keeping them to themselves. Back in the Industrial Age, knowledge hoarding was the only way to get ahead in your career. It worked because you could impress your boss and your peers and rise to the executive committee by having your own methodologies. It was easy to become a hero. All you had to do was implement a few ideas along the assembly line and you made the company profitable.

New leadership is not about hoarding ideas; it's about sharing them. (But note that it isn't about management by committee, either. Waiting for each and every person to have their say before a project gets out the door only slows things down.) This new way of doing business requires something that Industrial Age alpha managers disdain: being involved with and evaluated by the people you are leading.

The college degree an information-hoarding Boomer earned twenty-five years ago is obsolete, given that 75 percent of the things you have to learn today didn't exist back then. To lead you have to stay up to date. In order to keep pace with change, remember:

~~~

**Knowledge hoarding is out.
Knowledge sharing is in.**

Today's leaders are an integral part of companies' successes and not a separate anomaly looming at the edges of day-to-day production. For leadership to work these days requires leaders to be more approachable, more flexible, stronger decision makers who show respect for every member's contribution to the organization. Even the weirdest member of your group is now a vital contributor. Decision making must include input from the bottom contributors for implementation to be sound. After all, do you even know how your products are made? Seriously! How much time is involved to build it? Why do software coders take so long, while hardware is always on time? How about visiting that one store out of 3,600 that is the leading producer in a seemingly shrinking economy? What makes that store tick? What's their magic? If you haven't spent time at the bottom, it is just a bunch of numbers on a page . . . and nothing more than an educated guess. Real-time, up-front, in-the-customer's-face feedback may be the only way to get an answer.

Skills and knowledge must be constantly updated, and what better way than knowledge sharing? It will also make you think twice about just looking at a resume when choosing your people or just looking at a spreadsheet. What is really going on? We must be on constant alert for the next big thing. Assumptions do not work. Never have, never will.

Here's an example of what can happen if you neglect to share, ask questions, and get some real feedback. Two scientists who happen to be friends of mine showed me a manuscript they had been working on for five hard years. I didn't say a word as they explained their breakthrough to me. Since both of them are well-respected chemistry professors at a local college in New York City, their ideas were backed up with PhD research and field-tested. But they had spent years keeping their big idea hush-hush.

Slowly we continued the discussion as I walked with them to Barnes & Noble. I listened intently, but I didn't have the heart to burst their bubble, so I just brought them to an *entire section* of published books that were already talking about their "unique" breakthrough. Their shocked looks said it all—their ideas weren't that unique. What they assumed was a proprietary idea had already been beaten to death by dozens of other authors over the years. They hadn't realized that working in a closed world had been dangerous to their research. They had hoarded their supersecret knowledge, assuming it was so unique as to be worth millions. These two scientists had to abandon everything they had worked on for a half a decade for the book project. If only they had discussed their ideas and researched the industry outside of academia, they might have discovered their faux pas in time and changed direction slightly.

Shaman or Sherpa?

Like an ostrich that wakes up to find its head in the sand, today's executives must realize they can no longer assume their ideas are unique or even sufficient to take the company to another level. What you think is a unique idea may be a business norm in another country. And Generation Y knows this!

Knowledge sharing, on the other hand, keeps everyone within the team up to date and ready to attack the new frontier. Since young people have this type of "seek out all knowledge all the time" mentality, you will need to start listening to their input. Their accumulated knowledge base will make sure you don't waste your time reinventing the wheel. After all, Gen Y's perspective is unique, and many are working with technology that didn't exist ten years ago. With that in mind, the first step to new leadership on your part is to realize you have more to learn each day. As Alvin Toffler wrote in *Future Shock*, "The illiterate of the twenty-first century will not be those that cannot read and write, but those who cannot learn, unlearn, and relearn."

Millions of jobs have been phased out over the past ten years because they are no longer relevant. Key positions have become extinct, relics of the twentieth century, because the technology and methodologies they supported no longer exist. At the same time, there is a misalignment between those losing their jobs and the newly created jobs. This misalignment between jobs lost and jobs created exists because the skill sets don't line up. This is leaving millions of unemployed workers wondering what to do next, unaware that all they need is training to fill key positions in high-growth sectors like Green jobs or robotic repair.

Any sharp entrepreneur can see that there is a golden opportunity to build a training company to reposition the unemployed for the demands of a high tech job. This type of job training can't be found in college. It's just a matter of how the reeducation process gets actualized.

Being able to learn faster is the key to success in the twenty-first century. This means you must have not only the capacity to pick things up quickly but also the openness to let go of old methodologies while embracing new ones. Knowledge sharing works well when confronted with speed learning to learn, unlearn, and relearn in record time. Immersive learning has become the apprenticeship of the twenty-first century, and information-driven entrepreneurs—infopreneurs—are making a killing teaching new methods of learning. Citizens of the Information Age must be dedicated to being lifelong learners.

At first, knowledge sharing can seem counterintuitive. It's a matter of shifting from "me" language to "team" language. But if you make the switch, you will find greater innovation and productivity. And remember, you will only be as strong as your weakest link—the person who isn't receiving knowledge or isn't sharing their knowledge base.

What is the result of closing the distance between knowledge hoarders and leadership? With a flatter hierarchy changes can be implemented quicker than in an organization where the leadership is sitting in an ivory tower, disconnected from the front lines. By making yourself approachable and open to new ideas, you will get the inside scoop on internal innovation as well as problem solving. By giving power to the people on the front lines, you're assured that quality is managed *internally at the source*. Approachability assures that new ideas get funneled to the proper managers . . . and *implemented*.

In organizations where there is strict hierarchy and boundaries, management becomes the last to know when things go wrong—and the last to know they are about to go out of business. Innovative ideas are never brought forward in these types of organizations because no one is inspired to do so. Why bother? Silos begin to form, and knowledge hoarding begins to create redundancy. *This is wasting money.*

So do yourself a big favor—close the gap between upper management and work implementers, get rid of bottlenecks, redistribute decision making, and create an open door policy.

The hardest thing to face is that the weak link just might be you, the Industrial Age leader, still barking orders at your staff.

How do you start to manage diverse talents and knowledge in a multigenerational team? Management throughout the years assumed that lower-level employees were just task-driven and not capable of any real innovation. But today's workforce is far sharper. Technology has required a much smarter workforce at all levels. Think about how many software applications you have had to learn to use, along with system diagnostic knowledge. Knowledge workers have had to upgrade in order to be employable. So why not start an open door policy and invite people to bring their ideas to you personally? Instead of being the last to know, now you can be the leader who is in the know.

Today's young workers act more like entrepreneurs and expect to be treated as such. They see themselves as a business partner–slash-consultant who is directly affecting your bottom line. They want to be rewarded, and they know they are the ones making you look good. You may not want to hear this, but it's the truth. They also view leaders who don't contribute to the bottom line as a bloated waste of time. This requires leaders of tomorrow to be more dynamic, personable, and involved.

In this new paradigm, everyone gets to share the leadership role throughout the day and management is just the guide, a Sherpa on this sacred journey. Of course, someone has to make the final decision, but the new workforce expects to be included in the decision-making process. They are confident, knowledgeable self-starters, and if you listen to their contributions with the same respect you would give a thirty-year business veteran, you may be shocked to find that their ideas could revolutionize your business and even your industry.

On the other side of the coin, if you're a member of Gen Y, you need to focus on deadlines and redefine what communication actually is. Cherry-picking the best projects has to be balanced with the basics of business and actually getting some work done. We can't all be working on the next big breakthrough—someone will have to actually do the task-driven stuff no one wants to do—you know, the *real* work.

Texting, emailing, and instant messaging are ways of speeding up knowledge sharing while eliminating the face-to-face meeting inertia. This definitely helps eliminate stopping and starting on a deadline. It's just that now, technology can be used to speed up production, with simple questions being answered over the network in a five-minute window instead of hours of meetings.

Understand, though, that your responsibility doesn't end just because you click the SEND button. Using technology to touch base or get answers over a network is only a small part of the communication paradigm. The dynamics of interpersonal, interoffice communication will still require face time. What needs to be managed now is when an actual meeting is necessary and for what purpose. And who best to learn this from? Boomers.

For some strange reason there tend to be multiple training sessions to get Baby Boomers on board with how to handle Generation Y. Yet no one is training Gen Y on how to work with Boomers.

This is part of a serious communication gap in most organizations. As Boomers retire, their legacy of knowledge and methodologies isn't getting passed as it once would have. In the past, such generational gaps were naturally filled in, thanks to similar shared experiences. Everyone had similar skill sets and common experiences to eventually bridge the gap. But generations born after 1985 have a technological skill set that no other previous generation has, as well as a completely different ideology for how to live life. And this is causing Gen Y to look at Baby Boomers with mild disdain—as if Boomers are dinosaurs, simply to be tolerated. Hence the failure of generational knowledge to be transmitted as it used to be.

To counter this attitude, and to encourage more openness on the part of Gen Yers, you as a Liquid Leader must stress the knowledge base that Boomers bring to the table. Remind everyone that the technology we are using today was invented by Baby Boomers and that soon the younger workforce will be on their own without a compass. We need to really take the time to bridge that knowledge gap, or otherwise we will be living in a modern technological version of *The Lord of the Flies*.

Change Is the Only Constant

If you are scared by all this, you should be. Change is here. But you should also be excited. For the first time in history the workforce is brimming with incredibly talented self-starters more than comfortable working in a global marketplace and eager to prove themselves.

How does one stay open and handle the transition that is taking place? Look back at history: What would have made life more palatable for the farmer as his son went off to join the Industrial Revolution, leaving the farm for the factory? What would have prepared the horse-drawn carriage manufacturer for the explosion of that newfangled device called the "automobile"? Companies like Studebaker went from making horse-drawn wagons to making cars—and were damn good at it for a while, because they watched for trends and adapted accordingly.

Now look at what big companies like IBM are doing, sinking serious money into 3D online virtual worlds. Or how about the US military? They are sinking big money into Serious Gaming technology. Meanwhile, NASA is looking at building robots with artificial intelligence for missions beyond our galaxy. Think they are adapting, or wasting their money?

Because change is happening so rapidly, the world that our grandchildren will soon inherit will not look at all like the world in which we've grown up. The last 235 years of explosive advancement will look juvenile compared to the hypergrowth about to take place. To be in line with it and capable of seeing it requires a new set of skills. Being closed and incapable of being on top of the changes will only leave you struggling back in the Industrial Age. Challenge everyone to reinvent a completely new business model for you to evolve into. Build it, create it, and be the leader in your category. Hell, get a team involved whose sole mission is to destroy your current business model in favor of a technology-driven global powerhouse that runs lean and mean! Get as many young people on that team as you can. Why? Because they aren't bogged down by the traditional thought process. They also have a natural propensity for searching out new applications to make their work easier (besides, they are using technology online right now that you aren't even aware exists).

Change is the constant overall arc that will define the twenty-first century. Once you know that and expect it, will you continue to sit back on your laurels, or will you get ready to change your entire organization knowing full well that your current business model is being threatened by technology?

As the digital revolution continues to grow, will you be ready to make the leap, or will you stubbornly cling to old business models with a "wait and see" attitude?

***

Gather your best and brightest on a Friday afternoon, bring in the pizza and beer, and roll up those sleeves. Talk with them about how to catch the competition with their pants down.

To shake up their status quo, Netflix announced a competition with a $1 million reward promised to any team that could improve their movie recommendation service. Is it that Netflix is too close to their internal workings to come up with their own ideas? Or is it something bigger?

Cinematch was Netflix's movie recommendations engine. For years, it did an efficient job of matching movies with users' past choices and historical favorites. Then, suddenly, it seemed to plateau. So Reed Hastings, Netflix's founder, chairman, and CEO, turned to the public for fresh ideas—and upped the competition by offering a million bucks. Almost overnight six hundred teams, totaling one thousand people from thirty-one different countries, registered to participate. The campaign has been so successful, reaping thousands of revenue-generating ideas for immediate use, that Netflix held another contest immediately after. These new ideas will make a company like Netflix cutting-edge and keep them solidly entrenched in the future of content on demand.

So how are you going to take your company from a Model T to a space shuttle? Open up your organization to new ideas. And as you conduct these brainstorming sessions, pay close attention to happy accidents that just might change your industry.

Take a look at the most explosive technology-driven companies over the past thirty years, the ones that made larger, established companies rethink their business model: Microsoft, Apple Computer, Yahoo,

Google, Netscape, Facebook, MySpace, Dell, Electronic Arts, Twitter, etc. All of them were started by twentysomethings frustrated that their ideas were being ignored in favor of the status quo, by old farts in suits who wouldn't listen. These upstarts felt their big ideas were better than anything currently in use. They decided to do something about it, and they turned those ideas into billion-dollar companies.

If you don't start listening to the youth in your company, you will miss the next big idea that is right under your nose. This young generation has been trained as children—through video games, karate classes, lacrosse, and micromanaged scheduling—to see risk taking as normal.

How do micromanagement and karate classes as children translate into risk taking as adults? Simply put, today's middle manager had a Day Runner–style organizational schedule as a youth and thus an enriched lifestyle. They were raised without winners and losers. If they did fail, their parents didn't acknowledge it. Because of this they see life as bold and adventuresome, filled with one experience after another—a dynamic world to be embraced and to leap into, not one spent sitting in a cubicle all day, typing. Video games taught them to take risks and not worry about learning each part of the game; you'll learn that as you go forward. In other words, Gen Y has been raised on taking action before they have the knowledge. (This is the opposite of Boomers.) This has made them ambitious adults not bogged down by status quo thinking or so-called proper behavior. These young people are all looking to invent the million-dollar idea that will allow them to retire before they get old, like, before *forty*, dude. It is impossible for a Millennial to sit still for too long.

So I ask, are you listening to the youth of today? The ones on the front lines who are constantly looking for new software to automate their jobs and your business? You might want to start asking them what they have discovered—and listen to the answer.

Looking for the Next Big Idea

The hardest part for anyone is trying to stay open to new and fresh ideas. I'll be honest: The first time I saw the Internet, I was cynical. *What is the big deal? How do you make money on this thing?* I wondered. I had friends who were already talking to people all over the world via ham radio. Boring. But then the dot-com boom happened, and everybody wanted a website. It just took off, and I had to eat crow. Either I was right and it was a waste of time, or it was me who didn't get it. No one was explaining it to me.

If someone had explained to me that the World Wide Web was a media channel, a publishing site, a storefront, a communications tool, a web log, and a social network all rolled into one, that had low operational costs and had far greater reach and influence than television, then I might not have been so cynical.

So take a page from my failures, and listen to your younger tech experts. Not only because they have the potential to start their own company and compete directly with you (many of my former employees have done just that), but also because the horrifying truth is that someday soon *you* may have to work for *them*. Many companies are reporting a shift in team management, with twentysomethings leading a Baby Boomer team. It is happening now.

Our entire Industrial Age model will be reworked as we begin to understand that it doesn't apply anymore to the way we do business in the Information Age. From small mom-and-pop stores to large hundred-year-old multinationals, technology has leveled the playing field. Rethinking and retooling your core business may be your only strategy.

I predict a surge in businesses that continuously create new online businesses, sell them off, and reinvent another and another, all according to the marketplace and its needs—idea factories specializing in creating products for a new Internet marketplace. This disruption of traditional business models is a normal part of the twenty-first century, and companies like Google, Atlassian, and Oracle push the boundaries by building an idea incubation farm within their company culture. All they do is give their people the freedom to create something amazing.

Try being adaptable to new ideas, flexible to emerging models and those already in existence, or try creating an entirely new model. After all, what do you have to lose? Oh yeah, your Industrial Age business model and its limitations.

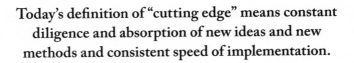

Today's definition of "cutting edge" means constant diligence and absorption of new ideas and new methods and consistent speed of implementation.

We can no longer afford to believe that our knowledge accumulation ends once we get a college degree. The idea of coasting once you hit forty is over, as today's graduates hit the ground hungry and eager to prove their worth. And they have new tools at their disposal that we Boomers barely even understand how to use!

The depth of knowledge that your team brings to the table is what determines success these days. The dirty little secret of all this is that no one can fool you by sitting on their past accomplishments, nor can they attempt to razzle-dazzle you with old ideas. Someone with a PhD from twenty years ago may not necessarily be the smartest person in the room. The only way to stay ahead is to commit to a lifetime of learning and challenging our own interpersonal status quo. Skills and knowledge must be constantly updated for everyone's career survival.

Leaders will need to be open to the newness of technology, leverage the fresh perspective that Gen X and Gen Y bring to the table, and spot the "Aha!" moment when they realize how that technology can be used to create a new business paradigm.

You want to be the wise sage who can spot the future in a five-minute, badly presented PowerPoint presentation. To do that requires someone who is open to new ideas and willing to ask a lot of questions that might make you look stupid. But you can laugh all the way to the bank. Remember, many billion-dollar ideas have been scribbled on cocktail napkins by college dropouts.

The Rise of the Transient Workforce

This is the story of how K2 was called upon to do the first live event on the Internet—the IBM Deep Blue vs. Gary Kasparov Chess Challenge—and of what this experience taught us about the value of transient workers in a new era.

Doing an event of this magnitude on the Internet meant that we had to build a website with dynamic interaction and, more important, to be the support channel for a live, real-world event . . . like covering a party, a rock concert, or an event live. This was also a time when the World Wide Web had just stepped out of the static page era and into a more dynamic experience with QuickTime and JavaScript. All this interactivity and video was so brand new at the time and a hallmark of the Web 1.0 dot-com boom.

Known for his crazy antics, cell phone usage, stall tactics, and ability to play multiple opponents in a single match (and beat them all), Garry Kasparov was the eccentric Russian chess master for a new generation. IBM asked Mr. Kasparov to play against their supercomputer, Deep Blue, over several days of intense chess. The competition was very high-profile, very lucrative, and very challenging.

The first thing K2 did was hire the best programmers possible from Russia. Why? Well, chess to a Russian is like baseball is to an American. Our event had to be accurate, and we needed people who knew chess like the back of their hand. If Garry started off with the French Defense, every Russian in the room would smirk and look at each other with that silent look that says, "The French Defense—brilliant." Meanwhile every

American in the room would look around as if to say, "What the hell is the French Defense?"

Second, we set it up so that court stenographers would cover the blow-by-blow action as if you were ringside in Philadelphia. This event was going to be covered by the *New York Times*, so accuracy was paramount. When someone starts printing in the newspaper that Garry Kasparov moved his knight, our website had to reflect it with graphical precision—after all, the Deep Blue site would be the press's first resource for research. We also threw in GIFs (Graphics Interchange Format files, if you're not a techie) on the fly. Move after move had to be posted on the website with a minimal delay, along with never-before-seen moving banners that would post chess trivia. All live. Years before JavaScript and QuickTime would become industry standards, we used every trick in the book to make a static page look as though it was streaming.

I had just gotten back from my honeymoon when one of my business partners, Doug, asked me if I wanted to meet the new programmers from Russia. Apparently, they were amazing and seemed to live for code.

"Sure," I replied.

He just laughed.

"What?" I said.

"You'll see."

Nicholai had been our best programmer for almost a year now. Although Russian born, he moved to the West after high school, and after five years in the United States he was 100 percent Americanized. His evenings were immersed in the whole New York cultural and club scene. Nicholai preferred hand-rolled cigarettes, espresso from Starbucks, and a black turtleneck sweater and black leather jackets. He always looked like a secret agent in a bad spy thriller. He had hand-picked the Russian programmers, so it became his immediate job to be a full-time interpreter, explainer of all things American as well as their manager.

As I was ushered into the new office, someone introduced me as an owner, boss, whatever; I forget, it all happened so fast. As I extended my hand, three men leaped up from their chairs and stood military style at attention.

I almost fell back, I was so startled. "Whoa, what the hell is that?" I blurted out. It was as if I was aboard a submarine and expected to dress down the troops. Other K2 staff just stood around to see my reaction. My face must have conveyed my shock, because Doug just looked at me and laughed.

I was dumbfounded. Nicholai, wearing his black turtleneck, stepped forward and began to explain in his thick Russian accent that in Russia most bosses were treated this way. I learned later that the reason for their fear was that executives in Russia usually received their financing from the Russian mob, and it wasn't unheard of for them to shoot insubordinate employees. No wonder the programmers had moved here.

"Gentlemen, it is a pleasure to meet you all. Thank you for working for us on this project. At ease," I said. It was so military. I could have sworn I heard the Russian national anthem in the background. They blinked. "Please sit. I don't want you to ever do that again. You are in America now. You don't salute your boss." Then I made a nervous joke out of it. "And let that be a lesson to the rest of you employees on how to treat your superiors."

Everyone laughed, but I couldn't help but be thankful that I live in a country where I won't get shot for forgetting to salute someone.

Scary Numbers

Back then, the Internet wasn't the tried-and-true network it is today, and TV coverage was still the norm. Many people thought IBM's Deep Blue computer with its artificial intelligence playing chess against a human being was going to be a nonevent. Apparently IBM thought this too, because they had given us only one server, with a capacity for 250,000 hits—not nearly enough for this event.

We saw it quite differently.

The event would set a new world record, and we knew it—but we were the only ones who did.

We tried to convince IBM that the Deep Blue site was going to get vaporized with hits, but they refused to believe our warnings. "Hits" at that time was a new term for the number of users coming to each page of a website. Even our original contractor, the prestigious ad agency Ogilvy, couldn't sway IBM. But we felt the IBM Chess Challenge was the first live event to really utilize what the Internet was all about—broadcasting up-to-the-minute information.

The first day of the Deep Blue Chess Challenge was a Friday, and the site received 5 million hits that day. Whoa, Nelly! The server was crashing constantly, and if you were lucky enough to load in one page, you never could download a second one. Chaos reigned.

The Internet can only work if the rate of delivery from a server is fast enough and capable enough to handle large amounts of traffic. The other side of that coin is your ISP's ability to receive and deliver the content back to you. Anticipating this interaction requires simple calculations and a little guesswork as to when will be the moment of capacity overload. How can I explain it in today's Web 2.0 environment? Think Twitter's server capacity at 7:00 PM Eastern Standard Time, and add two billion users, and you'll get it. Five million users on a static site in 1996 was beyond anyone's imagination.

Once IBM saw the numbers, we got five servers by Saturday morning. Over the weekend, it was my job to update a few graphics from our office in New York City. The mirrored sites needed to be up and running by Sunday night. The on-site team was pounding out the code and updating on a daily basis. By Monday we were able to handle the capacity.

Bringing In Da Funk

From that moment on, K2 was the new standard for live Internet events. We handed out posters at events that advertised K2 as the Internet live broadcast company. Videos were hard to watch over a 56K modem back then, but no one seemed to care. No one knew what the Internet was about yet. Was it for video broadcast? Was it for posting on a bulletin board? Or was it a giant library? One big marketplace? No one was quite sure.

One of K2's producers, Matt De Ganon, was able to attract some high-profile clients because of his background as an agent in the entertainment industry. The online video broadcast of the after party to celebrate *Bring In Da Noise, Bring In Da Funk* making it to Broadway was done by us.

The Broadway musical *Rent*, needing a website for its New York and Boston debut, also called on K2. We became *the* studio for Broadway events, especially after the *Noise, Funk* party, when K2 made it onto *Entertainment Tonight*, with Matt and Cecilia Pagkalinawan, one of our interactive producers, interviewed for all the world to see. We had gone way past anything I could have strategized. These amazingly talented individuals were forming a close-knit group; they were becoming the culture of K2. Because of Matt's work, we decided to make him a full partner at K2.

This was a fantastic time, and it was also a crazy time. (That sounds like the beginning of *A Tale of Two Cities*.) I started to really take a good look at how hard everyone was working. Our company was truly international: programmers from Russia, code jockeys from England and Germany, art directors from Jamaica, accountants from Japan and Israel. We were truly a global melting pot.

But what made us financially sound in the chaos of building websites was a model that would fit the design industry for years: one that uses a transient, freelance workforce. They are independent; they pay their own taxes, retirement, and insurance; and when they are no longer needed, they are let go until a future date. Not only is it cost-effective, it is a win-win situation. Consultants make a higher day rate than an employee does, but the company doesn't have to maintain a support staff, handle their payroll taxes, pay their insurance, or sustain their existence over time.

The other great part is that consultants must be on top of their game to stay competitive. Only the best survive in a dog-eat-dog industry. Pick someone who has been doing it a while. They'll be the alpha, and you'll get some seriously experienced talent.

Once the IBM Chess Challenge was over, so was our need for most of our programmers. Nicholai was full-time, so he stayed on for many more years, but otherwise, freelance workers were the best fit for our business model.

In the world of the Information Age, technology makes it easier to consider who on your staff must be permanent and who can fill temporary positions . . . and who can work from home.

Have Laptop, Will Travel

But how will you manage productivity or necessary face time or even morale when your staff is spread out over five continents? Technology is the answer—or rather, those who can handle the technology and people at the same time are. Perhaps those who were raised on this technology would be the managers best able to understand its potential? Or its reach?

Back in 2007, to get a greater grasp of Gen Y, I decided to do some research that was off the beaten path. I took a flight from LaGuardia Airport, New York, to Madison, Wisconsin, to attend the third annual Games + Learning + Society conference, or GLS 3.0, a three-day get-together of the best innovations and discussions between academia and game designers. The key discussion was about how to create teaching games that could be used in the classroom—from kindergarten to college.

This may sound like silly nonsense until you begin to realize that every computer's graphical user interface is based on the intuitive design learned from the use of gaming technology. From your ATM to your MacBook or PC, from your iPhone to your cable television remote and onscreen interface—all have been designed and influenced by the video game interface. It is information architecture at its best.

Now here's an idea of how gaming technology will be applied to the future of teaching. Imagine taking a city-planning and economics course in college using a *Sim City*–style simulator to track taxation, capital improvements, bureaucracy overhead, and labor factors within the model. This type of simulation along with task-and-reward model is already being utilized in more progressive schools and is the central ideology of the GLS conference. How can games be used to teach or to implement dangerous tasks, or, in general, be integrated into our everyday life?

Self-running simulations and simulators all come under the heading of Serious Games, and it is changing the way we work. Remote robotic units can be sent into extremely dangerous situations and locales: a battlefield, a bomb disarming, and a scientific analysis of volcanoes, or the surface of Mars. If you think this is some future you will never see in your lifetime, think again; remote surgery is already being performed using this type of technology right now.

Upon touchdown in Madison for the GLS conference, the prop-driven plane droned ever more slowly as we taxied slowly off the runway, even as my excitement began to build. In my research, I'd had a sense I was missing a big piece of the puzzle, and I was hoping I might finally find out what it was.

I was to be indoctrinated into the world of gaming, but more important, I'd have a chance to see firsthand how gaming and computers were impacting people's behavior, especially Generation Y. And, in fact, I half suspected the implications would extend well beyond Gen Y, into my own world of family, friends, and work—the world of all of us impacted by technology. I decided to keep my mind open.

The first really intense event I attended was a fireside chat. As I entered the darkened room, a computer screen was running a loop of perpetual fireplace footage to keep us warm, even if it was just in our minds. Author and professor James Paul Gee of the University of Wisconsin played host to Charles Herold, video game critic from the *New York Times*. The topic was storytelling in games. It was a well sought-out session. You could feel the excitement in the air.

When the fireside chat started, Professor Gee introduced Charles. The depth of Charles's knowledge was apparent, but the focus of this discussion was just how effective rich storytelling was to the success of a game—both commercially and for general satisfaction among game players.

My first shock came when several twentysomething gamers in the audience confessed that as children, when playing the video game *Planetfall,* they were pushed to tears by the death of the lead character, a robot companion that befriended you throughout the entire game and eventually sacrificed itself so your character could live. No matter how you played, in order to win, the robot would *always* die. When they had been under the age of ten, a video game had forced them to make complex choices that before only adults had made.

This was obviously way beyond *Space Invaders*. I learned that the recurring theme "moral compromise" kept cropping up in the video game world. It seemed to be a very important concern; the squatting students were only the first to reveal their feelings about killing opponents within a game only to hear the dying character proclaim, "Don't kill me; I have kids!"—making the guilt more intense.

The audience complained that few of the game engines allowed a choice; kill or be killed was the norm. Surprisingly, Tom Clancy's *Splinter Cell* in fact did give players the choice of killing the enemy or knocking them out and tying them up. This was an improvement, but it made the player vulnerable, since the knocked-out character could awaken and sound the intruder alert. One must do what one must do to assure survival in these games.

Even a Boomer Brain Can Play

That the players were often confronted with moral dilemmas was my first shock about gaming. *Pong*, *Space Invaders*, and *Ms. Pac-Man* weren't that complicated. Yet here was a group emotionally engaged in a virtual world that could move them just as easily as my generation could be moved to tears by movies or television. And in a step beyond anything my generation had ever experienced, this new generation of video game players was being forced to make not just choices but life-and-death choices in order to win.

My second shock during the GLS conference came on Saturday evening. After all the talks and the black-tie dinner, I grabbed a couple of sodas with two friends and business colleagues my own age: Richard Carey, of Richard Carey Associates, and Lee Wilson, of Headway Strategies. We headed back to Lee's hotel. He had one more thing to reveal to me before he felt comfortable that I "got it."

He set up his laptop and began to talk me through the creation of an avatar in *World of Warcraft*. An avatar is a digital representative of a player that interacts within a 3D environment. My head was spinning at this point as I began to realize the ramifications of twenty years of gaming technology and its influence.

As I began to move my character through the 3D world, it became apparent that this was not only fun, it was addictive. All I had to do was master a few navigation skills and the ability to toggle between the types of weapons and things I could acquire. After an hour, I had accomplished seven different quests and earned 150 points to be traded in for various weapons, magic spells, and supplies. I could move on to the next level.

And then I asked Lee the obvious question: "What got you into *World of Warcraft*?"

"I wanted to spend time with my kids."

Whoa! Again I was blown away as Lee began to explain how his schedule had him flying all over the country several times a month. He decided that in order to spend time with his children, he would log in to *World of Warcraft* with them. If you can't beat 'em, join 'em. It didn't matter what city he was in; they could all enjoy some time together and chat a little as their characters. It was a great way for dad to be with the kids, and when he returned home, they had shared adventures that they could talk about. It was as if he never left home. Mom, Dad, sons, and daughters could discuss shared experiences despite Dad being in another state or on another continent.

If this is how people spend their free time, no wonder people want to integrate gaming technology with our work a day world.

It was fun and exciting, and with each level I was engaged and challenged and learned more skills.

What was even more fascinating was that my mentors Richard and Lee were real Baby Boomers and yet were clearly living in the future. How come they had adapted while most people their age did not? It's because the majority of Boomers were taught to ignore games as child's play rather than see them for what they really are: multilevel training environments that are teaching twenty-first-century skills.

In this topsy-turvy world today, where twenty-three-year-old executives are running billion-dollar corporations, forty-year-old millionaire skateboard athletes have their own video games and clothing lines, and business meetings are now done on laptops with a webcam, it feels as though we are living in a Stephen King novel with a gaggle of creepy children running the show while the adults react in fear, pretending to keep up and wondering who will be next to get the ax.

Something today is very different from the world of our grandparents. Video games and computers have changed everything.

Unhooking from Time and Place

Because of virtual worlds, remote servers, and open-source technology, the linear time-management ideologies of the twentieth century no longer apply. Today's workforce can work wherever and whenever they want . . . and they do. But there is another paradigm to consider: Generation Y is loyal to their own talent and abilities, and they have become selective about who they give their time and attention to. The idea of working from a single place is becoming a foreign ideology, like listening to your grandparents tell stories of drive-in movie theaters, ice-delivery wagons, or Bobby Darin ruling the airwaves.

Think about it for a moment. Most of us were raised as linear thinkers, and therefore we approach time the same way. It worked for centuries because our time was based on going to work and then coming home. Time management was easy because all you had to do was look at your environment to know what you were supposed to be doing. Where you spent your time determined what task you focused on. If you felt a little too much stress in your life, just spend more time at home and less time at work. If you wanted that promotion, simply spend more time at work than at home. It was linear, purposeful, and less stressful because one could easily manage it.

If you are like me, you *still* define your time by where you spend it—at work, at a club, at a friend's house, driving, etc.—despite the fact that most of us are no longer bound by our location. Our thinking was shaped from birth by the ancient framework of places in which we occupied our time: Work was where we worked, and our house was where we ate, slept, played, and lived. Forty years ago, no one would have dreamed of a computer in the house, but today many of us have a computer in the living room. Laptops are a symbol of this shift from time defined by location to time defined by whatever and wherever we decide it to be.

This is why a transient worker will be in demand in the twenty-first century. It is a more efficient use of the corporation's needs, yet it fits into our new time-management ideology of being able to take our work with us.

Since pure Internet businesses like Amazon have proven that brick-and-mortar storefronts are no longer a necessary cornerstone for a multibillion-dollar company to exist, the model of efficiency going forward will be the time-management methodologies of remote workers—workers fully capable of doing their work at home, emailing a PDF, and attending that Monday morning meeting via Skype. Without having to spend money on a storefront, with heating bills, lighting, cash registers, and other necessities, companies of the twenty-first century will be looking to leverage more and more of their staff remotely and spend less money on fancy mahogany offices.

Lounge Lizard, formerly of Bohemia, Long Island, in New York, does just that. With twenty full-time employees, company founders Ken and Sharon Braun see only one-third of their staff day in, day out. The rest of their staff makes a pilgrimage to the office about five times a year for brainstorming sessions, face-to-face pitches, and company celebrations. Most of these remote employees work from home yet remain in touch with the Long Island headquarters 24/7. The amount of money Ken and Sharon are saving on office space is amazing. And the money they save this way goes back into their employees; their virtual designers get trained in the latest software innovations, and Lounge Lizard can put that money into attracting better talent and promoting their business. It has given them the ability to move their headquarters into New York City.

Today the boundaries of time and space are no longer clear. As life speeds up, we are expected to speed up with it. If you are a linear thinker, this will only lead to an overwhelming feeling that you can't keep up. Multitasking is expected and has created a world where linear time-management becomes an antiquated way to work. Beginning, middle, and end no longer have value in the new business world. It is just as normal for me to work at 1:00 AM as it is for someone else to work from 10:00 AM to 6:00 PM, or to work from 10:00 AM to noon and then again from 6:00 PM to 11:00 PM. Time management is more about managing the self than managing time.

The greatest danger of this type of work is that a remote worker will be expected to be on call twenty-four hours a day, seven days a week, to do what is needed, no questions asked. For any sense of sanity to be maintained from an "always on" style of work, a new set of boundaries will need to be established. Otherwise early burnout will become another ubiquitous part of the twenty-first century.

Advances in hardware such as laptops, cell phones, PDAs, webcams, and home computers, along with networking technologies like global satellites, fiber optics, wireless hubs, and high-speed Internet connections, have given even a small company the ability to dramatically manage a remote staff and increase what an individual can accomplish from anywhere.

Look at the iPhone. It not only answers the problem of having too many devices to carry by converging email, phone calls, applications, and entertainment into a personalized PDA-style device, but it also makes several generational leaps in technology: touch-screen access, a robust operating system, vertical-to-horizontal sensors, gaming software, intuitive interfacing, large icons, motion sensors, data management, data accessibility, and, of course, sleek design.

Smart developers realized a long time ago that a cell phone was much more than a phone. It was a device that gave the user access to data and networks in real time. Answers to questions no longer needed research when a PDA-style cell phone could get you an answer over the network in minutes. Many a sales force is already armed with these types of cell phones and is able to stay constantly in the field, filling orders and tracking inventory. Apple store employees can check a customer out from a cell phone–like device with a built-in credit card reader. No need for a bank of cash registers—it's all virtual now.

Technology smooths our way and gives us greater reach if properly applied.

As of the time of this writing, 2010, technological information will be doubling every seventy-two hours. You will need to eliminate what is wasting your time, what isn't helping your bottom line, and ask yourself how a transient workforce can help maximize profits and increase production.

The Information Age is about working smarter, not harder. Ask your IT pros what is out there that can save you money. Technology, when used properly, can increase profits, increase your reach, and increase your speed to conversion—in other words, sales! At each level, learn what's possible and implement what works—just like in a video game.

The Bridge to Generation Y

Back in the midnineties as we built K2, I began to feel like the lead character in the movie *Gattaca*, Vincent Freeman. He's a regular guy who assumes the identity of a genetically altered man in a futuristic caste society, a society in which mentally, physically, and emotionally superior, genetically altered humans rule over the naturally born humans whom they are slowly displacing. Vincent's efforts to keep pace with the genetically manipulated group seemed laughable—the illusion was upheld by his need to put in extra efforts. In like manner, Boomers are trying to keep up as well. Gen Y on the other hand goes about their business as if life has always been filled with big-screen TVs, HD video, Nickelodeon, and the video game *Rock Band*. The idea of picking up a real instrument is a foreign concept.

I began to realize that the generations I was managing were just the beginning of the first wave, and a new, more tech-savvy group was coming forward to claim their prize. This generation is very comfortable and unafraid to take on the reins of management at a young age.

**Believe it or not, if you are forty-five or older,
eventually, your son or daughter's college roommate
will soon be your boss.**

It is not that Boomers will become irrelevant, but in order to stay employable, most will have to learn how to keep abreast of trends that are fast becoming a normal part of the business landscape—things like free desktop videoconferencing, 24/7 availability, Internet television, and the idea of using a credit card anytime, anywhere. With an app like Credit Card Terminal, users can turn their iPhone into a mobile credit card terminal. Take a moment to realize how that will be impacting small business owners, and you begin to see why you need to stay aware of new technology.

I used to think I was unique for my generation. I started my first business at sixteen, gravitated toward NYC after college to become a part of the corporate theater sector of events, and started another business, and then another, and then another. I used to believe that I ran circles around most. Now here before me was an entire generation that ran circles around me. It was intimidating at best and exhausting to keep up. This isn't a fad; these people are here to stay.

Isn't it time we bridge the knowledge gap? Isn't it time for us to create tools and methodologies that work time and time again, while retraining and repurposing those eager to make the leap? The creative energy of your workforce is a strong force; they're just dying to show off their expertise, so why not give them a chance? It isn't one big idea that makes things happen; it is giving talented individuals the working environment to create big ideas on a consistent basis.

Just look at the A-list of übersuccessful companies such as Apple Computer, Ben & Jerry's, Dell, Tesla, Google, Facebook, MySpace, PayPal, Twitter, and Netscape. How did they go from start-ups to multimillion-dollar companies in what appears to be a short amount of time? And how do they continuously survive and thrive, no matter what the economic climate may be?

It's not because of soft management—not by a long shot. These founders surround themselves with other like-minded people capable of seeing the original vision but also engaged completely in pushing the boundaries. This internal competitiveness has a consistent impact on the bottom line and destroys the inertia that status quo can create. You better be ambitious if you want to work for these companies.

And that is what leadership has always been about: balancing the collaborative, creative workforce by nurturing innovation but dramatically affecting output, the marketplace, and the bottom line. What drives these types of companies is that they give their people the ability to be contributors to the overall vision and profitability of the company.

A revolution is happening. Not a physical revolution with guns ablaze, but one in which the battleground is our entire way of living, working, and playing. I am talking about something that has been forgotten for a few millennia and is now being reintroduced—the very human and quite disruptive side of the business paradigm is being included in the sales cycle. People at every level are starting to realize that for business to get done, you have to get connected with as many people as possible in as many strategically chosen networks as possible. This need has created a socialized business environment where people are treating their careers as an integrated part of their lives, not a separate thing they do just for money. Technology allows us to tap into networks that at one time were hidden and obscure. Leisure time is no longer without purpose or intention, as technology extends our reach and creates a borderless, dynamic lifestyle.

Like an archeologist who discovers the ancient city of Troy long after the history books claimed it to be a myth, I too feel as if there is more to be added. The story of the human race is never-ending, and we truly are at a crossroads—where one age meets another. The scope of the story keeps expanding with each new piece of data.

As business leaders, we need to weed out the bad habits, malinvestments, and hubris that have piled up over the years, and face the simple fact that a shift has taken place and we can no longer return to the land of our innocence. The balance between what is right and long term is at odds with quick profits. The Information Age will leave most companies buried under the weight of their own status quo management principles. Only the *flexible and swift* will survive.

It will be tempting to fall backward into old-fashioned management methodologies, especially as this global economy takes a hard hit. But waiting and hiding won't work. If instead you commit to becoming a true Liquid Leader—an adaptable business commando, capable of survival in any environment—you will be able to build a better, stronger, and more adaptable company, one that kicks the old corporate ideology up a notch, breaks the mold, and makes your work environment a once-in-a-lifetime experience.

A Liquid Leader Cultivates an Environment Where It Is Free and Safe to Tell the Truth

A good manager doesn't try to eliminate conflict; he tries to keep it from wasting the energies of his people. If you're the boss and your people fight you openly when they think that you are wrong—that's healthy.

—Robert Townsend

Why a Truth-telling Environment Is So Important

The only way to stay ahead these days is to come up with bigger, better ideas, all day long, every day. The most innovative companies do this by creating an environment where best practices include supporting even the most outrageous idea. Walking the halls of these organizations, one can see an immediate difference from other companies—the environment is fast-paced, loose, and creative. The reason for such a rich experience is that creative people can create only in environments where it is safe to take chances and make mistakes without being penalized, and where it is safe to tell the truth about what isn't working.

Ever work with a particular piece of software and find that management doesn't want you to discuss its limitations or even suggest workarounds? This is the type of scenario I am talking about—people are afraid to state the obvious for fear of retribution. Time and attention are wasted when these types of problems aren't solved.

Management can set the tone by letting people know that it is okay to be truthful and constructive. It is okay to describe problems as part of coming up with solutions. The bad news needs to be delivered so the good news can be written.

However, in an environment that allows truth telling, you must make sure each team member understands how to present a sticky subject without destroying a fellow colleague's contribution. In other words, speak properly and respectfully when critiquing. Speaking the truth should not be used as a way to get even or to make a coworker look bad. Making someone feel as if they are under attack leaves angry feelings and creates a hostile environment. But when everyone is supportive and nurturing, people feel safe to admit their weaknesses. The common goal is to get better. Be sure to let people express how they could do better or what support is missing for them to get their jobs done more efficiently. You'd be surprised how aware people are of what they need to work on.

The higher the anxiety in an organization, the lower the creativity; the lower the anxiety in an organization, the greater the creativity and the innovation. Leading companies understand that to stay on the cutting edge, creative people must work in an environment free of draconian management and strict hierarchy. Despite a lack of perceived hierarchy, this isn't loosey-goosey management; these environments are fast-paced and dynamic.

These are not environments where mediocrity is rewarded. Each team is made up of strong, smart, talented individuals from multiple disciplines, and many of them wear more than one hat in an organization such as this. The weak get eaten alive by their own team if they don't get excited about the work they are doing.

Putting intensely creative people together in the same room can be dangerous, especially when strong personalities are involved, but corporations have figured out that strong leadership is the way to manage it. HR in these companies has been instructed to look for the best, with quirky backgrounds and even quirkier resumes. Leadership positions are earned, and they are rotated over and over again through team support, evaluation, and opportunity. New team members know that they, too, will eventually be asked to take on a leadership role—because they earned it.

The key for leadership in the Information Age isn't to try and dominate and demoralize, but to learn, listen, and improve the quality of the products or services you make. Expect greatness, and people will deliver it.

Grandpa, What's a Hierarchy?

Near the end of the 1970s, I heard about something called "child-centric parenting." Led by guru Dr. Spock, child-centric parenting flipped five thousand years of parenting on its head in favor of raising children to have higher self-esteem instead of survival skills. Self-esteem was managed by getting rid of winners and losers and just enjoying the game. Scoreless baseball games became the norm as everyone began to drink the Gatorade and children began to tell Mommy and Daddy what to do. My father gave it his stamp of approval: "What a bunch of crap!"

This type of parenting had previously been found only within an only-child household, but with the onset of the child-centric parenting craze, an entire generation was raised to be on equal footing with their parents—more precocious, independent, and familiar with the world of adults at an early age. And they were encouraged to be this way.

Eventually these kids grew up and entered the workforce. Wonder why your organizational chart has flattened today?

The family organizational chart was collapsed in the eighties.

The erosion of corporate hierarchies started with Gen X entering the workforce. Because of child-centric parenting, Generations X and Y do not look up to authority. Actually, they see authority as their peer group. When the parent-to-child paradigm was flip-flopped, children began to see themselves on equal footing not only with their parents but also with all other adults. Their parents became their friends, and as they grew into adulthood, they confided in those "friends" about everything from relationship advice to career consulting. The apron strings remained attached. John Hughes' movies *The Breakfast Club, Sixteen Candles, Ferris Bueller's Day Off,* and *Pretty in Pink* began to give this new generation a voice—one of angst and cynicism.

And the close relationships with their parents continue in full force. Many HR departments have had to deal with Gen Y parents storming into their offices demanding to know why their child, now in their late twenties, didn't get a raise at the last review. The flattening of the family hierarchy has led directly to the flattening of the corporate hierarchy because of the changed attitudes of the youngest, most vital workers. These are the same people who see themselves running your company in a few years.

Flatter is Faster

There's another reason hierarchies have flattened—the inevitable acceleration of technology has shrunk the world faster than was once thought possible. Computers themselves work in a peer-to-peer network; it is faster, more efficient, and self-managing.

Think about how recently and how quickly the world has sped up. Maybe you are old enough to remember that when Fred Smith started the Federal Express Corporation in 1971 most people were thinking, "Why would anyone want a package delivered to them overnight?" It was a reflection of the slow pace of the seventies. But Fred was a visionary, able to see that someday our world would shrink and speed up at the same time. The company that today we call FedEx spent years bleeding money, just waiting for the world to catch up to the vision. But when it did, they became the standard in overnight delivery.

FedEx, then fax machines, and then email changed our expectations on when and where we should get information. They made our world borderless. They also demanded that we speed up, doing more in one day than our parents did in a month. And so these days we can hardly wait for an email to be delivered to our inbox, a PowerPoint presentation to be finished, or a microwave to beep without thinking, "What the hell is taking so long?"

I am willing to bet real money that you can't survive one day without the Internet. Think I'm exaggerating? Ten years ago, if your email went down, you probably could have still finished your work. Today, losing an Internet connection might create such chaos that some businesses would lose a billion dollars overnight.

As a society, we no longer talk the same, work the same, romance the same, or commute the same. E-commerce has driven fifty-year-old companies out of business, and remote working has redefined what it means to commute or to get the corner office. The cost of business is coming down because we no longer have to spend astronomical amounts to build a new brick-and-mortar store and then hope the costs will be made back in five years. Our business world is becoming virtualized, no longer married to a singular location.

And here's another year for you: 1984, when the personal computer first entered the home en masse. Sure, there were companies that tried before but failed. But when Apple introduced the Macintosh, and Nintendo introduced newer, more dynamic game consoles for the household, it all took off. The Computer Age began.

And then there's the new speed and prevalence of air shipping and air travel. Today even the most common person on the street has access to coffee from Africa, rugs from Turkey, and automobiles from Germany. We also have the ability to travel to these lands and experience them firsthand. For most of us, a six-hour flight can leave us off on a new continent.

So with the shrinking of the world, and the access of the young generations to all the world's information within seconds via the Internet, the world has changed dramatically. But remember—it's not just technology that has changed, but the people using it, especially the young people who understand this technology best.

The Computer Age has brought us The Information Age. And those with the power to access the *right* information make the rules.

Gen X and the Gen Y entered the workforce demanding more from their HR departments than anyone before them had. I immediately noticed this shift at K2. The majority of my staff were only three to five years younger than I was, but they might as well have been a race of aliens. They lived on their laptops, worked remotely, and at the same time went to fabulous parties that seemed like a big extension of college. They answered cell phone calls in the middle of movie theaters, letting everyone else know just how *important* they were. And those cell phones were paid for by me.

They loved every minute of it because the press was documenting every move this generation made. They acted like rock stars because they were attention junkies and the media was giving them that fix.

Technology, along with their helicopter parents, has made these generations more comfortable with peer-to-peer thinking than with hierarchy. They see computers and the Internet as the way to solve all problems. Their generation has been taught that, without much effort, they should be CEOs within a few years. They aren't about to be slaves to the corporate way of life as their parents were. Since "thoughts are real," given the chance, Gen Y just might pull it off. Ever notice that people who believe in something—no matter how weird—eventually manifest it?

But where does this leave the aging, techno-challenged Boomer? If new and old generations are to work together in an atmosphere not of hostility or cold bafflement, but of mutual trust and discovery, then someone will have to adjust. The question is, who, when, and how?

How Technology Influences Behavior

One way to get over mistrust of another group is to learn more about them—what forces have shaped their lives and made them who they are today. So to understand Gen X and especially Gen Y, let's go back to another favorite year of mine, 1977.

That was the year Atari introduced the first home gaming system, the VCS—later renamed the Atari 2600—and transformed the gaming industry overnight. As a Cusp Baby Boomer I got a taste of this new form of entertainment; it was addictive. Despite being the most incredible business success story of the seventies, for some strange reason Atari decided to shift from the newly formed electronic gaming industry that made them successful to the computer industry, competing directly with industry leader IBM. They failed miserably.

So in the early eighties, home-based video game technology took off once again as Nintendo and Sony took the lead away from Atari, creating more robust games and consoles with faster response and better gaming engines and, of course, better gaming systems.

Instead of focusing on getting their games into the arcades, Nintendo focused on creating a unit that would be in the home. This was a unique business model for a new industry and at a time when games were mostly found at malls and arcades. This move was visionary.

By being in the home, video game consoles gave 24/7 access to the new entertainment medium. Video games for the home created an entertainment choice that, for the first time in human history, required 100 percent of a player's attention. The user could spend hours mastering a single task before being rewarded so they could move up the ladder to the next challenge.

These video games for the home caused younger generations to start learning in a completely different way through immersive, repetitive tasks with multilevel goals that took weeks to master. The games were engaging and always challenging, and they kept users interested because the more a player advanced, the more challenging the game became. The artificial intelligence of an ever-increasing challenge kept users engaged for thousands of hours. This also changed their behavior.

In an article in the *Atlantic* magazine,[1] writer Nicholas Carr (author of *The Shallows: What the Internet Is Doing to Our Brains*) cites sociologist Daniel Bell as claiming the following: "Whenever we begin to use 'intellectual technologies' such as computers (or video games)—tools that extend our mental rather than our physical capacities—we inevitably begin to take on the qualities of those technologies."

Immersed in Technology Since Birth

As the generations born after 1965 began to pick up video games, and then a computer, and eventually the Internet, their behavior changed. They adapted to it all.

Since this generation saw themselves as equal to adults, as peers not needing permission to learn when and where they wanted or to obey someone else, they learned to use their own wits to find an answer to their questions through technology. As new generations started to turn to technology instead of parents for answers, parents' roles changed to that of friends. Now rich, exciting video game play made working with a computer almost a ubiquitous part of a child's world, as easy to access as building blocks were for other generations. After all, video games— although using a different type of computer—trained them to do so. I am not talking about *Ms. Pac-Man*. I am talking about deeply complex, rich storytelling and task-driven games.

Another thing video games do is make the users the heroes within

---

1. This article, "Is Google Making Us Stoopid?" can be found in the July/August 2008 issue of the *Atlantic*. I highly recommend it if you're interested in the behavioral impact of the Web.

their own stories. Instead of *watching* Bruce Willis shoot everyone and get the girl, gamers actually get the chance in a game environment to get the girl all by themselves. In other words, in a single-person gaming environment, they *are* Bruce Willis. They can be any hero they want to be—Luke Skywalker, Tony Hawk, Lara Croft—for a few hours a day. It's safer than facing a real girl in the real world. They don't need to *become* famous or heroes; they *are* heroes in their own reality. When your brain has experienced hundreds if not thousands of rescue attempts and accomplished tasks, what kind of self-esteem would you have? This distinction is important to understanding Generation Y self-esteem issues and the main reason they act like rock stars today. Telling them that they are anything less is met with shock and awe.

Success was also being redefined by video games, and it was no longer based in the real world of trees, grass, and sunshine. Instead, it existed in a virtual gaming environment. Children started having gaming parties where each could show off their gaming skills and knowledge of a particular video game. The star quarterback was losing ground to the video gamer. Magazines started to publish shortcuts called "cheats," and Gen Y learned how to get around the system.

Any of this behavior sound familiar in today's work environment? Throw in a global connection to their peers, and you have a child of the Information Age, a peer-to-peer parallel thinker who assumes they are capable of processing multiple thoughts all at once and, unbeknownst to the individual, just like a computer. These kids are now adults, and they have been using this type of technology at college and in the workday world for the past thirty years and more.

So, to a Boomer, why does any of this matter? I am sure you are tired of hearing all about Generation Y and how wonderful they all are . . . blah, blah, blah. But here is what you should be aware of: All the check cards, ATMs, online banking, Web transactions, Google, texting, PDAs, iPhones, BlackBerrys, iPods, and e-readers came about because of an entire generation that feels entitled to the best and latest technology.

And that's not all. Just watch any show on HGTV and see how picky young homebuyers are. They demand the best because they were raised to do so, and every market in the world followed. "Why?" you may ask. Well, first off, the generations raised on video games make more money than we did at the same age. They feel entitled, just as Cusp Boomers (the original "me" generation) did after the economic recession of the late seventies. With that said, youth are the fastest group to part with their money on silly purchases. Now take disposable cash, a need to have electronic doodads, a need to upgrade all the time, and the decision-making properties of youth, and you have a simple answer to all your curious questions about Generation Y.

They part with their money easier than any other generation because they have it to spend.

Youth is the jugular vein of quick cash, and marketers know it. This is why marketers and corporations have retooled all their efforts on Generation Y—DVDs at the local 7-Eleven, Netbooks, iPhones and iPods, Kindle, etc. To sell to a Boomer takes real work, and many companies don't have time for that.

On top of that, many of these young folks were introduced to incredibly dynamic technologies while at college—like T1 connectivity, Internet-based communication, and online feedback—long before it became the norm in our households. The way we work, the way we communicate, text, and buy, is because of Generation Y's methodologies and ease as an early adopter . . . all supported by companies that know if you market to youth, and their habits, you can make a killing. Want to invest in the next big thing? Ask a college student. What is normal on college campuses eventually becomes the next big industry within ten years—like that thing called the personal computer or the Internet or open-source Wikis. All these were originally rolled out and tested on college campuses.

In contrast, Baby Boomers use computers in entirely different ways than younger generations do. Boomers' brains adapted to computers as a secondary set of skills later in life. In other words, computer skills were added to an already formed adult brain.

Another point from Carr's *Atlantic* article came from Maryanne Wolf, a developmental psychologist at Tufts University and author of *Proust and the Squid: The Story and Science of the Reading Brain*, who claims that speech is an instinctual skill that we pick up, while reading is something we have to be taught. This is how Boomers learned the computer—someone taught it to them years into their career, and years after their brains had finished growing.

By contrast, most of Generation X and all of Generation Y were born with and immersed in some form of computer technology since the day they were born. Most of them haven't known a day without technology whether it's a Speak & Spell, a video game, or a VCR.

If you haven't noticed, the majority of computer operating systems are visual-driven systems, just like a video game. And unbeknownst to us older generations, Generations X and Y were already practicing business tasks in their games. They worked with a team, failing over and over again until they mastered one skill, seeking out mentorship to help them advance. They would figure out the rules and politics at each new level, and always upgrade their skill level in order to get ahead. The more risks they took, the further they would advance, and the more points they would accumulate.

If you don't believe me, just pull aside your thirty-five-year-old vice president—the one who doesn't have kids yet—and ask him whether he owns a game console or plays an online game?

Today we notice that computers are primary to Gen Y's abilities, and they are the best explanation as to why there is such a generation gap.

> **Because of readily available technology in their toys since birth, Gen Y thinks, operates, and sees opportunities we can't. Their brains are wired differently than those of any generation that has come before them.**

Again, technology changes our behavior more than we may be aware of. A good example from Nicholas Carr's *Atlantic* piece is when Friedrich Nietzsche was given his first typewriter in an act of desperation. His eyesight was failing, and focusing for hours while writing on a page became exhaustive and painful, bringing on splitting headaches. His doctors recommend that he stop writing altogether. But with the typewriter, Friedrich didn't have to look at the paper; he just had to close his eyes and type.

But learning how to type actually changed the style of his writing. One of Nietzsche's friends, a composer, commented in a letter that he noticed a change in Friedrich's writing. Now more terse and staccato-like, it was as if he was writing not just *with* a typewriter, but *like* a typewriter.

These young generations do not know of a world without color television, computers, the Internet, cell phones, instant messaging, texting, Twitter, and the Cartoon Network. Pretty soon no one will remember eight-track tapes or film. As with Stone Age tools, you will eventually have to go to the museum to see examples of our past, because they won't exist anywhere else.

Multitasking as Myth and as Metaphor

If Baby Boomers are linear thinkers, then every generation born and raised using a computer has developed a parallel thinking brain—only comfortable with a world of multitasking. Although human beings in fact are not designed to multitask—and many experts with more degrees than me can prove to you that multitasking does not work—this method is the behavioral norm of Generation Y.

But let's not count out Boomers either—everyone's mental habits have been changed by the new technologies, much more than we might think. When was the last time you were able to finish reading a book? Even a book you love—even this book—was probably hard to read. Why? You have been retrained to read only a Web page worth of text. We've become accustomed to staring at a computer every day, not to mention reading on the Internet. Most of us get bored when we have to read more than a screen and a half of text—the exact amount we read when we scroll down just once in a browser. That is why, as you may have noticed, this book is divided into quickly absorbable chapters, each centered around a singular idea; to read much like a blog entry's worth of information.

Boomers are trying to keep up by adopting what they believe to be Gen Y's multitasking behaviors. This is where the gap is showing the most, as most Boomers are feeling overwhelmed. The Boomer brain is simply not wired like a parallel processor.

In fact, no one's brain really is. The multitasking brain is the result of a child raised on computers, video games, and the World Wide Web. Consistent overstimulation is all Millennials know, but it doesn't work quite as well as they think it does. Studies have found that even the young can only concentrate on one high-end task at a time. Where we get into trouble is when our brains tell us that multitasking works, that we are being as productive as we think we are: "Look at how much I am getting done!" Actually you are doing busywork. It feels productive, but it is not.

From generation to generation we are simply not cognitive of our own behavior or what has changed it. But behavioral specialists have known about the limits of multitasking for a long time. All of us are limited in how much we can take in, process, and accomplish. Anything beyond our biological capacity makes us short-circuit. I am sure somewhere in a top secret lab at, say, Virginia Tech there are experiments being done with biochip enhancements to push humans farther, but until we can pick one up at Wal-Mart, we will all continue to be overwhelmed with the constant bombardment of information that marks the twenty-first century. The more we attempt to do it all at once, the more we experience ADD-like symptoms. And with more distractions, we make more mistakes.

It's a Visual Future

The future is visual, and Gen Y has huge learning advantages over Boomers in working and living with technology. They are Digital Natives, immersed in this world since the day they were born, comfortable with anything that has a screen. The visual way of controlling a computer is something they picked up as children. And the risk taking and fast learning encouraged by computers and video games are on their way to becoming the norm in the world of business.

Gaming technology is being utilized by the military to train sharpshooters and to pilot remotely operated reconnaissance planes. It is also the same technology used to train airline pilots, astronauts, oceanographers, remote surgeons, etc.

The US military is putting millions of dollars into role-playing games like *America's Army: Special Forces*. Even the military's Predator program—unmanned drones that are flown by a remote operator from a computer console—is utilizing Microsoft's Xbox platform. The reason is simple: The video game generation has better hand-eye coordination than their forefathers, even those raised around guns, and video games helped make that happen. They make better soldiers, period. Each game focuses on missions that emphasize marksmanship, responsibility, teamwork, and training. Like it or not, this has been the most effective recruitment tool in the military's history.

What is also not so obvious is that video games, online games, and even Skype are being used to train our young people for adult situations such as warfare, remote work, global networking, and conferencing with a multicultural reach. Think about it for a moment—every computer interface is based on the intuitive design of a gaming interface. From your ATM to your laptop to your cell phone to your cable television remote, all new technology has been designed like and influenced by the video game interface.

Self-running simulations and simulators all come under the heading of Serious Games, and it is changing the way we work. Remote robotic units can be sent into extremely dangerous situations: to disarm a bomb on a battlefield or to conduct scientific analysis of volcanoes on the surface of Mars. Look at the 2010 BP Oil spill in the Gulf of Mexico; the use of remote-controlled robots a mile under water, while the human operator sits on the surface in a ship, has roots in gaming technology.

Now how do we apply this to the future of work? These interfaces change our thoughts and the way we perceive our reality as well as our reach. No longer are we limited by physical danger or slaves to our location. Those raised on gaming technology will adjust quickly to a global virtualized work environment; they are quite used to working with a gaming interface across multiple continents with multiple users.

If you are reading this on a Kindle or a Nook, just look at how many of the buttons on the interface are intuitive. The assumption is that you already know this, and the industrial designers built from there.

All this chaotic change because of video games, computers, and the Internet alters the way we think and do things. So what does the future hold? While interviewing Gen Y for this book, I posed a question: "What scares you?" Their response may surprise you: The children growing up today are freaking *them* out. The generation that will replace them is already scaring them. As a Boomer you may be feeling a bit happy about that news.

Getting the Generations Together

Here is the big disconnect between opposing generations: Young people don't see any value in what Baby Boomers bring to the table because most of today's inventions and ways of working didn't exist five years ago! So Gen Y sees the Boomer as a dinosaur, way past their prime, unable to keep up and ineffectual at understanding the newly emerging technologies. Worse yet, Gen Y sees the massive amount of information possessed by Baby Boomers as having no real value—after all, it's based on what Gen Y sees as analog data, out of date and inherently less precise. Many believe the Boomers "just don't get it."

Now look at it from the Baby Boomers' point of view. They see Gen Y as a bunch of spoiled and demanding "kids" who need to be put in their place. Boomers cannot see what makes Gen Y so damn special. They are just waiting for them to calm down, take on mortgages and kids, and learn how to get in line like the rest of us did for centuries. Currently Boomers are facing the very real tinge of age discrimination as many are being asked to retire early, with major cuts in their pensions during one of the worst economic periods since the Great Depression—while at the corporate level, they are being replaced with lower-paid and more demanding Millennials. This makes no sense to the uninitiated.

But this era will give Boomers an incredible opportunity to strike out on their own and start consultancies. It will not be an easy time, but if you are willing to work for yourself—perhaps for the first time in your life—to the risk takers go the spoils, I say.

Look, if Alec Baldwin can become the greatest comedic actor of our time, then anything is possible.

Generations X and Y have no guidelines for adulthood, so don't expect them to grow up anytime soon. Of course, someday (hopefully soon)

Generation Y will awaken to the fact that they will be getting older as well. Because Millenials have yet to fully realize this, Boomers see them as the ones who "just don't get it." But weren't we like that as well?

Without guidelines, you are just as likely to see a forty-year-old skateboarder as a twenty-three-year-old CEO. Digital Natives do not adhere to traditional, linear thought—or aging—because they can't. Sometimes the idea of the bigger picture escapes them. If this is all true, then wouldn't it be smarter to manage their weakness? After all, Boomers *can* see the bigger picture and the ramifications of certain actions.

Someone needs to get these two generations talking and working together. In an environment where it is safe to tell the truth without being insulting, the strengths of both generations can be celebrated. Boomers can see and drive deadlines, with an overarching understanding that pace and priorities have to be managed. Boomers will need to fully grasp the concepts of flex time, technological disruption, and time for research and development as well as moments for personal projects.

Generation Y, on the other hand, can learn to see the arc of the production process and use it to their advantage. Boomers see the ramifications of too much transparency, trusting in technology past the point of logic and the ability to monetize projects. Boomers can teach Gen Y that the dull and boring parts of any job can be balanced with the exciting work that seems to always be on the front burner. Back-burner work is just as important.

As for multitasking and the mistakes that are made because of it, this can be managed better by young and old alike. It's a matter of developing and celebrating better work habits. Boomers always tried to get the work done right the first time and make as few mistakes as possible. That way, the work gets done once. But Generation Y has learned that with so much to do and so much complexity, mistakes can be made and fixed later. This nonchalant attitude toward doing the same work over and over again until the mistakes are fixed drives Boomers nuts—but they need to understand that it is a natural part of almost every new digitally enabled activity, from building websites to coding software.

And it isn't strictly an age thing either. I have met Baby Boomers who can text and multitask circles around a Gen Yer, and I have met twenty-five-year-olds who act like a Baby Boomer—doing one thing at a time and checking their work even though they most likely did it right the first time. I don't judge either way of operating. I just see them as two different paradigms, both valid and both needing refinement for maximum effectiveness. Managing people requires an awareness and understanding of where each is coming from, whether the difference is generational or individual. Linear thinkers have value and so do parallel thinkers. Each can learn from the other.

Understanding the differences in the way each person and each group approaches their work is part of the job of a Liquid Leader. Leaders must get groups to share and transfer their knowledge base and wisdom across the generational gaps—not just one way, but both ways. The megabrands, the great innovators, and the groundbreakers know that the key to success is to get both Gen Y and Boomers working together on the same team—developing new ideas, sharing knowledge and workloads—while developing one-of-a-kind cool stuff.

Sit-Forward New Media and the End of Shotgun Marketing

One hundred years ago the external image of a company and their brand could be completely disconnected from the internal work environment: internally a sweatshop, externally "Wow! I love your stuff." Communication was slow, employees were loyal—out of fear, mostly—and customers were to be seen and not heard. Marketing was a new idea, and although it started out as a two-way conversation, it quickly turned into one-way marketing lingo. Those days are over.

Let's talk about the customer part of this equation first. The biggest surprise to have evolved from the Information Age is the social network, a peer-to-peer group of like-minded individuals who have banded together under a common cause—or just to chat.

For thousands of years people gathered in the marketplace to buy produce, meat, and coffee or to discuss the latest news with friends. People were comfortable speaking their minds. Buying a product was an intimate process, and most businesspeople guarded their reputations with their lives. If word spread that a particular vendor had bad products or was hard to get along with, that vendor's business would suffer. The one-to-one relationship was very important and was the norm for most of the history of business and commerce.

But then came the Industrial Age, and over a hundred-year period, this newfangled entity called a "corporation" started to change the marketplace discussion from a one-to-one conversation to a one-way conversation. This control of the marketplace discussion about the merits and qualities of one product over another became known as "marketing," a one-way conversation that was contrived and fake. A byproduct of the Industrial Age of mass marketing, the new conversation was usually about how great the company was and how cool their products really were.

It was a lot of noise, and even if a company had great products, the mission of the message was always to invest the product with a certain amount of mysticism: "Buy our stuff; change your life."

With technological leaps in printing, packaging, and advertising, companies could control their image even more. Whether it was true or not didn't matter; these tools were used to massage people's perceptions, to drown out the customer's conversation.

The Revolution Won't Be Televised, It Will Be Online

The marketplace conversation has always been there. Since time began, people have always complained or raved about the stuff they use. Those companies that actually dared listen to their customers' complaints and changed accordingly became the first megabrands. Bad things seem to happen to companies that decided *not* to listen—just as in high school, an unmanaged reputation can follow you around for years.

In the seventies, Jack Trout and Al Ries attempted to educate advertising agencies, warning them that consumers—not the ad agency or the advertisers themselves—controlled the brand. The customers' experience with the brand was what gave them ownership. If the manufacturer changed the product radically, the customer would reject it. In spite of such warnings, Atari, Studebaker, and Dairy Queen all made radical changes to their brand, with disastrous results and money lost. Who thinks of Dairy Queen when it comes to juicy cheeseburgers?

What was not apparent at first was that the consumer was getting savvier. TV execs put together shows to provide an audience for their advertisers, but unfortunately, the power was in the buyers' hands, not the advertisers. They just didn't know it or want to admit it. Their assumption was that any conversation about a product was controlled by marketing and advertising. Marketers assumed this conversation was ineffectual or even nonexistent. The school of thought was that if it was there, it could be manipulated or changed.

What is marketing, really? It's a one-way conversation from on high, always positive and always about how great a company's products are and how they can make your life better.

And then the Internet came along and revealed a conversation that was always present yet never heard before—consumers hate marketing. And thus, they ignore it.

Once again people were having two-way conversations. They gravitated to message boards, blogs, instant messaging, and then chat—although typed out, these were new forms of conversation from real people, complaining just as they did for thousands of years, but now out in the open for all to see. It was the return of the small town, the gossip mill, and the local barbershop/hair salon. People were connecting on blogs, in chat rooms, and in comment fields . . . rejoicing, complaining, supporting, and inflaming each other.

They didn't want to hear from a company. They wanted to discuss life, politics, diseases, survival, automobiles, etc. Everything was wide open. It was a freedom most didn't have in their own countries—even the United States. Things that couldn't be said in public were readily posted on the Internet. Transparency became normal in cyberspace.

For the first time since the Industrial Revolution, the consumers' conversation has started to drown out a very expensive marketing message. It is unpolished, real, supportive, and sometimes not; it is raw, angry, happy, sad, confused, and sometimes furious. Either way, most see it as a phenomenon of the Internet . . . when in fact it is normal human behavior—we like to connect through "conversation." It is filled with typos and emotional rants, and sometimes it is outrageous and dirty. When marketers enter the Internet world, they are met with disdain; they are seen as an intrusion. The Internet is the largest public opinion forum ever built, and marketing and advertising make many members of this forum furious. Marketing sticks out on the Internet like a plastic bottle floating in a pond. To true Netizens it doesn't belong there.

If you are a marketer, the flow of raw, unpolished chitchat on the Internet will come as a surprise unless you read *The Cluetrain Manifesto*: "That's the awful truth about marketing. It broadcasts messages to people who don't want to listen. Every advertisement, press release, publicity stunt, and giveaway engineered by a marketing department is colored by the fact that it's going to a public that doesn't ask to hear it" (New York: Perseus Publishing, 2001, p. 79).

In the world of social media, people gather to discuss their problems, their hopes, and their dreams. Places like Facebook give "friends" the ability to network and create a string of virtual friendships based on their primary group of close friends, a secondary group of buddies from work, or one of their social-networked games like Farmville or Mafia Wars . . . and strangers actually want to be introduced to one another because of common likes and dislikes. It's fun and it's human. Many gain hundreds of friends from the games they play, and 50 percent of Facebook users are over the age of thirty-five. There are already more users on Facebook than the population of the U.S. Imagine a corporation trying to start a one-way conversation in that network. Wouldn't it seem contrived and creepy?

Yet marketers are using the same old-fashioned marketing techniques they learned over the past hundred years from television, radio, and print. No wonder banner ads get less than a 4 percent click-through rate. Digital Natives see corporations as an invasion into their private space, as predators at best. An outsider with an agenda is not welcome.

Making Friends with the Marketplace

Today's consumer doesn't like to be sold to, nor do they like to be patronized. Marketing on the Web requires seduction. First, consumers must learn to trust you. Trust allows you to build a relationship. And then, if you've built up enough time and there is compatibility, you can wine and dine them to get them to buy whatever you are selling. This tête-à-tête is actually called "seduction marketing" and is a direct reaction to today's cynical, Internet- and computer-savvy buyer. Marketing to your target audience with the well-written copy from your marketing brochure will only get you in trouble. Companies must learn to do what was once unthinkable: make friends with the marketplace and build a relationship.

Seduction marketing requires companies to act human. This creates a brand that is subtle and woven into the fabric of our online communities. It is a brand that people start having a relationship with—a relationship created with a specific market that is not using the passive, one-way, shotgun approach of marketing, but instead develops a one-to-one relationship that is truly a two-way conversation. By creating a buzz in an online network, corporations join the online party. It's socializing and business together, much like multilevel marketing.

I like to call this new type of branding the "stealth brand," because it means staying below the radar, unpretentious, and quiet. Google, Facebook, and Twitter are good examples. Stealth brands spread their gospel through subtlety and word of mouth.

Conversions from 1-800 numbers on an infomercial show up instantly—so now adding a website becomes a must, as most people just want to order a product, not talk to a telemarketer or an actual live person on the phone. The Internet is the most discreet tool ever invented to create a seemingly private transaction. And it is a measurable world, thanks to Internet protocols, leaving us with a depth of options for even a simple marketing campaign.

Steve Jobs describes television as a lean-back medium: You lean back and enjoy it as you sit in your living room and veg out. The world of Internet videos, by contrast, is a sit-forward medium. As you lean into the computer screen, it gives the illusion of intimacy and a sense of closeness.

It is funny to see a large company create a successful presence online, dropping their hyper-controlled marketing language for an intimate Web relationship, yet still have their printed pieces reflect the old Industrial Age, one-way marketing message. They talk a certain way online, another way on the website, and another way on their commercials. It's as if we entered a late-night jazz club where everyone is using hip and cool language—but when the sun comes back up, it's business as usual, with everyone pretending to be as far away from that world as possible.

You can't be hip and cool in one arena while being a seasoned ultra-conservative in another. It's paradoxical. Only a handful of companies get away with it: Nationwide Insurance, McDonald's, Verizon, and Geico seem to be successful with double messages—one set of commercials for the hipsters and another for the oldsters. But it's the elephant in the room.

The shotgun approach to marketing, where companies broadcast the "I'm telling you how great our product is and you are gonna be so impressed" message, is now being ignored by their target audience. The online buyer is responding with "You know what I found out about so-and-so's products? They suck. Pass it on."

This has been a major shock across the advertising world, from Madison Avenue to every boardroom around the globe. Traditional marketing aimed at any particular audience is now typically met with hostility. Today's marketing involves a conversation among consumers, and it's not always pretty. This conversation was always there, but most marketers assumed that it was irrelevant and not really necessary for a company's success. No one ever realized that even if people like your products and use them, they are tired of being told about them all the time. Commercials bombard us everywhere—from television to radio to print ads to highway billboards. And online marketers wonder why people ignore banner ads! Marketing just talks at people, never once listening. This is why it is called "shotgun" (rather than "sharpshooter") marketing—90 percent of the message hits the wrong target audience. And now the Internet has let the cat out of the bag: Marketing is a hated though ubiquitous part of people's lives, and it's okay to ignore it, just as you pay no attention to the electrical power lines in front of your house.

But big companies don't know how to interact with an audience that is even a little bit hostile to their core message. It's as if they're still trying to give a sales pitch to an angry mob that's brandishing torches. So why do corporations continue to do it?

In this brave new world of the Internet, marketing and advertising stick out like a sore thumb. It's a false mechanical message from the halls of corporate Camelot. And the intended target is rejecting it. Instead of hierarchy and a canned marketing message, consumers want a two-way conversation like the one they get from their current social "friends" network with its one-to-one, peer-to-peer responses. They want to be treated not like a group of solipsistic consumers but as individuals who are quite knowledgeable about what they want and what they like.

So how do you approach an already existing online conversation about your products or service? Try joining in on the conversation that already exists instead of trying to change it.

Stepping through the Looking Glass

Now let's talk about the other half of the equation: your internal work environment. Connecting to the conversation in this environment is just as important as connecting to your customers' perception of your brand. Everything goes hand in hand.

Why, you may ask? Because there is no invisible wall anymore between the people who work for you and your customers. More and more they are one and the same. If you want to hear the truth as it is spoken outside the company, you need to hear what your employees are saying, too.

Here's a thought: If your products are good, shouldn't your employees be using them as well? Back in the seventies, major auto manufacturer executives couldn't figure out why their cars weren't selling. Then some of them looked in the parking lot and noticed company employees were buying the affordable Japanese imports. With all the incentives and employee discounts, they wondered why were their own employees were buying the foreign imports. Was fuel efficiency and affordability *that* important? D'oh! What do you think? The obvious was right in front of their eyes.

Don't wait until the pain of failure burns you. Try being a leader who listens, who makes it safe for employees to share what they know about the market's reactions to the products and services you are selling. If your own employees don't buy your products, why should a stranger?

Understand your brand and understand your internal process. It will make you a better leader. Practitioners of ancient Chinese medicine believe in fixing the entire body; the symptoms are just part of the larger puzzle. The same philosophy should go for your company. Take a look at the whole picture, not just the pieces, both internally and externally. If your brand isn't meeting your customers' needs, chances are, there is an internal reason. And if you have an internal hiccup, it will hamper your brand's ability to deliver a perfect product.

Internal excellence will be reflected in your brand and the quality of your products.

It isn't about eyeballs, or consumption, or enforcing commerce; it's a return to individualism. People inside and outside of your company are having a conversation about your brand and your products, whether you are marketing to them or not. So take a moment and listen to what they are saying.

True Lies

When I first started K2, a producer for the Caribiner Group called us in to help them win a pitch for BMW. I had worked with Scott for almost a decade at Caribiner as an independent contractor before founding K2, and he and I had learned to trust each other's skill sets. What he wanted me for in this case was my nontraditional approach to winning massive assignments.

BMW was handing out a $200,000 bonus to any corporate-events company that could come up with a totally outrageous event to launch a brand new type of BMW—a roadster geared toward the younger, newer, hipper car buyer. The Z-Class would look different from any Beamer ever seen—it was sleek, sexy, and shark shaped, and it would bring back the days of driving through the countryside with the top down.

The pitch was not going out to any of the traditional ad agencies, because BMW wanted out-of-the-box thinking. The firm that won the job would be given $10 million to do a nationwide event to promote the car, an event aligned with the advertising agency's vision. This was going to be a *big* event over a one-year period. Since Caribiner was the number one corporate-events company in the United States, it was assumed they were a shoo-in.

Because Scott had brought in K2 to help with this brainstorming session, Doug and I had assumed we'd get at least a polite welcome; yet the moment we entered the room, we could sense the tension and hostility. Apparently, we were seen as a threat. We learned later that Scott had been getting flak over our presence. Perhaps it for the very reason he wanted us in the first place: He just wasn't that confident in Caribiner's own creative team.

Scott's intuition quickly proved justified. As the session got under way, Caribiner's in-house creative director, whom I'll call Paul, insisted over and over that the new roadster was being aimed at the eighteen-to-twenty-four-year-old market. Doug shot back, "Are you sure about that?" at which point Paul assumed an air of arrogance and assured us he knew what BMW was all about.

He began regaling the entire brainstorming session with one quote after another. In the midst of this he said something that gave us even more pause: that he was "pretty sure" that BMW's target-audience data was sound. Doug replied, "You're going to risk a $10 million pitch on a *hunch*?"

Doug insisted that we needed up-to-date market information, and of course he was right. By the next meeting, Paul had found out from BMW that the numbers had changed dramatically: The supposed eighteen-to-twenty-four market had shifted to fortysomethings who wanted to relive their glory days. Oops! Caribiner almost undershot the mark—by twenty years.

Show Up and Listen

There's a very large lesson in the Caribiner story: Companies that continuously refuse to listen to the truth—whether from their customers or their employees—are usually the last to wake up and discover that their company is in trouble. And no wonder. In environments where honesty is crushed and people are kept in line through hierarchy, employees learn it's better to give up than give ideas. Why be innovative in a suppressive environment, when a great idea could be viewed as insubordination? No one sticks their neck out in such a place. By nurturing an environment for truth, on the other hand, leadership can see problems early and turn them into opportunities.

How do you go about this? One way is to get down on the production floor during peak production and watch how your product is assembled. Ask the people on the front lines how they would do it better. Oh, and do yourself a favor—show up unannounced. The truth comes to the surface quicker when no one has prepared for your arrival. Or even go in under-cover. When everyone knows the CEO is in town, they put on a façade.

So get in there. Stop ordering and bossing people around. Instead, listen to the truth. Have a brainstorming session and ask what software is out there that could replace your business in a few years. Kick it up a notch. Don't punish people for speaking up; see it differently—people who speak up care about the company they work for! Listen to their ideas. In a safe environment, ideas start stampeding in, along with profits.

Not surprisingly, Caribiner went out of business a few years later.

Rebirth of the Badass Bike[2]

Early in the seventies, the name Harley-Davidson became synonymous with junk. American Machine and Foundry (AMF), the bicycle and sports equipment manufacturer, had purchased Harley back in 1969, assuming that the Harley name would assure a profit center.

Unfortunately, over time AMF drove the octogenarian company into the ground by streamlining production, cheapening the manufacturing process with inferior parts, and firing employees in an attempt to squeeze every penny out of its acquisition. At the same time, Japanese imports began inundating the United States with cheaper, café-style racing motor-cycles. Harley-Davidson became the laughingstock of the motorcycle industry, and even die-hard HOGs (members of Harley Owners Groups) were having trouble supporting a company whose motorcycles could come apart on the highway.

Something had to be done, or else Harley—at the time America's only motorcycle company—was about to go out of business. In 1981, a con-glomerate of investors and thirteen company executives led by Vaughn Beals and Willie G. Davidson, grandson of cofounder William David-son, bought back an almost-bankrupt Harley-Davidson Motorcycles from AMF for $80 million, and the Milwaukee-based headquarters had to get to work restoring the tarnished Harley name.

---

2 The content in this section was adapted from *Forbes Greatest Business Stories of All Time* by *Forbes* Magazine Staff and Daniel Gross. Copyright ©1996 by Byron Preiss Visual Publications, Inc., and Forbes Inc. Reproduced with permission of John Wiley & Sons, Inc.

The "new" owners had been with the company for years, so they knew the Harley brand and what was needed to turn it around. The first mission was to change how their bikes were made—increasing quality while keeping costs low. One way they did this was to shift decision making from the top of the organization to the front lines, putting quality control in the hands of assembly workers during any and every stage of the manufacturing process. If a part or a weld didn't meet the new Harley standard, any worker could stop the line and correct the final product.

Innovation can thrive only in environments where it is safe to tell the truth.

Harley faced the truth quickly and implemented a quality-over-quantity attitude. Pride in workmanship and a sense of purpose returned to the factory floor and the work that employees were involved in. Word began to spread that Harley made great bikes again. Once the internal part of the company was reworked, it was time to change customer perception about the Harley-Davidson brand.

The executive team at Harley is rare for another reason: They don't just work for the company, they live the motorcycle lifestyle. By participating in racing events and HOG rallies in Daytona and Pennsylvania, they could meet their customers face-to-face. This is not an easy thing for a company to do if its customers feel angry and abused. Yet even though it hurt to listen to painful and honest complaints from customers, it helped give the company still more direction for recovery—and clout.

Meeting Harley owners head-on helped these executives for another reason: It let them show off new products while building brand loyalty. After all, if the guys at the top were riding these cycles, they had to be good. This went a long way to bringing the brand back to life.

As a result of all of this, Harley's demographic evolved. What had been an affordable motorcycle for a small group on the edge of society became a high-end brand that started to attract doctors, lawyers, and college-educated wannabes who could afford the new bike lines but also wanted to get back in touch with masculinity. The affluent who worked in homogenized offices and courtrooms were suddenly interested in dabbling in the rugged Harley-Davidson lifestyle on weekends. The nine-to-five office worker became a weekend warrior Friday at 5:00 PM.

Since Yamaha, Kawasaki, and Honda had chosen to inundate the United States with their modern café racer look, Harley did the opposite in order to recapture their brand—they deliberately returned to the macho, "retro" look of the past.

But that didn't stop the development team from looking into the future. Today's Harley-Davidson brands encompass traditional touring bikes such as the Fat Boy, female biker–focused brands like the Sportster, and cutting-edge bikes like the café racer–style and retro-inspired V-Rod, along with a macho-inspired apparel line of jackets, T-shirts, and helmets. This is part of the strategy that made them strong enough to go public. The lesson here is to give the customer a lifestyle-changing product that is built to last, and support the hell out of that choice.

It's an amazing turnaround story, but it couldn't have gotten off the ground if the executive team hadn't taken a good hard look at their company and faced the truth about the internal and external problems of the Harley-Davidson brand—it was dying a slow and miserable death.

They didn't live in the glory days, and they neither blamed nor complained. They simply faced the reality of what had destroyed their products and took steps to turn it around and make an even better product that would keep customers coming back.

Truth is the cornerstone of great leadership, and great leadership faces the truth—head-on. Even if it is uncomfortable.

I am always astounded when companies refuse to face facts. Making money during boom cycles in an economy is easy. Making money during a down cycle requires brilliance.

Jack of All Brands, Master of None

A few years ago, after I had finished a speech on branding, a young executive approached me from the crowd. Her name was Yuan. (Yes, her parents named her after money. She found this to be hysterical. So did I, for that matter.) She confided in me that for the past five years she had worked closely on every brand at General Motors, but she was now unemployed. She began to tell me that she just couldn't understand why GM wasn't doing better in the marketplace (this was before GM's meltdown and government bailout). In turn, I explained to her that GM wasn't listening to their customers, nor was the company providing them with great products that met their needs. People didn't want bulky gas-guzzlers anymore; they wanted intelligently designed vehicles with the technological advances they were used to elsewhere: fuel-efficient hybrids and responsible SUVs with doodads such as iPod docking stations, onboard computers for GPS navigation, fuel-efficiency monitors, and hands-free phone systems. Stuff like this had been in Hondas, Volkswagens, and MINI Coopers for years.

"The consumer is someone GM stopped listening to," I told Yuan. "And while GM continues to manufacture mediocre products, other companies that *are* listening and adjusting are eroding their market share."

I added that GM had become a jack-of-all-trades—or in this case, brands—and a master of none. In an attempt to please everyone, they had created too many brands in too many categories, offering too many choices. The resulting brand dilution meant that to car buyers, GM now stood for nothing. Yet they kept manufacturing and manufacturing, and the inventory kept piling up.

It's a fact that once the consumer has a strong opinion about a company and its products, it doesn't matter what the company tries to put out into the marketplace; it won't be able to overcome the inertia behind an already existing perception. Anything that doesn't align with that perception is being force-fed to a customer who doesn't want what you are selling.

Your opinion from inside your company is not what matters—it's what your customers think that matters.

GM was wasting mounds of cash, when all they had to do was ask the consumer what they hated and what they wanted. How many companies make the same mistake? How many brands out there in the market are based on hope that the consumer will grow to like them? Hope is not a strategy.

Facing the truth—and I mean the real truth, not your personal opinion about your company—will help you to see what is holding your organization back. And once the truth is out in the open, brainstorming from that reality will bring about great ideas that can change your company. It's about leadership that is willing to listen.

Most American car companies have left themselves vulnerable to foreign imports. And their success is well deserved—they seem to try harder. Companies like Korea-based KIA have spent serious money building their brands over the years by providing car buyers an affordable mini SUV that stands for quality. KIA's Sorento gives active soccer moms plenty of room at an affordable price. This is the new KIA, luxurious, affordable, and family oriented. It is family adventure in an incredibly well-designed package.

American manufacturers have to stage a comeback . . . but first, they have to figure out why everyone seems to be buying affordable imports. KIA has at least four family-focused SUVs and minivans. Hello? Anyone in Detroit paying attention?

Ignoring your customers leaves you vulnerable to those who pay attention. May the best company win.

3RD LAW

A Liquid Leader Nurtures a Creative Culture

A little nonsense now and then is relished by the wisest men.

—Gene Wilder as Willy Wonka in *Willy Wonka and the Chocolate Factory*

Isn't Creativity Just for Artistic Types?

To find creative cultures in today's world of business, we need to look no further than start-ups. Start-ups are great resources for innovation because, in their pursuit to make their brand a household name, they take risks and chances that may make established companies cringe. Start-ups thrive on rejecting assumptions that a market is this way or that. They simply try as many models as possible, keeping what works and refining it while dumping the rest.

This is the big difference between an entrepreneur and an executive, especially when it comes to methodologies and thought. Executives thrive on systems and processes, whereas entrepreneurs attempt to disrupt the status quo and create new markets. If you have ever walked into a start-up, you know what I mean—there is electricity in the air.

Yes, a lot of start-ups go out of business, but every once in a while a start-up survives because the founder straddles both worlds of leadership—entrepreneur and executive—and creates such a dynamic company that we stop and go, "Wow." Even while running a big, established organization, such leaders find ways to cultivate the hunger, drive, passion, and talent of a start-up, while destroying established models that otherwise would get in the way. Every product from a company managed like this catapults the organization into consistent market leadership and the role of industry innovator.

And here's the key: Such companies engage every individual personally in the drive for success. Every contribution is taken into consideration and rewarded. The excitement in these organizations is contagious.

But don't take my word for it. As cited by Daniel Pink in his book *Drive: The Surprising Truth About What Motivates Us*, studies done at the Massachusetts Institute of Technology and the London School of Economics discovered that when a simple set of rules, goals, and tasks was laid out to for people to follow—as long as each task involved rudimentary mechanical skills with a basic set of achievable tasks—bonuses worked as expected. There's nothing new there. But when a task required more developed cognitive skills, out-of-the-box thinking, or creative breakthroughs, a larger reward actually led to poorer performance!

The studies reached the conclusion that when the task gets more complex and requires more conceptual, inventive thinking, traditional motivators do not work. Now, this flies in the face of every assumption common in management circles!

But here is the "Aha!" moment that both studies revealed: When they removed the issue of money—by paying people really well in the first place—smart people started thinking about the work instead of competing for bonuses. They started using their free time to do things that "made no sense" from the corporate perspective. They would hang out together, write poetry, take guitar lessons, or enroll in cooking or art classes. But what was even more surprising? Productivity in the work environment went up!

Through these studies, behavioral scientists discovered that three factors (discussed below) lead to better performance and personal satisfaction in creative working environments.

The Intuitive Desire to Be Self-directed

Traditional management works great if you want people to simply obey and follow the rules. This is especially important when the tasks are simple and achievable, such as "We need to bag three hundred thousand loaves of bread per day." Not so easy, but achievable.

But when it comes to higher complexity and creative work, such as overseeing the design of a new green energy system, giving people the freedom of choice to give their time over to the company changes their output levels. They become completely engaged in their work and the mission of the company. Remember when your parents would say, "You know, if I made you do it, you wouldn't want to do it?" Well, as it turns out, that's true. When we offer people the autonomy to self-direct their work, they start giving over more than their time; they give their heart, mind, and spirit.

With people doing more complicated and sophisticated work these days, the sensible model—the one that provides rewards to all involved—involves self-direction.

People Have a Built-in Desire to Get Better and Better at Something They Like to Do

Again, according to Daniel Pink in his book *Drive*, the second finding of the MIT and LSE studies was that people have a natural urge to get better at stuff that they like. Whether it is becoming a better musician, video gamer, or athlete, people like a challenge. Now, when that challenge is automatically built in to a great work environment, people will work non-stop to get better and better at something.

To economists who study human behavior, this makes no sense. Why learn how to play a musical instrument? It isn't gonna make you rich or get you ahead at your job, so why do it? Yet since economists believe people are driven by money, they simply miss the point; economics are about people's behavior, not about money. At some levels, yes, people who are struggling to put food on the table or are raising kids are driven by money. But we all know this; it is just common sense. Once again, Daniel Pink states it best—if you don't pay people enough, they won't be motivated. Simply put, if you aren't willing to pay your people well for what they do, they will not be engaged in the company's mission.

The simple and wonderful thing about us all is this: Once we are making enough money, we are free to engage in all sorts of challenging things.

And what escapes most behavioral scientists is that people are driven to get better at something because it gives us a sense of accomplishment.

It seems that facing a challenge and mastering that challenge over time enriches us beyond the printed page, beyond even our sense of logic. Why did I enroll in Shaolin Kempo at forty-five years of age? I wanted a bigger challenge. It also gave me a sense of contribution to my nephew's world—a sense of "This is bigger than me"—and that led me to the next finding.

People Yearn to Do What We Do Best in the Service of Something Larger than Ourselves

More and more companies, in order to create a certain level of engagement among their employees, have created a transcendent, purpose-filled work environment where everyone feels as if they are a contributor to something bigger than themselves. That makes coming to work more enjoyable, and it is also a way to attract and retain talent.

When people have a sense of purpose built into what they do, you don't just get an employee—you get a person's talent, passion, and full attention. Most people around the world just show up to a job and do what it takes to get ahead. But real engagement—real, 100 percent commitment—requires a workplace that isn't just making stuff but, in some way, changing the world. On the other hand, when a company doesn't have a purpose, they lose their direction and start making both bad products and bad decisions. Like I've said before, change begins within.

Companies that are flourishing in this economy are the ones that inspire their workforce, both inside and out, with a sense of purpose! And the little secret is this: Purpose and profits go hand in hand.

In short, companies that nurture a results-only, creative culture trust their people to be self-directed and give them the training and the challenge so they can do so. Try putting that in a mission statement.

From the Mail Room to the Boardroom and the Power of Systemic Alignment

For the majority of my career in corporate events management, I specialized in two sectors: automobile companies, such as Ford and Lincoln Mercury, Mercedes-Benz, and BMW; and big pharmaceutical companies such as Merck, Roche, Pfizer, Novartis, Bristol-Myers Squibb, and Johnson & Johnson. And in both cases, through years of meetings, I worked for some of the top production companies in the country: Caribiner, Roger Wade Productions, Meeting Makers, and Drury Design, to name a few. This was long before I cofounded K2.

What always impressed me about the pharmaceutical meetings in particular was the degree of training required for the sales reps in that industry. Upon the release of each new product, they required four days of intensive training and knowledge sharing to prepare for all sorts of rejection from doctors and hospitals. Mini-plays, mentoring programs, and even flash cards were used to get every rep up to speed.

There were actually two goals to these extensive exercises. The first was, as you might expect, to make sure the reps were well versed in both the negatives and the positives of the product. That way they could remain comfortable within potentially confrontational situations, and respond with confidence and candor instead of panic and confusion.

The second goal was less obvious, and yet at least as important—if not more so. It was to get absolutely everyone aligned to the goals of the company and the brand. The better the alignment, the more creative the sales force could be without straying from mission or message, and the greater the company's chance of success.

So how do you go about getting aligned? Here are a few pages from my playbook, with information I learned from the inside, privy to every new drug launch and FDA question—a fly on the wall at every conference, watching in amazement at the intensity and cleverness of the training.

Stonecutting Can Be Contagious

Remember the story of the three medieval stonecutters? A man came upon them and asked what they were doing. The first one replied, "I'm cutting stones—what does it look like?" The second one said merely, "I'm cutting these stones for a cathedral," then fell silent. But the third stonecutter looked the man in the eye and replied firmly, "I am part of a five-year project to create the greatest cathedral ever seen."

Although there weren't any structures in place just yet, the third stonecutter became so excited, he continued to explain: "Here will be the doors. They will be made of the finest oak. And here will be the altar. And the main tower will stand here." The more he explained, the easier it became to imagine just how beautiful the structure was going to be. He could see it clearly, and so could his inquisitor.

This story explains well how attitude can determine one's direction in life. If you had workers like these three stonecutters, which one do you believe would be the most creative? Which would get the most done?

The energy and enthusiasm in an organization is paramount to its success, especially during tough times. Imagine working in an organization where the entire company is excited to be working with a singular vision—a vision of greatness, bearing with it a profound sense that once the goal is accomplished, not only will everyone get a bonus, but also the world itself will be a better place.

As a leader, you have the job of spreading this kind of contagious fever throughout the company, in every office and every conference room. Instead of spouting convoluted mumbo jumbo, communicate a clear goal that gets everyone fired up, just as the third stonecutter did. What I am talking about is inspiring a sense of engagement in everyone involved.

Stay away from multiple or tiered goals, stated in weak or overly qualified language. You need strong dynamics and a single objective. Oh, and take out "Our goal is to make $35 million by the end of next quarter." That sort of language is for the sales reps and their meetings. Try having a goal like "Our kick-ass products will change the way people do business." Okay, so it's not my best marketing slogan, but you get the picture.

Great companies stand on one great idea. Anything more confuses the message. Here's the last line from one of my favorite advertising slogans, "Think Different," created for Apple Computer in 1997 by advertising agency TBWA\Chiat\Day: "The people who are crazy enough to think they can change the world, are the ones who do." It is inspirational and falls in line with Apple's brand. They design computers for the non-nerds, the quirky individuals who apply the same discipline to a video project as an engineer would. That is Apple's audience, the nonbusiness types.

By knowing your brand well—the good and bad, the internal and the external—you'll find less inertia to overcome.

Back to the pharmaceutical industry: A few years ago I was called in to oversee the speeches and videos for one of the top pharmaceutical companies in the United States. This company had spent years overcoming some very bad press about their proprietary drug cocktail that, unfortunately, caused deadly heart attacks. To get the company over this hurdle, the CEO put together a multi-tiered strategy to get the company back on track over a seven-year period. But he didn't stop there. He took this strategy statement and reduced its essence to a pyramid, a diagram you could scribble on a napkin and immediately understand. He made sure it was repeated and understood, from the boardroom to the mail room, via every PowerPoint presentation within the company.

This CEO's mantra was to make better products, and he made sure everyone knew it and lived it. As I stood in this company's eight hundred–seat auditorium outside Philadelphia, surrounded by enthusiasm and excitement, I realized that they had come through the worst and that they were a stronger organization for it. This pharmaceutical giant reignited their passion for helping people instead of selling.

To redirect your company, start training your best trainers in the new direction. Changing people's minds may take years, even in organizations that have positive environments. But remember, this type of training is not from the top down but from the bottom up—from the mail room to the boardroom, not the reverse. When a company makes the mistake of training from the top down, they are attempting to force people to go in a direction that those people may resist. This is in part due to the fact that the new direction is seen not as organic but as mandated by disconnected management. But when the new direction begins from within, the vision and idea become an organic part of the company's overall vision. Your mission statement shouldn't be just a plaque on the wall—it should be something that engages everyone's participation.

Remember, too, there is no such thing as a company man or woman these days. People have the option to leave companies quickly, to further their own career. Staying more than two years has become the exception, not the rule. If people are consistently opting to leave, eventually your competition will know your deepest, darkest secrets, because people always talk—even with ironclad non-compete clauses.

This makes talent retention even more important as you reposition your organization. And it is not something to leave up to HR—you must take charge. When shaping a vision, ask yourself, "Will this vision be as exciting to others as it is to me? Is it a worthwhile trip to make? Is this something for the long term, or is it more short term? Is this a vision that I would personally get behind if I wasn't a leader? Is it in line with what our brand represents to our customer? Is it true? Or am I ignoring the facts in order to make Wall Street happy?" Try inventing a no-BS zone in your company. Asking these sorts of serious questions will bring about a very serious and exciting vision for your company. And people who are fired up about a vision that is simple, true, and emotionally engaging are unstoppable.

It's not magic; it's coaching.

Now is the time to get everyone in the organization on board. Let them know the intention. Set clear and simple goals. Answer questions like "How will this affect us?" and "What are the dangers?" and most important, "What are the rewards?" And make sure everyone has the elevator speech down pat.

Did you know that when you are flying in an airplane, the pilot is off course 90 percent of the time? By readjusting and listening to his or her navigator, the pilot can make the tiny, periodical micro-adjustments that assure that the plane and all its passengers will land in Zurich instead of Zimbabwe. Periodically ask yourself, "Do we make cool stuff?" or "Are we enriching people's lives?" It is your job as a leader to stay on course and continually remind your people of the direction of the company. Alignment doesn't happen just once. Like a great pilot, you need to check alignment over and over until the destination is reached.

And remember: from the bottom up, from the mail room to the boardroom.

The Right Tool
for the Job

Back in the nineties I watched one production company after another go under because they didn't know that their slide projector–based business was being upgraded to a laptop-driven business. Portable, easier to work with, and less costly, the laptop destroyed those who didn't move quickly enough and adapt to the newfangled invention. It also meant a CEO could make changes right up until showtime.

Today there is technology available that can make even a small company competitive with a larger company. This has forced larger corporations to scramble, while smaller companies are able to nab already existing business from them, starting with what big companies would see as low-hanging fruit. Smaller companies are willing to take these smaller projects off the hands of the big boys by simply giving more attention and better customer service.

Technology is lowering the barrier of entry for one-person boutiques to compete with midsize companies. It is also flattening the criteria that define small, midsize, and big-cap companies' size and potential.

**Internal hierarchies are collapsing,
and so are external ones.**

Look at Skype, a free online videoconferencing tool that works over any high-speed Internet connection. It allows small companies to partake of global meeting and videoconferencing technology that at one time was extremely expensive and only in the hands of production departments with money. Now even a small company can set up a videoconference with an international clientele for free.

So when thinking in terms of what technology is available to make your company more creative, get on board with your tech people as quickly as possible. Ask them on a consistent basis to be on the lookout for business-altering technologies that your company could utilize.

And do yourself a favor: make sure you aren't married to one type of technology. Too many companies have failed by putting billions into technology that became obsolete. Just remember, eight-track tapes and cassette players were replaced by CD and MP3 players; the computer replaced the typewriter; and DVDs replaced VHS tapes.

You might be surprised with all this hi-tech talk that a very low-tech company is the biggest thorn in the side of Netflix. Redbox—a very low-tech vending machine, fully loaded with DVDs for overnight rental and located in thirty-five thousand supermarkets and stores across the country, is giving the big three movie rental companies a run for their money.

Ironically, it is the most disruptive piece of low-tech equipment ever to confuse the technologically elite. It is as old-school as you can get. So why is it so successful?

Much like alcohol and gambling go together, movies and "what should we make for dinner tonight?" are the pastimes of the modern American nuclear family. Experts are analyzing the why behind Redbox success, yet no one is actually facing the truth that's right in front of them: it isn't a cultural backlash against technology or an in-between resource, or even an alternative to Netflix. It is a point of purchase display that happens to be in the right place at the right time. Period.

Think about it for a moment—two thirds of all movie rentals in the United States happen between four and nine p.m. What else are people doing during that time? Coming home from work and trying to figure out what to make for dinner. Redbox simply intersects two impulse purchases at the same time: food buying and entertainment. After a hard day's work, most Americans, whether they have kids or not, want the evening to go smoothly and want entertainment that they can sit back and just watch.

Redbox makes the point of purchase as cheap, easy, and convenient as one can get. Emblazoned across the top of the kiosk it says "$1 DVD rentals," meaning if you keep a movie one night it's one dollar and if you keep it five days, it's five dollars. It also means people will take greater chances on movies that they might not normally watch. At one dollar, what do you have to lose? It's easy and convenient and perfect for a customer that doesn't want to pay a monthly fee. When you are done with the movie, simply return it to any Redbox vending machine.

It is not magic—it's about placing a kiosk at the exact location where people make an impulse decision. The simplicity of Redbox's success is confusing people who only think in terms of technology. How can something so old-fashioned be so disruptive to companies like Netflix who have carved out an incredible business model using hi-tech efficiency?

But don't be fooled by Redbox's simplicity. It utilizes the Internet to keep inventory up to date and to track a customer's tastes by ordering and keeping their favorite titles conveniently in stock. The Redbox system is a very sophisticated inventory management system that stays in touch with local customers and communicates those requests to the Redbox technicians. It's where high-tech inventory management software meets old-fashioned vending machine systems.

Reed Hastings has called Redbox one of Netflix's most challenging rivals. He also told The Hollywood Reporter in March of 2009, "It's really scary." Probably because Redbox just doesn't look that sophisticated.

And this is without a single dollar spent on advertising. This makes Redbox a stealth brand—below radar and one of those successful companies you've never heard of.

How can you simplify things to reach your customer? What technology is available right now that closes the gap between you and your customer? Can you utilize the right combination of tools to be a thorn in the side of your competitor?

Be visionary when it comes to technology . . . and remember, it is always evolving. Howard Hughes understood before anyone else seemed to that the future of television was to be in the satellites circling earth. So he founded the company that later created DirecTV, long before anyone else could see the future of digital TV or telecommunication satellites.

Disruption will be the norm for the next twenty-five years. As the Internet takes on a new life and evolves into a more robust, open-source network with smart nodes, be prepared to evolve with it.

Throw away the briefcase, set up your home office, and prepare for a virtualized workforce without brick-and-mortar office spaces or cubicles. The Information Age is filled with young folks immersed in developing applications and methodologies unencumbered by tradition. Memories of going to an office will become stories you will tell your grandkids. After all, a real office costs money to heat, light, and make comfortable for human occupation. A virtual office requires only a steady stream of 220-volt electric current and a programmer to make it "real."

What should scare the hell out of anyone in business is that I can migrate an entire company online. The receptionist, the sales force, the products you manufacture, the retail space, marketing department…all gone in favor of a fully automated website that imitates the real-world version of your business. A website with the proper software and the right network can automate an entire company. That should scare you enough to wake up to the potential of generations raised to think in terms of automating everything—even the simplest task—with an application.

Actual work as well as business is being redefined.

The hourly-rate job is transitioning into an independent virtualized workforce because technology frees us up to work wherever and whenever we want. It is the return of independent craftsmen, each offering their services to a company, except now their toolkit is kept on a computer or a network of servers.

Today's Transformer

I really enjoy when my seminars shift people's thinking and illuminate their old paradigms. Those "Aha!" moments are great, but honestly, most people forget what they learned by the time Monday morning rolls around. To truly implement change and make it sustainable requires consistent training and a systemic, supportive environment. Otherwise the old status quo will creep right back in.

So you need the proper training, plus an oversight team to shepherd people through to the promised land. But that's only part of it. As Emeril Lagasse likes to say, *"Bam!* Let's kick it up a notch!"* To get more alignment from your people requires more than just training; what's needed is the ability to see talent in your staff that isn't apparent on a resume or in a half-hour interview.

Look in particular for skill sets that may be best suited for different departments. This is especially important when a company is really changing direction. Before you fire people or reposition them, take a good, long look at their resume, and then arrange a face-to-face and a copious Q&A session about how they see themselves.

To get past conventional thinking, try asking the person where and at what they would ideally see themselves working. You'd be amazed at how many people are at first unaware of their core competency. Give them the opportunity to do what they do best and be who they really want to be, and you'll retain talent that would otherwise have been wasted and redirect energy to where it can best benefit the organization.

A client of mine, a small-business owner, experienced this for herself with one of her key employees. He had been hired to deliver the IT portion of their presentations, but he wasn't very good with face-to-face communication. As polished as that young man was, and as well as he could talk the right tech talk, he couldn't feel out the direction a meeting was taking, and so he missed a lot of visual and emotional cues to finish up or make his presentation more exciting. Yet he was an integral part of the team.

What my client began to see was that this young man was an incredible writer. His ability to write was far greater than his speaking abilities. So she agreed to repurpose him for writing proposals. My client didn't eliminate him from pitch meetings; she simply nurtured his innate abilities. And coincidentally this enabled the company to land larger and larger projects.

Spotting and nurturing talent in this manner is essential to your organization's health. Don't get bogged down by what you think of an individual. Instead, look at the skills they bring to the table— even skills they may not realize they have. Try to repurpose people according to their natural abilities.

Of course, bad leaders tend to be threatened by talented individuals. Over time, unbeknownst to themselves, such leaders make the road harder for their employees. Many in the workforce may quit, only to have amazing careers somewhere else. And the dysfunctional leader can't understand why they did so well at another company.

Evolved leaders don't make the way any softer either, but they do provide the knowledge, training, and support to point out the stepping-stones along the way. These types of leaders are secure in their positions and welcome new talent with open arms, knowing that with enough time, training, and experience, each individual will deserve to stand in the same winners' circle. They respect each and every individual's contribution to their organization. So be an evolved leader. It saves a lot of time and energy, and it helps retain your best talent.

Remember that when people's enthusiasm isn't 100 percent, their work becomes like a chore to them. Their energy just isn't into it. It's like asking a teenager to take out the garbage; it would be easier to just do it yourself. In contrast, when you move a person with enthusiasm and talent into a department that aligns with their skills, then you have the right person in the right position. Try stopping a company where the executives have done this for every individual. It's like trying to stop a teenager from playing a video game. Good luck with *that*!

What it boils down to is supporting the individual. When you do that, appreciation will be reciprocated, as will loyalty. No one leaves a company that is run well.

Becoming a Peer-to-Peer Communicator

Technology is changing rapidly; we've seen more inventions in the past twenty-five years than in the previous 235 years. Everything is moving faster and faster. What is happening? We've seen this sort of economic boom throughout history, but previous booms were small, self-contained, and short lived. Yet they were always the result of freedom, support from a structure of law, and access to a long-term sustained economic system, such as the Roman Republic or the Ottoman Empire. The difference today is that this boom is global, affecting everyone on Earth—and it's the first time this has happened in six thousand years. What we are experiencing is like compound interest; we have reached maximum velocity and are entering an era of infinite possibilities. The only thing missing from this joyride into the future is a brand-new DeLorean.

Now add to that a global marketplace. Emerging industrialized nations have spent the past two decades building the same style of infrastructure that the United States built over the past one hundred years. Emotionally, mentally, and physically these countries will be skipping the Industrial Revolution altogether and going straight to the Information Age. But can they handle Western-style economics, digital banking, and Internet economies?

The majority of these emerging nations are hungry to experience the same prosperity that Europe and the United States have enjoyed for centuries. As our Western economies take a pounding, we may be surprised to see that the rest of the world has risen to our standards. We are no longer the leader in a multitude of sectors.

As other countries and cultures speed up, what do you want to do in this fast-paced, explosive, globally connected environment: slow down and micromanage, or loosen up and speed up your organization?

Such speed can seem impossible for an individual to keep track of. And that's where your internal talent pool comes in. By making your company a place where it is safe to share even the weirdest idea, you make yourself approachable, a confidant and an expert at the same time. Most employees, even in upper management, are afraid to approach executive teams when it comes to ideas and changes that are happening outside the corporation, for fear of being fired. By making everyone fearless, you get the real person and their real thoughts—unmoved by your presence as "the boss."

This is especially important if you've achieved any degree of fame as a leader or an innovator in your industry. For a new employee, meeting someone with that aura can be very intimidating. Most employees in this situation try to be perfect instead of being natural. Nip this in the bud immediately. Take these employees out for a drink or a few golf outings with upper management. Give them a chance to see you with your hair down. Ask them to be themselves. Let them know that perfection is not what you want to hear about, nor do you want just a bunch of safe ideas. You may just see them breathe a literal sigh of relief right then and there.

By opening up communication and creating an environment where communication is a two-way process, something that takes place between peers, an organization can navigate with mercurial speed and spot business threats a mile away. Knowledge sharing keeps your organization moving forward, on the cutting edge, and fearless, with everyone on the lookout for up-to-date technology, practices, methodologies, and software developments.

Some companies use instant messaging to allow everyone a chance to be in constant communication, and some go so far as to have an instant messaging network for their *clients* to critique them in real time. Scary, perhaps, but it's incredibly effective and efficient in a world so fast-paced, it can seem hyperactive.

By taking in peer-to-peer and peer-to-client feedback, you can adjust to changes in the marketplace almost instantly and stay relevant in the New Economic Order.

Measuring Productivity without Becoming Big Brother

With all this trendy talk of collaboration and teamwork, you are probably wondering how to measure people's output. Fortunately, a far better answer is available than ever before.

For almost six decades, experts at statistical analysis worked at refining a specialized type of number crunching into full-blown digital sleuthing, allowing companies to discover fraud that can't be detected with a simple overview of a spreadsheet. Such analysis has since been extended via proprietary systems and 3D computer imaging to measure human output, via what has become known as operations research.

The 3D models created by operations research look like an exercise in mind mapping, with one circle representing an employee interconnected to other employees. Each circle has multiple layers in various colors that represent how much work is done and how much intercommunication is taking place. Peer-to-peer communication can be measured, and so can peer-to-group communication as well as productivity.

Operations research offers a far quicker and more accurate account of who is actually pulling their weight in an organization. When it comes time for a promotion, it is easy to see in living color who the winners are and who needs to be fired. These models can even be used to see which departments are failing and to reduce redundancy. Compare this to the old-fashioned way of determining where the axe will fall, based on nothing more than a look at salary and an arbitrary decision. How many times has a department head or regular employee been let go, only for management to discover a month later that the person in question was vital to the success of not just one but several departments?

A friend of mine was laid off recently, only to be rehired a week later—the executive team suddenly realized that without her, communications had become nonexistent between them and the rest of the company, as well as key construction people located on several job sites. Oops.

> Now human analytics models can be applied for a
> more fair and balanced decision-making process, by
> showing 3D, real-time analysis of individual output
> and compliance.

Strong managers should be monitoring completion and updates from their staff. This data can be handed off to your HR department for an unbiased overview. Let HR draft the progress reports for executives and department heads.

Get your best people on this. By establishing a training program with measurable results and benchmarks, your organization can start determining a system of best practices. These should be visible at any time during the production arch on any given project. This also cuts down on the amount of meetings managers will need in order to determine project status. No matter how complex your process may be, there are plenty of software choices out there for tracking a project and employee output.

Tomorrow's Goal: Autonomy

Bear in mind that statistical studies of employee performance are a form of data mining and can be extremely Big Brother–ish, requiring employees to always be "on." So you need a way to defuse the anxiety and turn it into something that is competitive, but also healthy and productive.

Accenture has done this by transforming performance evaluations via a Facebook-style program called Performance Multiplier. Employees can post status reports, photos, and both weekly and quarterly goals on their profile pages, where they can be viewed by their peers and managers. If an employee leaves this area blank, the lack of goal setting is visible and an email alert goes out to their managers. Such visibility may at first seem nitoring, but really it is about self-motivation and partici- goals over a peer-to-peer network gives a sense of trans- d with bragging rights. enture's network is internal, but they are working to de their clients as well. There are plenty of companies internal system for you. Toronto start-up Rypple lets witter-length questions—140 characters—about their performance in exchange for anonymous feedback. Companies like Great Harvest Bread Co. and Mozilla have signed up for the software. Employees seeking a response can ask, "How was my presentation?" Their query goes out to a select group of peers and managers, or to anyone else the user selects. This makes employee evaluation more dynamic and democratic while keeping the feedback short, to the point, and anonymous.

No matter how you choose to develop better performance evaluations, or even if you have a results-only environment, don't forget that you still have to reward your top performers.

In task-driven environments, people are competitive when they know they are going to be rewarded for their efforts. The accolades that come from success are intoxicating, but more important, they are motivating. It's truly amazing to watch someone step on stage in front of all their peers, where they receive a cash bonus and a plaque that tells the world, "For going above and beyond the call of duty, and for achieving sales goals for 2010 . . ." The crowd goes wild and another year begins.

Implement such a program today, and you'll see healthy internal competition before you know it—and like you've never seen it before. And do yourself a favor: Make the program big and engaging. If you give $50 dinner certificates, don't expect much. The same effort you put into a rewards program is the same effort you will see from your sales staff; it will affect the bottom line.

Think in terms of incentives; profit sharing programs; an employee stock ownership plan program; an all-expenses-paid "vacation" to Costa Rica for your top regional sales reps and their spouses, with the CEO and a day of private trainings; promotions; and company cars. Whatever works for your people, do it. Make sure your best and brightest get acknowledged for taking the company to another level. If you fail to do so, don't expect them to stay.

Big salaries alone don't motivate people anymore; people want to gain dynamic experiences by working in companies that give autonomy, challenges, and a sense of purpose. A tall order, yes, but when you expect people to think out of the box, so must you when it comes to a rewards program. Think about what makes your people tick. Loosen up the workflow. Create built-in flextime and creative initiatives for big ideas. Brainstorm over cake and coffee. Give your teams a week at the Yankees spring training camp in Florida, complete with a meet and greet. Or how about a week enjoying the World Cup? Or perhaps an evening at the Hard Rock Cafe Casino, complete with an employees-only Battle of the Bands? Run a weekend competition to see who can come up with one groundbreaking idea that could make the company more profitable. These are actual rewards and operational programs that I have seen work quite well.

We're in a new era of productivity, and the trick to harnessing it is to put the systems and analytics in place, measure compliance, and motivate your workforce by giving them self-directed engagement.

Waste nothing, and remember that the larger the ship, the longer it takes to turn. Create a strategy from the data you're getting from the front lines. Get your organization aligned with a great vision, and train for the goals within that vision. Take the time to get there, and once you arrive, give back to your people in a big way.

The key is to create the kind of company *you* would want to work for.

Kirk and Spock and the Fantasy of a Productive Team

As you nurture a culture of creativity, alignment, support, and teamwork, remember, you're doing this for success, not for touchy-feely reasons.

Hollywood has given us a barrage of images on how the right team can work against all odds and create miracles; consider *The A-Team*, *Mission Impossible* (the original), and of course, *Star Trek*. But truth be told, this is a myth. Teams are most effective when each member is the best in their field and demands that all contributions come up to the group's standard. When a group's standard is low, the result is mediocre products. In those industries where teams are successful, the standard of excellence is so high that many newbies pull out all the stops to stay in the group. In these kinds of teams, you have to earn your position. Technology, advertising, and the military are sectors where teams are trained to work best for the greatest results. But these teams don't leave much room for accidental breakthroughs, the sort that change our world. Think tank environments like the one at DuPont, on the other hand, leave room for play.

I could write an entire book about the accidental breakthroughs that have created some of the most innovative ideas on Earth. Just look at the telephone; Alexander Graham Bell was trying to develop technology to help deaf people hear. Watson spilled some chemicals, and *then* the darned thing worked. Imagine that: An accident brought the phone into our world.

How about microwave ovens? Teflon? Plastics? All discovered by accident. There is a market for each. But to have a breakthrough requires room for an accident to happen. The point is, real innovation is almost always accidental, so we can't make it happen directly. All we can do is increase the chances of such accidents occurring, by creating the right kind of environment for them to happen in. Teams must be given the right environment to come up with great work.

I know what you are thinking: Enough already about "teams." It's the latest and hottest buzzword out there, as overused by now as *paradigm*, *synergy*, and *maverick*. And honestly, depending on the type of business you are in, teams may not be appropriate. The majority of companies out there are deadline and production driven—get it done and out the door—so forming teams would be a waste of time. Not everyone will be fortunate enough to work with cutting-edge technology, film production, or robots, or get to wave to their mom from Skype in the weightless vacuum of an orbiting space station. Not everyone will be a knowledge worker in the New World Order.

If your goal is to create innovative one-of-a-kind products and solutions, then teams are for you.

I have worked with and within teams for more than twenty years, long before they became a popular notion in corporate America. That's because I come from a graphic design and advertising business, where teams are ubiquitous and have long been the key to creative work. Such creativity is highly competitive and cutthroat, but it's done that way for a reason, and in most cases it's done well.

By contrast, in the corporate world, teams are only just now getting a foothold. As much as I hate to say it, the majority of such teams aren't properly managed, so naturally they *don't* work well. A big reason for this is that teams generate unpredicted outcomes, and managing them isn't a simple, linear process. But there is a way to drive productivity and innovation without destroying the creative spark that can make teams incredibly productive.

We'll spend the remaining chapters in this section going over some of the team management ideas I've learned and refined in nearly three decades of creative work. You won't find any of this in a textbook; if everything worthwhile about managing could be found in a textbook, we'd all be rich by now.

You Gotta Earn It

We've all been in a brainstorming session where everyone has an idea, and most of the ideas are useless. Usually, 90 percent of the group shouldn't even be there. The painful truth is, not everyone should even be on a team. By filling a room with a bunch of mediocre people, you defeat the purpose and potential of teams. Too many incongruous ideas waste time.

Remember when Avis went gaga over the employee-owned fad and let anyone who wanted to do so present their idea on a PowerPoint deck during the annual stockholders' meeting? Six hours into the meeting, management realized it was a bad idea.

I suggest that only those who are capable of self-managing their own output be allowed on a team. The cream always rises to the top, so why not reward them with a team position? For breakthroughs to happen, complex, creative thinkers need to be given a place to thrive. That's why you're hiring smart, creative people in the first place, isn't it?

To create greatness, you put your best creative types from multiple disciplines in a room and watch them play—it's like bottling lightning. These are people who are not comfortable with the same old, same old. These are people who love the process that makes their work better. In the corporate world this is called "whiteboarding" or "mind mapping," and in the design and Internet arenas, it's called "brainstorming." What makes brainstorming special is that we get so many more pieces of input from so many different backgrounds. Where else would you see marketing pros sitting alongside designers, programmers, software developers, network specialists, and project managers? Everything gets addressed: the user experience, the technology platform, behavioral insights, and the branding that plants a high concept in the user's mind long after they've logged off.

Whether you call it mind mapping or brainstorming, what you want is synergy—different people, with different concerns and thought processes, coming together to give their contributions. Think of it like jazz. When a great band gets together, the sum of the parts is never equal to the output. It's much greater, as if the best and brightest individually push one another to another level of performance.

I once saw Huey Lewis and the News at Madison Square Garden. A third of the way through the concert, Paul Schaffer, David Lettermen's sidekick, showed up on keyboards. The crowd went wild. But the real kicker came a few songs later when Tower of Power, one of the most progressive brass quartets ever, showed up to help kick Huey's brass up a notch. The show went to a completely different level after that. The energy and musicianship were off the charts—the sum total was greater than its parts. It was a googolplex above what I had assumed I was going to see. After that, I became a fan of Huey Lewis and the News, Tower of Power, *and* Paul Schaffer.

On the other hand, imagine spending good money to see a group of mediocre musicians muddle through an hour-and-a-half-long set. Painful, huh? Unless it is your kid's sixth-grade recital, you would probably try to get your money back.

Set up a system with criteria and guidelines. People on teams must earn the right to be there; otherwise it is a waste of everybody's time.

Many companies have a method of choosing their best team members based on talent, and then they whittle choices down to an A team, a B team, a C team, etc. The A team is the best in the company and has earned the right to cherry-pick their projects.

But try to keep your teams from competing against each other. Arrange to have them compete *alongside* each other instead. What's the difference? "Competing against" is counterproductive and can sabotage output. Arguments can erupt. "Competing alongside," on the other hand, empowers teams to impress and inspire one another. It becomes contagious and competitive. Make no mistake about it: Competition like this creates teams that are self-managing, self-motivated, and excited to come to work.

Over time you will be able to see that some team members have earned the right to be moved up to the A team, while others are moved down to the minor leagues of the D team. But try not to let people know you've labeled the teams this way. Let them realize it through observation. Who knows? Over time you may have to create more than one or two A teams.

Make sure each and every member of your organization understands the company's mission, where the company is going, and how it plans on getting there. Try to make the vision exciting for everyone. Team members need to be crystal clear as to goals, purposes, and intentions for the group. Keep the mission of each team front and center, and they'll stay on target, and your employees will understand how to earn their place on the team.

High standards will guarantee greater output.

A Safe Haven

Getting people of different disciplines to respect one another can be hard. In the early days of the Internet it was a struggle at first to get software developers to see graphic designers as equals, yet they had to, because it was the designers who were anticipating the user's experience both psychologically and graphically. They simplified the experience for the average Joe.

In the early days of the Internet boom, I actually had an argument with an IT professional who couldn't understand why anyone would want graphics on a website. Last I heard, he now lives in a cabin in the middle of nowhere in upstate New York—off the grid.

This IT pro forgot why Henry Ford was so successful. Ford understood that selling to the elite wouldn't make him very rich, but making his products available to the common man would assure dense exposure and massive sales.

Respecting each member of the team requires that egos be put on hold and a healthy air of teamwork and support be present in your work environment. Over time, each team member should be able to earn the respect of their coworkers. Once this happens, people become loyal to their peers and trust their peers' constructive criticism. These teams should be multigenerational, not "We older participants are wiser, and younger people know nothing." These are team environments where every person is involved and engaged. At this stage, the work becomes paramount. The team begins to feel as if they are a part of something extraordinary and are following a greater vision.

Unfortunately, a team can become nothing more than a mutual admiration society, where individuals are petrified to criticize one another's weaknesses. This can be true of interaction between teams as well. The underlying fear is that if one team starts critiquing the other, it will open up a can of worms in each, and no one wants that. Or do they?

In mediocre companies that support the status quo, no one makes waves and no one cares enough to make better products. Healthy organizations, on the other hand, critique their work; it's just that someone needs to get the ball rolling and make it contagious. Start with a system that encourages constructive criticism for the betterment of the group.

Companies like W. L. Gore & Associates, the makers of GORE-TEX, operate and thrive very well in a team-driven environment. When new hires are brought on board, they are encouraged to use their own judgment, wander from team to team, and see where they think they can fit in and contribute. The exploration goes both ways: New hires are allowed to pick their own projects if they wish, while teams can seek out new hires to help shake things up.

This apparently loosey-goosey management style has brought about hundreds of major multibillion-dollar ideas and made W. L. Gore a leading incubator of consistently great ideas and products for more than fifty years. To an outside observer it looks as though the focus is on having fun. But to the initiated, it is about hiring intense self-starters who contribute wholeheartedly to what they are doing and to the team, and most important, who can self-manage their time and skill sets.

W. L. Gore's company motto:
Internal fairness, external competitiveness.

Young talent is also encouraged to offer as much input to the mature, established team as possible. This assures the company that their ideas stay fresh and won't get stale. Some types of businesses *must* have an influx of new talent in order to stay innovative. New blood is sometimes what it takes to make consistent breakthroughs a company-wide habit.

Darwin without the Danger

One big idea might make you rich, but only the companies that consistently nurture a stable of creative, talented individuals succeed in the long run. These companies consistently develop multiple great ideas, over and over again.

Creative individuals in such settings have learned to trust and respect one another's contributions. Constructive criticism in these environments is intense, but accepted as the support structure for each member's vision of a better product. These types of people do not need hands-on managers. They need the opposite: a manager who respects them and expects the best from them. Teams do not thrive in companies with controlling HR departments, micromanagers, and thick employee handbooks.

What keeps these team-driven environments deadline oriented and productive? Consider the Darwinian concept that a herd will kill off its weakest member to ensure the group's overall survival. Survival of the fittest is what real business is all about. And in team environments, everyone is a peer unfettered by politics, free to give serious contributions without fear of losing their job because they didn't agree with the boss.

At the same time, Darwin-style self-management needs a forum for constructive criticism and critique that won't bruise egos. There must be a safe haven for teams to develop and interact.

When you get a number of really bright people in a room, you are bound to encounter egos, hubris, and sensitivity. Try running meetings without placing blame on an individual, instead asking the sort of questions that lead to a better work environment: "How can we make production better?" and "Lucy, how did you and David do with the new software?" and "Jackie, what do you think were our best practices on this project?" and "What would you say are our worst practices?" and "How can we all improve?" Even let people critique themselves once in a while.

These groups understand it is better to get criticism from colleagues at an early stage on a project than when it is too late to solve any problems. Honesty goes deeper the more time a team spends together. To an outsider, some members may seem a little too brutally honest. But this is the norm in an intense team environment.

Some people on your team may need to be trained to control their reactive mind. Emotional intelligence training can go a long way, but it would be even better to create an environment of trust, where people feel safe even if they lose their temper or disagree. This is healthy and a sure sign that your people are passionate about the product and the output. Complacency is not passion.

Always remember, anger is a secondary emotion, not a primary emotion like joy. Anger is when someone feels fear, a reaction to danger. Put a *d* in front of that "anger," and you'll see what I mean. Ask yourself, what is this person afraid of? Chances are, they are afraid of looking bad in front of the group. Once you make the environment safe and uncritical but constructive, people will give up their fear, and with it their competitive streak toward self-preservation.

Intense people will create intense work environments, so be prepared. As they say, to get to the fruit on a tree you must go out on a limb. Your job is to make it safe to go out on a limb and harvest those great ideas.

Smaller Means Mercurial

think people believe big teams work because we've all been taught that many hands make light work. The more people, the more gets done, right? The next time you are thinking that, come visit New York City's Department of Motor Vehicles.

I have often wondered where the mystique of big teams comes from. In my case, I have a few guesses. I grew up in Pennsylvania, and I saw on several occasions a large group of Amish workers successfully build a house or a barn in an afternoon. And then there were all those movies about the Roman Empire I saw as a kid. Plus, there was that book report I did in junior high on General Omar Bradley, who was in charge of two million troops on the day U.S. military landed on the Normandy beaches during WWII.

Still, the reality is, the larger the team, the harder it is to manage. The more there is to manage, the more ineffective the team gets. And though I hate to say it, the larger the team, the longer it takes to discover all this.

Conversely, small teams can get an amazing amount done. I believe small teams are the way to go. Take John Lasseter, the director of Pixar's *Toy Story*. So successful were the standards he set for his creative teams that he won a Special Achievement Academy Award for his "inspired leadership of the Pixar *Toy Story* team, resulting in the first feature-length computer animated film."

Here's how it works. To handle such groundbreaking undertakings, a company like Pixar assigns small, creative, multidisciplined teams of smart people to each project. Each person represents their department and has, over time, earned their right to be there.

Working at an animation company requires that multiple departments work in unison like a well-choreographed military operation, taking hundreds of people from many different backgrounds—character developers, background artists, set builders (who can build entire cities and town landscapes using virtual brick and mortar), sculptors, writers, creative directors, software developers, lighting directors, and character designers—to iron out how a character will move and show emotion. This all happens long before the voice-over talent is recorded. Watch the credits at the end of an animated feature film, and you'll get an idea of how many individuals it takes to get the product to the final stage and in the theaters. Only our military works with comparable precision.

Companies that promote these sorts of small, competitive teams create a sense of excitement, creativity, and healthy competition. It's built right into their corporate culture. Yes, they are budget conscious, too, but that's not what's in the forefront of their vision. Creating consistent breakthroughs is.

My own experience is similar. Depending on the size of your organization, I find that teams consisting of five to nine people will ensure smooth workflow and short meetings. Encourage input that isn't about one-upmanship. Keep meetings on-topic and on-agenda. Short and sweet, with purpose and intention, is what encourages people to attend each and every meeting. By contrast, when meetings are long and bogged down with pedantic chitchat, people start to disband and miss parts of them or stay away entirely. Multiple nine-person teams can come together for a companywide meeting once in a while, yet still keep meeting inertia to a minimum.

And once a small team gets used to working together, keep them together. Statistics have shown that teams that have been together for years trust one another and make fewer mistakes than those that are trained well but haven't gotten used to one another. Trust is at the forefront of their work, like a well-trained team of astronauts, each aware of their strengths, skill sets, and assignments.

Team-driven companies aren't thinking about crushing the competition; they're thinking of products so great, consumers *have* to buy them. They look for the "cool" in everything they do. Emotions are why we buy, and these companies seem to know that. Crushing the competition is merely the bonus result, a by-product of one of a kind innovation.

Name one great groundbreaking company, and I can guarantee that their success is due to the way the teams work.

Cool Digs

As I mentioned earlier, in the nineties K2 Design acquired new headquarters in the New York Technology Center at 55 Broad Street in New York City. But what I did not mention is that when I gave a tour to our underwriters, they didn't get how we had remodeled the office space. These were hardened Wall Street financiers, and they had seen a lot of offices in their time, but what they saw at K2 made no sense to them.

They had a million questions about the space. For example, they asked why I left the HVAC ceiling with all the ductwork and iron suspension bare and why there weren't any cubicles. They especially questioned why had I created such big, collaborative work areas.

I explained to them that I had designed such areas so that our people could brainstorm in unimpeded fashion. This made no sense to our underwriters, who had never worked in a creative environment. I pointed out that we weren't getting paid for our accounting abilities; we were getting paid for doing the best creative work in the business. So building a creative environment was paramount to our style of workflow.

And this is true for all creative teams. Real breakthroughs require a physical environment that supports team collaboration and training, integrated into a cultural environment that promotes intensity, healthy competition, and emotional support.

Leadership includes nurturing your staff in this manner—building an environment where a creative culture can thrive, a place where people want to work and care about the work they do. Places like this inspire and make work contagiously exciting to be a part of.

In the summer of 2008, I happened to be visiting MIT with my nephew and noticed that all their buildings are connected by the "Infinite Corridor," a single hallway running through the center of each building as if linking them all together. When I asked why this was, our tour guide explained, "It's in the hopes that a chemistry major will bump into a biology major and somehow, through intellectual discussion, lightning will strike and the two will come up with a collaborative solution that impacts biochemistry."

Take a tip from MIT. If the leading institute in America thinks multidisciplined collaboration is the key to great breakthroughs, who are we to argue? They do it because it works, and so should we. We can take a page from their playbook and get multidisciplined people in the same room to collaborate.

Remember my saying that happy accidents and out-of-the-box thinking are the real source of innovation? Well, accidents are more likely to happen when people from different disciplines are given the chance to run into one another and share ideas.

It's not just MIT that knows this. Google has open cafeterias that foster accidental collaboration. Pixar has a daily staff meeting where everyone comes together to show their team's work.

Environment and culture can be a sanctuary for ideas that need incubation. When these ideas hatch, the people on board will know they are revolutionizing the business world.

I don't know about you, but I want to work for a company that is revolutionizing the business world.

Me? Get Involved?
Are You Serious?

I recently sat down with Tim Davis, a behavioral coach. Tim is more than six feet eight inches tall and is of Italian and Irish decent. A native of Brooklyn, New York, he paints an imposing figure even when he is sitting down. I asked him to tell me his best Gen Y story. As he leaned forward to answer, his intense gaze was softened by both his reading glasses and a huge grin.

"Oh, that one is easy. I've been coaching an IT manager who just got the 'Boomer wake-up call.'" By now, you know what this means. It takes time, but eventually some Boomers are forced to realize that their old dogma is useless and the old paradigms are over, especially the one that says age and seasonality automatically earn the top position.

Tim explained to me how a Fortune 500 client had hired him to coach Nathan, a Baby Boomer in his late fifties with a few years to go before retirement. An IT veteran of more than twenty-five years, Nathan worked for one of the top insurance companies in the world. With the company headquarters in New York City, it went without saying that day-to-day operations were busy and cutting-edge.

Nathan was under great pressure from the CEO to go digital across the board, starting with the New York City office. And to get the job done as quickly as possible, Nathan had been given carte blanche. He could hire as many Gen Yers as he felt were necessary, with HR fully prepared to expedite the hiring. Nathan was ecstatic about this opportunity to take the company's technology up a level.

Nathan decided to hire four IT specialists ranging in age from twenty-four to thirty and put them to work. Things seemed to go well for the first couple of weeks, but over time, Nathan started to notice that his young protégés weren't exactly following orders. They started to ignore major deadlines and prioritized workflow according to what *they* wanted to work on for the day. Many of the smaller tasks began to pile up, and Nathan was getting short-tempered with his team.

In Nathan's Boomer world, younger generations were supposed to listen and obey their superiors' commands without question. These Gen Y tech-heads didn't seem to get it. He felt strongly that they must answer to him since he was the boss. In his mind set, *they* were the ones who were out of touch with reality.

When Nathan finally sat down on a Friday morning to make sure all the deadlines would be ready by five o'clock, he was met with an empty conference room. After twenty minutes of waiting, he stormed down the hall to the IT department.

Nathan couldn't hide his anger. "Why didn't anyone come to the meeting?"

"We had a defrag emergency."

"All four of you needed to work on it?" They looked at Nathan, dumbfounded. Why was he so angry?

Nathan gave them a piece of his mind and a list of every single complaint he had amassed since Day One. Months of frustration had welled up. "None of you get it! I have deadlines to meet, and you have been puttering around for days on nothing but crappy, self-indulgent projects that, quite frankly, aren't going to get us any closer to our goals!"

Nathan continued to berate, complain, and threaten. The entire team—Gary, Rob, Ken, and Nancy—stared back at him without speaking, like deer caught in the headlights.

After Nathan ran out of things to shout about, he went to complain to his superior. In the world of twenty years ago, Nathan would have been justified. Work styles fit into a black-and-white paradigm: Work hard; get rewarded. Screw up; get terminated.

As Nathan sat in front of his director, Valeria, he was running on adrenaline. Maybe that added to the shock he felt when he heard her answer, "Nathan, I need you to go back down there and apologize to your team."

"What? Valeria, they are missing major deadlines."

"I understand your frustration, Nathan, but . . . How can I put this delicately? Times have changed. Gen Y has an innate skill set and comfort with technology. Not only that, but they aren't into traditional hierarchy. This is hard to say, but I need them more than I need you.

"Managers who have your skills are a dime a dozen, Nathan, but the technology that those young IT specialists have in their brains is what I need now. So, you have two choices: You go down and apologize to them. After that, I want you to get some coaching that teaches you specifically how to speak to Gen Y."

"And my second choice?"

"You can clean out your desk, and I'll have your last check mailed to you."

Nathan of course said yes, he would apologize, and he immediately called Tim Davis, the coach recommended by Valeria.

As he started the coaching sessions, Nathan began to see that Valeria was right. He needed what so many Boomer managers need: an *upgrade* in his management style. Originally the term for the process of updating business software, "upgrade" became a common word in the gaming industry as well. It wasn't long before it became a metaphor for updating just about anything, including people who needed to learn new skills and attitudes.

Someday Generation Y will need a major upgrade. But an upgrade starts with your oldest components first, which means guys like Nathan. Those who don't get it drag organizations down. To a Baby Boomer, taking classes to learn how to get along and communicate with Generation Y makes no sense whatsoever. Shouldn't it be the other way around? It would be, if Gen Y didn't have us backed into a corner: their skill set of technological expertise has been timed perfectly to meet the demands of an ever-expanding Information Age.

Like it or not, the new kids on the block have money and freedom, and that equals power. They are also hardwired differently from the rest of us.

What Boomers *do* excel in is this: They have better communication skills, empathy, and life understanding, skills that Gen Y lacks completely. And it is these very skills and understanding that need to be taught to anyone under thirty-five. It can be hard to explain to someone that IMing, texting, and fielding over a hundred emails a day may not be real communication. Only with the help of Boomers can Millennials achieve the empathy for others that they so often lack and learn that every member of an organization is valid.

When someone has sat in front of computers all day for their entire life, they lose the ability to communicate with an actual person. Boomers can teach computer-immersed generations that text messaging, instant messaging, emails, and Twittering might *seem* like communication, but aren't necessarily so. Just as several hours on Facebook lulls one into a false sense of having a rich social life, this type of staccato interaction through technology is not communication; it's only an aspect of it. Worse yet, all this texting and Twittering and Facebooking can give people the illusion that they are actually spending "time" with friends.

The best communicators rise to the top in every organization, political arena, and endeavor. Communication as skill set is awarded top dollar. Each generation needs to be proficient at it on all fronts.

There are two things a manager like Nathan must learn about Gen Y workers before he can hope to manage them effectively: why they are so eager to work on their own stuff, stuff that may seem unimportant to the business, and why these workers may ignore their manager.

First let's delve into why Gen Y only works on what they like. Whether they wanted it or not, Baby Boomers were given a well-rounded education; meanwhile, the later gaming generations could cherry-pick their curriculum. They picked what they liked best, and teachers designed their teaching around a child's skill set. Learning by memorization was tossed in favor of kinesthetic learning. These young wunderkinder also grew up with a micromanaged schedule of karate classes, soccer practices, and dance lessons. They have logged in more than ten thousand hours on video games, where they self-managed their time and direction, and now you expect them to sit in a cubicle for nine hours at a time? Hello?

Yes, this has created one generation after another that only specializes in what they *like* to do rather than what is *necessary*. Boring work is either placed on the back burner or outsourced or, worse yet, rushed over by cutting and pasting someone else's previous work. Gen Yers choose exciting careers and shun the mundane . . . because they have been taught to do so. While Boomers were trained to do something once, and do it right the first time, Generation Y was trained to hurry up and get it done and fix the problems later. Now do you see why there is such an informational gap in corporations around the world?

On the other hand, your thirty years of experience means nothing to young people, for one big reason: In their view, the only knowledge that counts has to do with technology, and the majority of the technology that is being used these days, such as Facebook, Twitter, and iPhone apps, didn't exist five years ago. In their view, you can't possibly know anything about new technology because Boomers have no experience with most of it . . . and no understanding of its worthiness.

Another cause for their disdain is that they have been raised to see an authority figure as a peer, not someone to look up to. They simply do not see hierarchy at all. Their ideology is "If you can do it, so can I, but unlike you I won't take thirty years to get the corner office." If you try and boss them around the way you are used to bossing your staff, they'll stare at you as if you've lost your mind.

Peers don't obey peers.

Nor is Gen Y into listening to you talk about how awesome you were back in 1977 or some other dead year. (Note to self: Stop talking about your 1974 Duster, Brad.) They see this behavior on your part as arrogance. Your boasts mean nothing to them because they themselves are always "on," and they expect everyone else to be on top of their game too. Like professional athletes, Generation Y is into improving and upgrading constantly in order to stay employable. Stopping to rest and reflect is not built into Generation Y. They just want to get to another, cooler level in the game.

Using these concepts, Tim started coaching Nathan on the finer points of managing Generation Y. Instead of calling meeting after meeting, throughout which he barked orders, it was time for Nathan to integrate his knowledge base into the young workforce he was managing and set the example for leadership. Tim encouraged Nathan to drop the hierarchy he held in his mind, along with any assumptions that his seasonality meant he was "boss." Instead, he taught Nathan to ask his team how they wanted to work, within limits. The goal was to create an environment of genuine engagement, communication, meaningful deadlines, support for goals, and company loyalty.

Second, Nathan stopped his twice-a-week meetings. He started to understand that his meetings had only wasted people's time and inter-rupted their ability to work toward his deadlines. Instead, Nathan insti-tuted social network–style instant messaging software to keep his crews in constant up-to-the-minute communication during the day, whether for ad hoc communication or one-on-one meetings. As Nathan's staff expanded, face-to-face meetings became irrelevant and IMing could speed up each department. When he did have a meeting, it was packed with people who understood that this must be something important.

Third, Nathan encouraged each team member to set their *own* goals and tasks, rather than look to him all the time. Each employee was required to post weekly goals on their own home page on the company's intranet. Their direct managers were instructed to manage and support these goals by publicly viewing the pages and privately offering support, checking in on what each person needed in order to accomplish their goals as well as monitoring deadlines. Teams were encouraged to support one another and pick up the slack. Each member was required to handle two high-level projects and four lower-level ones during each work cycle. If someone needed help to meet a deadline, the whole team was encouraged to help. All Nathan had to do was check each team member's goals and where they were at in terms of accomplishing them.

This approach changed the way Nathan's division managed their time. Each member of a team could get their work done whenever and wherever they decided, as long as deadlines were met. This meant that if someone wanted to work later in the day, fine. If eight hours' worth of work could be finished in four, then the reward was that they could move on to the next task. Also, eight hours during any given week were to be used for one's own personal projects. These projects were posted to the person's goal page. The personal project could be something as complex as designing a new app to make the company work more efficiently, or something as simple as planning a company ski trip. Either way, the personal project had two criteria: It had to be something that the employee was passionate about, and it had to benefit the entire group.

These steps freed up Nathan to manage just his managers instead of trying to manage the entire network by himself. He eliminated the bottleneck that had inhibited communication and decision making—which had mainly been caused by him. The result was increased productivity and newly responsible employees. No one missed a deadline after the new system was implemented. Nathan had shifted his management style from "angry parent" to mentor and production shepherd and had gained his people's respect.

Look, Gen Y doesn't understand linear time. It doesn't make sense to them: Why sit at a desk for eight hours when one can get the same work done in four hours and then go home? This may sound outrageous to Baby Boomers—flexible work time?—but see it from their perspective: Come up with a great idea at 2:00 AM, work on a proposal until 7:00 AM, print it out, bring it to the office, show it to the right people, and expect to go home at 10:00 AM. Workday done.

Younger workers think and operate more like entrepreneurs than employees. They have had parents who managed their schedules and were involved in their school life. They have had thousand and thousands of self-directed video game missions, where they chose every single aspect of the adventure; in other words, they aren't watching the video game as if it were a movie. Instead, they are engaged and involved in it. They are rebelling, if you haven't noticed, by doing things their way. So instead of fighting it, why not treat them like entrepreneurs and get the most out of their quirky behavior and technologically driven ideas?

Sitting in an office and having everyone report to a boss is an incredibly inefficient paradigm, especially in today's chaotic environment. Leadership must learn a different route. Show respect and support for your people's initiatives and skill sets, and you'll get the most out of today's workforce. Everyone must be involved in order for a company to stay relevant and cutting-edge today.

By trusting in the fact that people are self-managing, you can be free to lead effectively.

There Can Be Only One

"Collaboration" is the hot buzzword these days. It seems so cool to get everyone on board, working in the same direction, sort of like the Knights of the Round Table, working for a cause bigger than oneself. But without ground rules, these collaborative teams can lose direction—especially when members work alone for days at a time—and spiral down into the mutual admiration society, the fast track to losing direction.

My sources have reported that the number one complaint of working in such collaborative environments is people become afraid to speak out and rock the boat. Major problems stay buried until eventually they can bring the entire organization down. There's an elephant in the room, and no one wants to talk about it.

The first three businesses I owned taught me about personalities and how getting along doesn't necessarily mean you will be successful. My business partners in those first ventures were fun to work with. Everyone was dynamic and skilled, and we all got along incredibly well. Yet the companies didn't do that well. I couldn't understand it then, but I do now. Our skill sets were too similar; we didn't really challenge one another. It was like being in a canoe and paddling on only one side. The best we could do was to turn in a circle. This has been proven by behavioral psychologists who analyze corporate teams. Teams that are harmonious and polite put out mediocre work at best; by contrast, when there is some disruption, team members push each other to another level. People who are challenged in this way are happier for it—and their businesses are more successful.

When I started K2 Design, my fourth company, I learned something powerful: Having a few members on the team to shake things up pushes people past their comfort zone. It makes them question the quality of their work from the inside out.

Although Doug and I had similar backgrounds when we started K2, we had very different ideas of how to approach our work. This created some dynamic tension and competition that brought out the best and sometimes the worst in each of us. With solid training in graphic design, multimedia design, and Swiss-grid methods, and with Bauhaus sensibilities, our creativity had a solid basis in the traditional print world. But we would argue as to the direction of the creative elements. What made us get any work done is that our first rule of business was to create the best possible design product every time. There could be no shortcuts, no excuses, and no sitting on our laurels.

It also helped that we both had that so-called Protestant work ethic.

In the crazy Wild West world of the new Internet, that dynamic tension between us pushed our firm to become second to none. Our high standards helped us become a leader within the design industry. And another pleasant surprise developed: We became internationally noticed as well.

Plain and simple, the most productive teams question their work at all times. They push the envelope, never accepting the same old choices. They are passionate and argumentative, yet still productive. Now, how do you apply that to your work? Every team needs at least one special person to play devil's advocate—a naysayer, a rabble-rouser incapable of just accepting the group status quo. This type of paradigm puts the work first. "Never be satisfied" becomes the battle cry for a great product.

Rocking the Boat without Going Overboard

Every great leader has someone behind them who questions everything to the point of being annoying. They do this to keep their leaders on their toes, to compel discussions about the bigger picture. The King of Wu in ancient China had Sun Tzu, Jesus had Doubting Thomas, and General Eisenhower had General Omar Bradley.

Unfortunately, these disruptive types are not always liked by the group. I realize that I just said that harmony creates mediocrity, while healthy disruption can create amazing work. But too much disruption will destroy productivity. There must be a balance. Someone must be the referee—which is where team leaders come in.

If everyone understands the goals at each meeting, and the team leader is trained in interpersonal dynamics and the goals of such personalities, then the disruptive individual will be seen as the one who brings something incredibly valuable to the table—a different opinion.

Encourage dynamic questions that challenge the group and their output. Discourage like hell those who want to fit in and not make waves. Encourage people after every satisfying meeting to challenge the final outcome by questioning it.

The group members need to push one another, and the team disrupter has that job. Neither the group nor the disruptor may know this. Without the disruptor, the team's work is usually just okay. With the disruptor, dynamics occur that may not have been seen before.

Great leaders know they can only get real answers from people who disagree with them. They want their orders questioned because they know that no one person can have all the answers. And when people's lives are on the line, they listen to their smartest.

Some of you may think that having a disruptor on your team makes you look as if you are a leader who is unsure and weak. Au contraire, people who listen to their advisors and then take action based on input are seen as brilliant. Leaders who listen to no one are egocentric and dangerous to an organization. We have plenty of examples of these types of leaders in the news these days.

But decisions are not always about following every single piece of input from advisors. Many a leader has listened to their cabinet and promptly done exactly what they set out to do from the beginning. Just read about the tactics of General Sam Houston after the battle at the Alamo. Public opinion was so against his tactics that it's a wonder he was allowed to continue at all. Yet when he turned to attack, the Mexican Army was caught completely off guard and almost defenseless. They had assumed from his previous actions that he was going to retreat again.

So why listen to a board of advisors at all? Feedback is essential to understanding if you are going in the right direction to begin with. It takes a unique leader to utilize feedback, one who is in it not for their personal ego but for the group.

Make sure your team has one leader who can coach and one disruptor. It will make all the difference.

The End of the Mutual Admiration Society

One of my favorite rituals when I worked in the corporate events field was to have routine postmortems. After a project would finish up, I would insist that everyone involved join me for pizza and beer in the conference room and take the time to ask hard questions. What could have been done differently to make things easier for the next time? What would make communication clearer in the future? What technology do we need to invest in?

Many times, though, a postmortem turns into a meeting of the mutual admiration society. Someone must oversee these meetings to make sure that *what was done right* isn't dominating the main reason for these sessions—to get to the root of *what was done wrong*, along with what could be improved and what worked smoothly or what didn't work at all. This is a chance for each department to share best and worse practices.

Of course, the reverse is true also. It's meant to be a learning process, not a "let's point the finger" session. Still, the answers that come out of these meetings should be taken seriously and implemented. The best way to keep them from turning into an all-out brawl is to ask questions in a way that is nonconfrontational. For example, ask an employee what he felt could make his job run more smoothly, how certain simple communications from other departments helped get his job done, and how this could improve production. Make it a safe haven by creating a sense that the constructive criticism is intended to help, not hurt. Keep emphasizing that it is not personal; it is about everybody helping one another improve product output. Someone can face the truth only when they are in an environment of trust, with colleagues they respect.

A recent consulting gig required a postmortem, yet no one wanted it. It was too painful for the company at the time to listen to constructive criticism and look at their flaws. The client I hooked them up with was frustrated with their lack of process, but I couldn't convince them to sit and figure out what went wrong and what went right and why. They didn't care, because the website worked, it looked beautiful, and the end users were ecstatic. So why bother?

They were sadly lacking in processes, yet they didn't believe they had a problem. It could have really aided in their hypergrowth, yet they kept blaming my client for micromanaging them. Eventually, in a year or two, they will hit a wall and wonder why they are having so many problems getting work done.

> Postmortems eliminate the prima donna attitude
> and myopic scope that all companies can suffer from.
> Running these meetings requires someone who has the
> skills of a coach, because postmortems can get ugly.

Do you want to sit around and tell each other how great you all are—the mutual admiration society—or do you want to roll up your sleeves and create even better products and systems?

Yeah, I thought so.

4TH LAW

A Liquid Leader Supports Reinvention of the Organization

You never change the existing reality by fighting it.
Instead, create a new model that makes the old one obsolete.
—Buckminster Fuller

But I Don't Want to Change

A century ago a company could come up with a dozen or so groundbreaking ideas and be an industry leader for years. But today, our world is moving much faster. Technology can give any individual with a dream the ability to take advantage of low barriers to entry, becoming a thorn in the side of larger, more seasoned companies.

This is creating disruption, and any organization that isn't paying attention will be missing the train as it pulls out of the station. By listening to each and every individual in their company, a leader opens up to new ideas, new directions, and new opportunities—early. In companies that have leaders who listen, brands may change to meet the demands of the street or to serve never-before-seen markets. These companies are eager to reinvent themselves without resistance. They evolve not because they have to, but because it is part of their internal process and what keeps them on the cutting edge.

Each of these successful new companies develops and improves upon products that made them industry leaders and household names. The breakthroughs these companies experience will force entire industries to rethink their own business models. The Internet has proven that just because you have an established brand in the real world doesn't mean it will translate well into cyberspace, an element that is essential today to compete and thrive.

Older, more established companies stay on the cutting edge with research, acquisition, or the creation of a separate brand. New blood is brought in to shake up the status quo and keep the brand and the company evolving. Either way, the key to both types of organizations is to stay open and accepting of new ways of doing business.

Insurance Claims and the New Customer

How do you reach a new type of consumer who can't sit still for two hours every night—the one who doesn't watch TV or read magazines? This consumer is a moving target, getting their news and entertainment on the go, whether through a DVR, satellite radio, Twitter, or YouTube, or via their mobile phone, iPod, iPad, iPhone, Kindle . . . I'm out of breath at this point, but you can be sure there are more devices on the way. These are the same people who sit *listening* to the TV while at the same time using their online social network for updates on the show; IMing with friends; and as always, surfing, surfing, surfing the Web. To get their attention, you've got to up your game.

Where there used to be four reliable media channels to use (radio, television, books, and publications like newspaper or magazines), today we have dozens of ways to connect with the consumer, and those are being fragmented into micro-markets. With so much interactivity, getting a single person's attention seems impossible these days, especially when they can download their favorite TV shows to their mobile phone to watch at any time of the day.

To keep up with today's on-the-go consumer, you have to learn the best way to be an influencer in your marketplace. What works for one company (or sector) may not work for another. Find a way to engage them, to disrupt previously held notions, and to take control of your leadership position by blowing their mind and exceeding their expectations.

But what has really made Nationwide stand out as a twenty-first-century brand is their latest idea, the Accident Toolkit—a killer app for the iPhone that immediately captures the respect of a younger audience—and their wallets. The premise is simple: A car accident tends to leave victims a little shaken and overwhelmed, so the toolkit helps the user stay focused as they gather the right information. It prompts them to exchange information with other motorists, provides access to insurance policy data, and automatically dials the local police, an emergency medical crew, and a tow truck. The Accident Toolkit also takes the user through each step of the picture-taking process and stores the photos as you start your insurance claim/accident report—all from your iPhone. A GPS tag also records the exact location of the accident, locating the nearest Nationwide agency. The app can even turn your iPhone into a flashlight. But the most amazing thing about this tool is that Nationwide is making the Accident Toolkit *free and available to anyone, even non-Nationwide customers.*

Nationwide has become an overnight leader by positioning itself as a company that is socially conscientious and by providing the tools that a new consumer is accustomed to. Now a whole new generation is into Nationwide Insurance. They live up to their slogan: Nationwide *is* on your side.

Nationwide was smart enough to get involved in the online conversation and go after a younger consumer without isolating their traditional customer. This isn't a onetime shot in the dark; companies like Nationwide continuously use technology to build a one-to-one relationship with their customers, making it a twenty-first-century innovator that has attracted a whole new customer base.

Just look at Nationwide Insurance. Years ago they ran a commercial on ifilm.com (now Spike.com) featuring iconic fashion and romance novel cover model Fabio. Humorously done, it received more than a million hits. Then, in order to attract a younger consumer, Nationwide started to feature commercials with Kevin Federline and *American Idol*'s Sanjaya Malakar on YouTube. Viewers were able to rate the commercials and give general feedback. This kind of new media exposure has opened a doorway for a new generation to Nationwide Insurance and their products.

YouTube "Stalkers"

Nationwide Insurance and other companies are shaking up their markets by engaging customers in any way that new technology allows. Companies willing to implement this sort of out-of-the-box thinking can exploit popular media such as YouTube to attract new consumers. Nationwide is consistently in the face of the online consumer, with humorous commercials that translate well to the viral video platform. Their *The World's Greatest Spokesperson in the World* series of commercials shows potential and existing customers that they can choose their own insurance package by calling Nationwide's Discount Finder℠, making Nationwide competitive with discount insurance competitors like Progressive and Esurance.

> What's even better about viral videos is that if used properly, they can shift the power center in an entrenched market.

Look at modeling. Strip away the glam and look at fashion as a business only, and what you get is an entrenched industry, with the advertisers calling the shots while modeling agencies like Ford, Wilhelmina, and Elite—the companies that provide and manage the modeling talent—are seen simply as service providers. A model's job, whether they are male or female, has traditionally been to act as a living, breathing mannequin on which to display products. Nothing more, nothing less.

But Ford Modeling decided to take their business up a notch by filming short segments of the most intimate moments in modeling—the photo session.[3]

The first of these videos was shot in the Ford offices, but they soon began using professional studios. Although the videos are well lit and professionally edited with music, they still retain a friendly and informal nature; the cinematography has a film-student quality, as if the camera is a fly on the wall in a girls' dorm. Nothing was scripted, and the models were

---

3 See the entire story in *Inc.* magazine's February 2008 article "A Digital Makeover for the Modeling Business," by David H. Freedman.

encouraged to be honest when commenting on the products they were using. As models try on a pair of jeans, they happen to mention that they got them at Express, Diesel, or DKNY. Since the models are not posing or glamming their way down a runway, the result is surprisingly honest and human—an inside look behind the curtain of fashion.

Surprisingly, these candid videos took off and have become an online phenomenon. Viewers range in age from teens to middle-aged women and have a tendency to spend like crazy; they come to Ford's YouTube videos looking for beauty tips.

As the Ford videos took on a life of their own, cosmetic and perfume companies, designers, and accessories companies started clamoring to have their products prominently featured by Ford on YouTube. Marketing coexists with the videos, and conversion is measurable, making this an attractive avenue for advertising. Clickable buttons can now lead a viewer to the brand's website where they can download a $20 coupon or some such. Just a little over three to four minutes in length, some videos have had more than six hundred thousand viewers over several days.

Now Ford has advertisers paying a fee to be part of the video production and have their products featured. But the company is aware that the non-selling approach to selling must be maintained. The main reason for the massive interest is that Ford's videos are shot so candidly, they don't come across as a branding campaign but instead sound like advocacy. Once the consumer feels they are being sold to, the glory days are over.

Ford's models have become neutral influencers of brands.

The thing most people aren't talking about, however, is the shift in the power structure vis-à-vis established ad agencies. Advertisers are now scrambling to be in Ford's videos, and voilà! Ford has shifted the methods of an entire industry. Oh, how the tables have turned.

How do you plan on getting your company into the twenty-first century viral conversation?

One of my all-time favorite viral marketing campaigns is Will It Blend? One lazy Saturday evening, my nephew Sebastian turned me on to this . . . and let me tell you, it is hysterical. Will It Blend? centers on a Blendtec blender, the über line of industrial-grade blenders for home as well as business use. You may have seen a few of their commercial blenders behind the counters at your local Starbucks or Planet Smoothie outlet.

While the point presumably is to prove that Blendtec blenders are the best in the business, founder Tom Dickson does nothing to promote or tell you to buy one of their blenders. Instead, in a Mr. Science–style documentary, he decides to blend something that no one would ever dream of putting in a blender. Items have ranged from his grandkids' Matchbox toy cars (because they left them around the house) to iPads, glow sticks, broom handles, and (my favorite) an entire chicken together with a can of Coke—yes, aluminum can and all. Look for the one where he blends a McDonald's Extra Value Meal. Lending an ironic sense of authority to the presentation, Tom appears in each episode in a white lab coat, safety glasses, and rubber gloves. These videos are campy, dry, daring, and funny.

The Will It Blend? campaign took off instantly, impacting sales and making Tom a cyber celebrity. The videos have gone viral and ignited the brand. They sell without selling. Tom's popularity has landed him on TV shows, blending anything viewers would deem impossible to blend. The viral videos have become so popular that Blendtec sells Will It Blend? merchandise on their site, including spoof T-shirts with the slogan "Tom Dickson Is My Homeboy" and the popular "Will It Blend?" logo.

This type of silliness has engendered an online audience for Blendtec and has flashed a big spotlight on its line of blenders. It has made them a leader in a niche market that is hard to sell in. Who says fun can't ignite sales?

Another favorite viral video series comes from Gary Vaynerchuk. Growing up around wine and liquor his entire life, the entrepreneurial Gary trained himself to be a sommelier. His passion for unusual wines and the rebranding of his family's liquor store in Springfield, New Jersey, as the Wine Library paid off—within a five-year period, the Wine Library grew from a $4 million business to a $45 million business. But it was the viral videos he created for his daily video blog that really helped his business take off and become an international sensation. As the star of Wine Library TV, Gary is quite the character; down to earth, sometimes loud, usually animated, and always impassioned, he makes wine simple. His popularity may be due to the fact that he is a regular guy who has burst the bubble on the snooty, pretentious world of wine. Anyone can watch Gary's videos in private and then sound like a connoisseur in public. Personal, approachable, and a New York Jets fan, he gives online viewers the real scoop on picking wine. I love his rants! This is what viral video marketing is all about: intimacy.

And Gary's show has excited more than just wine sales; the videos have attracted a cultlike community (more than eighty thousand viewers a day) of self-named "Vayniacs." They comment on an extremely active forum, post their wish lists, and have organized numerous off-line gatherings and wine tastings. Viewers have teamed up with Crushpad in the past year to create the first-ever community-created wine, called Vayniac Cabernet.

Gary has also appeared on such television talk shows as *Late Night with Conan O'Brien* and *The Ellen DeGeneres Show*, and his video blog's popularity and the resulting community engagement have garnered several book deals, including *Gary Vaynerchuk's 101 Wines: Guaranteed to Inspire, Delight, and Bring Thunder to Your World* and *Crush It!: Why NOW Is the Time to Cash In on Your Passion*. All this started from Gary's willingness to go out on a limb and create, in his own words, "the Internet's most passionate wine program."

Make a list of companies that are reinventing their brands for an online, always-on-the-go young consumer, yet not isolating their existing customers: Old Spice, Slim Jim, Timberland. Today, even CNN, Whole Foods, and Best Buy are using Twitter as a consumer gateway! My wife and I were able to contact CNN directly when the earthquake hit Haiti in order to check on family and friends. It was amazing to be part of this transparent process.

Companies that are using traditional ads can stay relevant by migrating online in order to influence a consumer who is, more and more, into the 24/7 connectivity of social networking. Those brands that lower their walls and become approachable "get" what an online customer is all about; these customers expect to be able to make contact with your company anytime, anywhere. So, what are you doing to be an influencer in your market?

As business management expert Tom Peters once put it, any idiot can sell a Rolex; it takes a genius to sell the Rolex lifestyle. Don't be satisfied with small-time or lag behind because you're stuck on the same old product through the same old outdated channels. Loosen up, and have a little fun with your advertising. Let customers get a little closer to you. It's about creating intangible value. It's about "getting" the lifestyle of your target audience. If you keep trying out new ideas and new methods, who knows? You might find an accidental fit.

Overcoming the Fear

I have mentioned this over and over again: Technology has allowed us to operate faster, getting more done in one day than our parents could accomplish in two weeks. It has extended our reach, giving us access to markets we could previously access only by plane, train, or ship. It has shrunk our world and virtually eliminated borders. Think about all the change that has occurred in the last couple of decades! Technology has changed our business landscape in ways that many executives cannot see yet. It has shortened the life cycle of our product lines while at the same time tightening our leeway.

How should a business leader handle things in the face of such rapid change? Surround yourself with people who are diligent at finding the next big thing. If you get it right, you can create entire new markets that could dominate for a hundred years. If you get it wrong, you could be out of business overnight. Executives are frozen with fear, not because they are afraid to move forward—these are smart people—but because their actions could put them out of business and into the limelight of corporate failure. I'm talking about career-ruining stuff.

This fear has created so much risk management and analysis that many companies are petrified, unable to move forward.

If you follow Traditional Business Strategies 101, by the time you figure it all out, you will be too late to the party. You must follow a new business primer. Action must be maintained at all times for an organization to stay up to date.

Whether with the help of a psychic hotline or with certain software, people are trying to predict the future while micromanaging the risk. For some strange reason, as human beings we like to think we are capable of figuring everything out. Our overconfidence is one of our major weaknesses.

Risk management is necessary, to a point. But instead of taking action, many companies are trying to micromanage the risk, cut back until the numbers add up, and then rehire for the same positions after the stock price goes back north. Quick fixes might make you a hero in the boardroom this month, but they will take you nowhere in the long term.

Managing the Intangible

Almost every business owner, entrepreneur, or executive I meet with nowadays is scared. Every one of these risk-averse executives is doing all they can to plan for a successful journey. Unfortunately all bets are off nowadays because technology, ambitious young Digital Natives, and fickle customers are changing systems businesses once relied on. Planning for success in this business environment is equivalent to fighting a guerrilla war. There is no defined target, and success has been redefined, yet leaders continue to act as if they know the way.

We are in a strange era of managing ambiguity. With its lack of clear boundaries, models, and direction, learning to be a leader in today's environment is a job for the courageous. With an ever-changing model and a lack of concrete rules and goals, many managers clinging to the old ways of management can be left with a fuzzy feeling of uncertainty.

If strategic planning, numbers crunching, and goal setting actually worked, everyone who crunched numbers and set goals would be rich and successful.

But part of the management journey is to figure out what works for you individually. By tightening the gap between actual methods that work and textbook models that appear to work, we can get closer to the truth.

We need to upgrade our skills as leaders until we are fit to lead on a hostile and ever-shifting battlefield, rather than act as if nothing has changed or as if things will return to the old ways if given enough time.

In such a disruptive climate of hyperchange, risk management becomes an oxymoron. When making parachutes, eventually you have to jump out of a plane and use one. A PowerPoint presentation on how the parachute may fail won't cut it.

If you want to be assured that your company will fail, all you have to do is two things: 1) Don't take any risks and just wait for the current economic storm to pass, and 2) Try your damnedest to make everybody happy.

So how do you stay up to date and cutting-edge? Like the most successful companies, you need to operate as if your company is an entrepreneurial start-up, with a hungry, innovative, creative staff that is excited about the work they are putting out.

Let's explore the 4th Law further by delving into a few tactics that will help redefine success and change your methodologies for a twenty-first-century refit.

Learn as You Go

Most people haven't ever experienced hypergrowth of more than 425 percent, but while at K2, my staff grew from two full-time employees to sixty in less than three years, while revenues exploded accordingly. To stay ahead of competing Web developers, I had to absorb as much information as was physically possible, then take action despite not being able to see the bigger picture. Why? Because if I waited for each and every little piece of data before I made my move, I could literally be the last company at the table.

To stay in the leadership position, I had to learn to do something I had never been trained to do: take action *before* I had all the facts. I learned to leap before I looked, trusting that the bridge would appear. It was like climbing a mountain on a foggy day when you can only see fifteen feet ahead at any given time. How do you navigate through that? Take a few steps forward until you see the next few steps. Readjust, then take a few more. Do this over and over again.

In the past I would have analyzed the market I was entering over and over again to make sure there was real money there. Then I would take action. But in this Information Age paradigm, I had to realize that I needed to take action with only four of the seven pieces of data, and trust that the rest would be there farther down the road. In other words, I had to react to basic market trends with creativity and intuition rather than research.

Each time I got more information, I adjusted my strategy. What really helped was that my business partners did the same, and we were surrounded by some of the smartest people around, from seasoned businesspeople and MIT MBAs to tech-heads and Wharton grads.

It isn't really a new concept. Adjusting your strategies as you go is actually a dynamic familiar to battlefield soldiers, firefighters, and video gamers—something Gen Y and Gen X are quite comfortable doing.

**Action gets results;
stopping to think about it does not.**

Adjusting to new data requires a mixture of intuition and logic, like driving through dense fog—best to do it twenty feet at a time, readjusting every thirty feet or so. Follow the GPS, but use your eyes as well. All the information says there should be a bridge up ahead, so you act accordingly. If you get to the chasm and the bridge isn't there, look around. It may be farther down. If no bridge appears, then either build one or hire a company that can build it. If they work out, buy the bridge builders.

Spartan and Speedy

As companies lay off more and more people, the corporation will start to change organically. Where there was once a thick layer of middle managers, the company of the future may have no such thing. Executives may find themselves sitting outside the bullpen. As each employee begins to take on more and more leadership roles within an organization, the number of people required to manage self-starters will begin to shrink.

When you shrink the distance between executives, managers, and producers, the time from idea to execution will shrink as well. Communication will be less discombobulated because the information won't have that far to travel. Think in terms of the telephone game: With fewer players involved, the amount of miscommunication will shrink, allowing smaller organizations to move faster. Speed, efficiency, disruption, and action are the hallmark of a twenty-first-century company.

The layers of communication found in large organizations will become a liability, as small companies take over the leadership position in a type of corporate guerrilla war. Speed is the advantage of the smaller company. And regardless of size, companies that are swift have almost no communication barriers between CEO, management, and staffers.

By eliminating the walls between you and the bright ideas, you'll be able to adapt your strategy to reflect new input. But no matter what, keep moving. Your survival depends on it.

Through your actions you'll start to see a strategy. Sit with your executive committee, and make this new ideology a reality. At the end of the road you will know what to do, but not before then.

Take on the tactic of a warrior, and adapt to the landscape.

Getting Out of the Way

To keep up in today's fast-paced world, you'll need to surround yourself with talented people who are always on the lookout for new ideas and cutting-edge solutions. You'll also have to redesign your management structure top to bottom in order to embrace new ideas and their implementation with the speed of a fighter pilot. And this may mean that you have to get out of the way.

Some of you may not understand the need for such seemingly radical actions. You may think or hope that it's enough to make whatever moves are necessary to wait out the storm: shoring up your company's cash, stopping the bleeding, cutting costs all across the board, downsizing (with even the executive suite taking temporary salary cuts). Yet as necessary as these moves may be, they are not enough to prepare you for when the sun comes out again. When it does, everything will be different.

Be smarter than that. Prepare now by putting as many irons as possible in the pot. The more new stuff that comes across your desk, the better your chances of finding big ideas and cutting-edge technology. This also applies to the ideas that cross everyone else's desk in your company. Think of it as a treasure hunt: The more teams you have searching for gold, the greater the likelihood you will find it.

Again, you may have to get out of the way to make it work.

Rub the Magic Lamp to Unbottle the New CEO

It may seem impossible, but all one has to do is think differently. Just ask John Chambers, CEO of Cisco Systems. Back in 2000, Cisco had the largest market cap in the world and 50 percent growth. They were the darlings of Wall Street, and things looked rosy—until the dot-com bubble burst.

Shareholders watched their investment go from $86 per share to $11 by fall 2001. John moved fast. He laid off thousands, shrank the number of suppliers, and, after in-depth analysis, eliminated entire product lines. But that wasn't enough. John had to change the way he managed the company. New times required new methods, so John dismantled Cisco's Industrial Age hierarchy, with its military-like command and control structure and slow approval process. In its place he installed a more democratic model.

John did this by shifting decision-making authority into three different types of democratic executive teams. Councils were put directly in charge of finding the $10 billion opportunities out there. Boards were given the authority to make educated decisions on $1 billion bets. And Working Groups were assigned specific tasks to target and complete.

The new hierarchy was integral to speeding up productivity and the decision-making process, thanks to the elimination of bottlenecks. The new, flatter communication structure allowed everyone access to more individuals in less time, thus speeding up communication and decisions. The internal structure at Cisco now acted more like a social network instead of a permission-driven hierarchy. This has increased Cisco's speed and reach when finding new companies and new products to add to their mix.

Many would be astounded that to this day, John isn't involved in the decision-making process of any of these teams. If he were, Cisco would not be the leader they are today, nor would they have survived the first dot-com implosion. Waiting for one executive to oversee hundreds of projects for a final decision slows down a company like Cisco too much. John simply eliminated the bottleneck in favor of speed to market. And that's what makes John Chambers a top CEO in my book. Not only was he savvy enough to see that he was the bottleneck, but he was also ego-free enough to get out of the way.

When decision making is spread out among your top people, you are freed up to just guide the process, and your organization can take full advantage of the opportunities that are coming at you at light speed.

As Vince Poscente puts it, we are in "the age of speed" (hence the title of his 2007 *New York Times* bestseller). When we resist, speed can look scary. When we embrace it, sometimes things actually appear to slow down and become more efficient.

Speed and Trust

Passing the baton to your key people says more about trust than power. It also frees each team from stagnation by giving them the responsibility as well as the autonomy to make key decisions in the moment. The concept may seem foreign at first, but it will free you up to guide the company into the new territory that is being defined by the creative decisions your teams are making. It's part of what keeps a technologically driven company like Cisco on the cutting edge, reliant on not one idea at a time but hundreds at once. No one person can see all the opportunities out there. The more eyeballs you have out there, the more opportunities will be available; these opportunities are absent from command-and-control hierarchies that must wait painfully for each decision to be approved.

It's Physics 101: Increase the number of opportunities at your fingertips, and you'll increase the number of possibilities for success.

Once you've given your company the ability to make decisions rapidly, the next step is to connect those decisions to intuitions about your audience and their future needs. Tons of ideas will fail, but it takes only one to win the day. Dyson, for example, had eight hundred patents before their first vacuum cleaner hit the market. Their innovation has made them a leader in what appeared to be a market already saturated and unable to grow.

At the same time, because of the increasing speed to market, you will have to cut your losses quicker when you see a dud. No matter how much money has been spent, if the idea looks as if it will fall flat, eliminate it as quickly as possible. Microsoft took too long to admit Vista was a dud. They tried as hard as they could to put an advertising campaign together to adjust public perception, but it was too late. People didn't like Vista almost immediately, long before the ads ran on TV. Quietly, Microsoft launched Windows 7.0 and abandoned Vista. The upgrade is free for Vista users.

Before you cut your losses, make damn sure the idea is definitely a dud. Remember, Xerox invented the idea of a user-friendly personal computer, but it was Steve Jobs who picked it up and ran with it. Give your new ideas, companies, or mergers time to develop. Incubate them, and if they don't bear fruit within a certain amount of time, eliminate them.

Rapid, firm decisions will make sure one of those ideas pays the way for all the ones that didn't work out. It just takes one great idea to create a new market.

Keep Your
Friends Close

Something strange happened during the dot-com era that turned my entire business acumen on its ear: Peers in Silicon Alley did not treat one another as competitors.

If a job was not within our skill set, we would pass it on to one of our competitors, and vice versa. Someone would throw us a new client one month, and we'd send a new client their way a month later. At first I thought, *What is happening?* But then one of my business partners at K2, David Centner, assured me this was the new way to do business.

At first it was weird. The creative team at K2 would show up at the same pitch meeting as Agency.com for PolyGram Records, and as they were leaving, cofounder Chan Suh of Agency.com would tell us everything we needed to know to do a better job.

I was a little blown away by all this. Everybody was getting along as if it were the Age of Aquarius or something. I knew there was plenty of money to be made by all of us, but it was like the buddy system of business, and it went against my entire business upbringing.

As it turned out, what I had thought was the return of the hippy mentality was really a new paradigm for success: Every competitor is a possible resource partner or an acquisition. You must expand your creative community to include your competitors.

Disney did this when they partnered with Pixar Animation Studios and released *Toy Story*. Instead of rolling Pixar under the bus, Disney integrated Pixar's expertise into their own and helped Pixar get backing for distribution and overall theater coverage. Disney later acquired Pixar but kept it as an independent company, and now the creative departments at Pixar are teaching Disney how to make a better product.

Pixar's key to success was to create the most brilliant work ever seen on the silver screen while making each and every film customized and groundbreaking. That newness and energy was missing from Disney; almost a century of industry dominance had left them stagnant and lackluster. Their formula for success was getting stale. Pixar, on the other hand, operated independently and made each new feature film unique to its own model, and they have the Oscars to prove that their ideology works.

Sure, it's easy to see the new kid on the block as a threat. But the reality is, they may have a piece of the puzzle that is missing from your company. Seasonality doesn't necessarily translate into innovation, but having a steady stream of young talent can bring new energy, new methodologies, new practices, or even new software that could revolutionize your industry. (This is something Pixar had, with their proprietary animation software PhotoRealistic RenderMan, now an industry-wide product.)

It's a bold new world, and seeing each and every competitor as a threat is an old model of competition—conquer and destroy— left over from the days of the Roman Empire. The new model for success is to see your competitors as opportunities.

Nowadays, even the simplest electronics installation needs a professional. Many smart people who thought they could easily install their HDTV 32-inch flat screen, Blu-ray DVD player, and cable box are having trouble. Because of this growing need for quick and easy installation, many electronic and computer companies saw a niche service just waiting to be exploited.

Best Buy wanted to enter this space. However, to do so would have been expensive and would have required duplicating services offered by existing players such as Geek Squad, a start-up created by master geek Robert Stephens. Instead, Best Buy bought out Geek Squad and made them a subsidiary, adding their unique suite of services to Best Buy's own—even a division for installing home theaters. Although Geek Squad can be found in every Best Buy store, they appear autonomous, offering services over the Internet via remote access as well as a 24/7 hotline. Their geeky brand image is accentuated by their uniform: black tie, pants, and shoes with white socks and white shirt, complete with a badge, à la *Men in Black*. They also arrive at your home in a black-and-white patrol car, a playoff of the 1950 hard-boiled cop image. Clearly this is a brand that takes pride in its image. A brand that knows what it stands for.

So when you think of the future of business, think of those smart moves by companies like Disney and Best Buy. And remember that it's about seeing competitors not as threats but as opportunities.

Looking for
Mr. Storefront

The beauty of leaving behind the Industrial Age in favor of the Information Age may not be so obvious, especially to those of us who have visited one empty mall after another, greeted not by the foot traffic of old but by the ubiquitous smell of Cinnabon in the air. Yes, we can blame the economy for all the shuttered storefronts, but if we are honest, we also have to look at a trend that has been growing for years, well before the crash of 2008.

You're thinking "Internet" when I say that—what else? But it would be a mistake to think that the changes of the past decade are only technological. When 70 percent of your foot traffic disappears, something else is going on, too. In fact, what is different these days is not just a new infrastructure, but also the new consumer purchasing habits this infrastructure spawned.

You and I and everyone we know have become more powerful as buyers, with many more choices as to how to spend our dollars and our time. Together we have created a new neighborhood to shop in, where brick and mortar matter less than bandwidth and accessibility, and where even the meaning of "shopping" has changed.

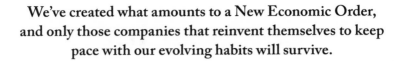

**We've created what amounts to a New Economic Order,
and only those companies that reinvent themselves to keep
pace with our evolving habits will survive.**

Not yet convinced? Let's look at some history. One of the first consumer sectors to be affected was the music industry. Take, for instance, Tower Records, whose iconic bright yellow signs and red logo were once as familiar to the New York City skyline as the Empire State building. With multiple locations around the city's five boroughs as well as Long Island, their brand dominated even the more established of the national music store chains.

Part of the reason they were so popular was that they always had every possible CD, in every genre imaginable, in stock at their flagship store on Fourth and Broadway—even bootleg stuff. I remember being able to find such diverse offerings as rare albums by jazz drummers like Buddy Rich and Billy Cobham, the greatest hits of Marvin Gaye, Léo Delibes' opera *Lakmé*, and rock classics by groups like Pearl Jam and my personal fave, Rush. Whether the music in question was pop, rock, jazz, classical, or so rare you didn't even know what to call it, Tower usually had it.

Over the years they extended that flagship store to the back of the building to accommodate even more inventory, plus the new and explosive market in DVDs. They even added another store, across the street from the back entrance on Lafayette Street, to accommodate the retro crowd, those who sought out old and outmoded VHS tapes and records.

To Tower, expansion like this must have seemed logical. After all, my Boomer generation would buy a record album, bring it home, and then sit on the floor, reading the jacket copy and absorbing the artwork while the music played. It was an event. Illustrators were hired to paint beautiful album covers that could absorb our attention for hours. The liner notes gave us a personalized taste of our favorite band members.

Yet though we didn't know it, we would be the last generation to savor and seek out such pleasures. The idea of browsing through a store on a Saturday or Sunday to buy stuff was already in the act of disappearing, as technology began to free us up, changing how we spent our time. The assumption we took for granted—that people liked browsing in a store—was soon to be phased out, dismissed as irrelevant by a generation that had no time or love for such experiences.

And so even as Tower Records was expanding to meet the demands of a market that now expected DVDs and VHS tapes alongside their musical choices, the seemingly unthinkable was happening: The company's cornerstone—their storefront business—was actually *shrinking*. Yes, people still walked through to marvel at the immense selection, but no one was buying like they used to. Although it took some time for consumers to trust online commerce, eventually the Internet reshaped our shopping habits.

As e-commerce became not just an *experiment* but a reliable and repeatable *experience*, people realized they no longer had to get up and travel to a mall and browse for things. Instead they could instantly download an album, preview a specific song, or order a book. Downloadable and disposable became the norm. People discarded media as easily as they tossed a tissue to the ground. They started to use the Internet to research price, quality, and availability—and the storefronts and malls suffered. Even when people visited such places, more and more they headed home and surfed for a better price.

And after a while, those visits to the mall became even less frequent. Why dress up, put gas in the car, and drive to the mall to buy something—say, the latest workout equipment—when you could relax in your underwear and order it over the Internet?

And remember, the Internet wasn't some monolithic, unchanging thing; it kept getting better, evolving, offering more on both sides of the purchase. Off-the-shelf software made building a website easier and put many a Web development shop out of business. Websites were no longer a bunch of linked, static pages, but transactional marketplaces capable of meeting the demands of finicky customers. Add to that increasing consumer trust in handing over credit card information, plus the bandwidth and infrastructure necessary to make those transactions seamless—no more waiting for a page to download. Consumers could order the latest knickknack anytime, anywhere. The future was casually happening in front of our eyes.

Retailers that didn't adapt fast enough to the shifting habits in their market missed the boat completely. They could only watch as companies like Napster and Apple changed the half-century-old model for purchasing music, Amazon changed how we buy books, and Netflix modernized how we watch movies.

Meanwhile, storefront foot traffic and the sales it generated, even during the biggest holidays, kept shrinking, year after year. Browsing in the mall was withering in favor of browsing online. And yet the reason for this, the underlying migration to cyberspace, was invisible to the companies that built mall spaces for a living. They just kept building one mall after another, ignoring the slowdown of foot traffic, chalking it up as a normal business cycle, hoping for a return by next election.

As for retailers, even the megabrands that appeared to acknowledge the Internet's impact either didn't see it as a threat or else figured their company was too big to be impacted by such a fad. But the mall builders and the megabrands were wrong. The New Economic Order had arrived, and it's still with us today. We see it everywhere, even in places we might not automatically think of.

Bookstores and similar businesses in saturated markets such as New York City don't have to worry about foot traffic ceasing altogether, for it remains a natural part of big-city living. But even these businesses must now be careful about what they offer. This is why Barnes & Noble has added magazine, music, movie, and café sections to its stores. Keep people in the store long enough, and eventually they will buy something. They may not buy a book, but the will buy a coffee and a scone. Truth is, the only way people stay in a bookstore these days is if there is a coffee shop attached with free Wi-Fi connectivity, or there's a book signing, or they're there to buy an e-reader.

The assumption of people wanting to come to a physical space to browse slowly and deliberately has been radically disrupted in favor of convenience and speed. Now people can order their books, CDs, and DVDs online, and then either download them or wait for the post office to deliver them to the front door. Meanwhile, we are free to pursue experiences that are more dynamic than shopping.

So the key to the survival of any company these days is to adapt and reshape its business according to these and other changes in consumer buying habits. Don't think of adding "more"; think of exploiting where consumers want to buy stuff. Your products and services must be as conveniently available as technology makes possible.

Thanks to cell phones, online product sites, and pass-and-go credit card terminals, the storefront is no longer a physical place but a transactional mecca that exists wherever consumers have access.

When the Internet first took hold, those brands that not only survived but also prospered had leaders at the helm who understood this. They could see the marketplace was dramatically changing, with new delivery platforms, increased product offerings, and dramatically different consumer habits. And so they changed their companies to exploit these new developments. They followed the money instead of clinging to old methodologies.

Here is where reinvention comes in. As I have said many times, even brands that have been in our minds and hearts for decades typically have no such track record on the Internet. This is a good and a bad thing. It's bad in that an established brand, one that exists in the real, flesh-and-blood world, will need to start from scratch to create an online presence. And yet it's good in that you *can* start from scratch, developing a completely new experience for a brand-new audience, perhaps even creating a separate online brand with a different name.

And the changes have only begun. With our data and work increasingly sitting on servers around the world rather than on a hard drive at home, even the idea of a PC-style computer has begun to die out in favor of smart netbooks that can access your data on an open-source server somewhere in the middle of Idaho. There will be no software ownership in the future, only software accessibility, a sort of pay-to-play model. That's just one example of how the handling of intellectual property is going to get ever more complex. Are you ready for the next leap, whatever it proves to be?

The Dynamic Reinvention of the American Mall

Now, not everyone is going to have to move to the Internet. Real-world experiences will still be relevant; it's just that they will be shifting both geographically and in terms of their purpose in our lives.

As we've seen, shopping as a socially acceptable recreational activity is changing, and the retail space it used to occupy is dying as well—that is, unless some serious changes are made to meet consumers' new expectations. In major cities like Manhattan, Chicago, or San Francisco, a steady stream of foot traffic keeps big stores like Kmart and Macy's full of browsers who buy. But malls that currently occupy rural dead zones—lingering between suburbia and extinction, where there exists virtually no foot traffic—are running the danger of becoming today's equivalent of an old ghost town.

Much like the roller-skating rinks and drive-in movie theaters that once dotted the landscape back in the fifties, malls are on their way to becoming an homage to the twentieth century, signifiers of the end of an era. The giant mall brands—names like Circuit City, Linens 'n Things, Bed Bath & Beyond, KB Toys, The Sharper Image—have either filed for Chapter 11, restructured, or disappeared altogether. Their formerly muscular brand names stand as empty shells waiting for someone to pay for the right to use them. To survive and draw a crowd once again, they'll need to retrofit the mall into something more like an amusement park than a store. To get Facebook users and *Rock Band* gamers out on a Saturday night, malls will have to rebuild with the goal of giving us dynamic, real-world experiences that we can find nowhere else.

Consumer spending for necessities is still strong in areas like food, gas, and clothing, but when it comes to spending an afternoon at the mall, unloading cash, those days are gone. For some strange reason, as unemployment rises, retailers still expect people to buy stuff. Small strip malls will still provide the necessary local fare—nail salons, fast food, dry cleaners, and such—but the behemoth malls that dot our landscape every few miles will evolve into something new. Unless your business is one gigantic indoor experience—an adult amusement park, so to speak—getting people to come hang at your boring twentieth-century mall will be hard. Especially when you are competing with the adult mega-experience of casinos like Mohegan Sun, or even an entire city of casinos such as Las Vegas, whose sole purpose is to get you to part with your money. To bring in families and to attract people who don't gamble, these large indoor spaces have turned into the indoor equivalent of Disney World, with bars, lounges, shopping zones, giant buffets, roller coasters, and hotels that rival anything in New York City. In the area of indoor entertainment, bigger is better as entertainment and retail come together into a new buzzword: retail-tainment.

Case in point: Years ago my wife and I spent a couple of lazy hours over a two-day period enjoying the Mall of America in Minneapolis, Minnesota. It was overwhelming, to say the least, boasting as it did an indoor amusement park, a shopping center, a recreational facility, and a family meeting place, along with first-class restaurants, a comedy club, and roller coasters. And this was only one floor out of many. The place lacked the sleaziness of Vegas, but it had the mesmerizing quality of Walt Disney World and the lingering smell of Cinnabon, cotton candy, and Starbucks. Every inch invited us to buy something, whether we needed it or not, and buy we did.

But here's the point: The Mall of America is not really a mall at all. Instead, it is a giant indoor refuge for families during the bitter cold Minnesota winters. It is a mecca of activity for those who lived in a state where the winter could make one feel depressed and shut-in for more than six months of the year.

Many malls are being repurposed like this. They have become megafacilities, providing people with rich experiences, movie houses, restaurants, amusement parks, and family gathering places. Some malls in Canada have even built realistic sandy beaches under a glass dome, complete with a wave tank to simulate an actual Caribbean beach, which wouldn't be a bad experience when it's twenty below zero outside.

If the Internet has stolen business, then smart businesses have upped the ante in return.

Look at the sports retailer and hunting outfitter Cabela's. They have become the leader in hunting, fishing, and outdoor gear by transforming the old-fashioned style of the dark, smoky gun shop with stuffed deer heads on the wall into a dynamic megabrand. Housed in giant retail spaces, Cabela's creates dioramas of hunters using equipment and families out camping—bigger-than-life outdoor experiences housed under one roof—and they've made the entire store friendlier to women as well. Cabela's has made their space a twenty-first-century event! I suggest you visit one near you . . . even if you don't hunt or fish, visiting Cabela's is an event.

And something else is happening to repurpose vacant mall space: Smart landlords are starting to retrofit these spaces into mixed-use environments. Shopping malls that used to be surrounded by parking lots have been transformed into pedestrian-friendly neighborhoods with tree-lined streets, outdoor cafes, and ground-level shops. The rest of the vacant inner spaces have been repurposed into apartments and office space. That's right, people are now living in *malls* in California, Florida, Colorado, and a slew of other locales where urban hotspots are close by. Even the ubiquitous food court, once a sure sign that you were in a mall, is being replaced with sit-down restaurants and nightspots, the better to cater to suburbia's growing population of empty nesters and young professionals.

The lesson here is that to compete against the cyber mall, brick-and-mortar retail spaces will have to offer more than just shopping. They will need to provide a community-based lifestyle, with socialization and camaraderie, to support a regular customer base used to living in still smaller, even more confined spaces. The mall of the future must be refitted into something less like a shopping space and more like a small town complete with a homeowners' association. Such spaces may seem at first like homogenized movie sets rather than naturally occurring communities, but at least they can be saved. But they will need to be repurposed quickly, for the glory days of mall-based retail aren't returning anytime soon.

For a brick-and-mortar storefront to thrive in the twenty-first century will require thinking outside the box. Leadership needs to keep their eyes on what has become the norm, and shift their business to meet the demands of a fickle consumer, who wants richer experiences than they've had in the past.

Imagine, all this disruption just because technology gave us another place to shop!

5TH LAW

A Liquid Leader Leads by Example

*A man who wants to lead the orchestra
must turn his back on the crowd.*

—James Cook

Why Be a Leader in the First Place?

The old method of the boss standing on a balcony of the factory floor and barking orders from on high doesn't get a company very far today. In newly industrialized countries where this is normal behavior, just give it time; the employees will eventually strike and form a union.

Even in the United States, the biggest problem I see is that the people working within today's corporation have evolved and so have their methods—but management hasn't. Even with technology having advanced to the point where big-ticket items like Range Rovers cost the same to build as lower-echelon brands like the Jeep Grand Cherokee, with the exact same quality, most management methods are still rooted in the way business was conducted half a century ago. Some companies have figured it out, especially those that work on the Internet or are already globally positioned.

Why has the bottom of the org chart shifted? Today's employee, through computer skills and an exposure to the new global social networks, sees opportunities that those at the top just don't have time to explore. What those employees need, however, is a new type of management methodology that addresses their needs yet understands and manages their weaknesses at the same time.

Call them what you will—Generation Y, Gamers, Millennials, Digital Natives, or Netizens—their demands have opened Pandora's box when it comes to how employees are expecting to be treated. Some are developing applications that may eventually make your business obsolete.

So who are you gonna listen to? Captains of industry who take companies public, or the tech-savvy programmer who is constantly looking for free applications to automate her job? (I say listen to both.) How about the frustrated designer just dying to start his own company? Or the smart MBA with a background in online marketing and SEO technologies? Or how about the branding expert who spoke at thirty different companies last year? "Listen, learn, and apply" is my motto. If something isn't working, discard it quickly before you lose too much money.

Something else has changed too. This new workforce doesn't stop working when they punch out. The norm used to be that employees tolerated one another during team-building exercises, even if those exercises were lame. They wanted to keep management happy, but that was it. Bonding took place only at work when necessary, usually at the annual holiday party. Today, however, many a workforce hangs out together. They join hockey teams, go on vacations together, even form rock bands. The corporation is becoming a socially acceptable peer network where people share not only their work, but also hobbies and just plain fun. The bonding doesn't hurt production, it enhances it.

So how does a leader fit into such an intense paradigm? Younger generations don't follow because they are told to. They need a reason, and since they choose whom they give their talents to, your job is to show them just how great you are to work for. Lead by setting the example and integrating your unique leadership style into the organization.

Setting the Tone

Years ago at K2 it was time for our first annual bonus meeting. Since the four of us—me, Matt, David, and Doug—made up the executive committee, naturally we would oversee the bonus process. We decided to pull in department managers and listen to their suggestions and reasoning for the cash amounts they thought their teams deserved. Normally we let our managers manage and very rarely interfered with their decisions. But these bonus meetings would be different. We wanted the managers to provide us with the logic behind their decisions.

As each name from each department was placed on the wall, big producers at the top and the lowest producers at the bottom, we started to notice a pattern. Despite the criteria being very clear, it became apparent that bonuses were being doled out according to how attractive someone was, how well they dressed, or how well they fit in to the clique. It was becoming an Abercrombie & Fitch runway show.

What stood out immediately for Doug and me was that a new female producer, Debbie, had been placed in the top bonus category despite having been on board for only two months, and despite working alongside employees who had been there for years and probably deserved the top bonus more. Debbie was glamorous and well dressed, and this seemed to have provoked both male and female managers into awarding her a big bonus. She was a delight to work with but certainly not worth the bonus suggested.

The selection of Debbie was only one example—there were plenty more. After twenty minutes, it became clear that our young managers were playing favorites. Doug and I were astounded. What the hell was going on? Did our managers not see who the real producers in the company were?

"What about Rochelle?" we blurted out in unison. Everyone in the room fell silent. Immediately they knew where we were going with this as soon as they heard the name. They were embarrassed at having entirely forgotten one of our key employees.

Yet somehow she wasn't on anyone's bonus list! Rochelle was the backbone of our entire company—*all* day-to-day production went through her. Not one job went anywhere without her approval. She never left the office before 8:00 PM, and she was back at her desk by 8:30 AM. How could they have missed her? Every single person who appeared in the top bonus category had to hand his or her job to Rochelle to get it produced, coded, printed, or rerouted.

I had my guess as to why she was not on the list. Rochelle was a quiet librarian type who raised her voice only when someone missed a deadline or a vendor didn't pay a bill. Red-headed, blue-eyed, and unglamorous, she would do things no one else had the guts to do, and she did it matter-of-factly, as if it was no big deal. Doug nicknamed her "Fearless," because she was. She focused on her job and did it silently and with maximum efficiency. This type of person is so rare that you want to keep them on board no matter what it takes.

We had a problem on our hands: We wanted our managers to make decisions based on facts, not opinions and acceptance within the mutual admiration society. We got our point across by awarding Rochelle the lion's share of bonus cash and giving her an award for going above and beyond the call of duty. Everyone from the executive committee to middle management agreed with our decision.

After that meeting, no one overlooked her again. Nor did they play favorites. Output was measured by diligently observing those who met their deadlines, client interaction, and bringing jobs in under budget. Period. As leaders, we had set the tone.

Setting the tone isn't about micromanaging. People are quite capable of managing themselves, but it takes unique leadership to see that certain actions, left unchecked, will lead to disaster. It is about becoming a shepherd of great ideas, methods, and best practices. Set the tone. Set a clear vision, with expectations and standards. Without them, no one can guess what your vision for the company might be.

The Rise of the Machines

Today, of course, technology has made it far easier to crunch truly meaningful numbers and thereby identify the producers in your organization. As I pointed out in the section titled "Measuring Productivity without Becoming Big Brother," this new type of number crunching is called applied mathematics, aka operations research. It really isn't all that new—it's been around since the forties—but what *is* new is that it's being applied to all sorts of models. This especially includes the measuring of outputs from both machines and humans.

Remember how in the past, many business decisions were based on a hasty numbers crunch done by hand, plus the occasional executive walk-through? Factories that *appeared* to be run well stayed open. Executives didn't really grasp the idea that every single employee had spent weeks cleaning and mending in anticipation of upper management's "surprise" visit. These factories appeared to be clean, efficient, and productive, but secretly they were hemorrhaging by the bucket. The executive decision whether to keep or close the location was euphemistically called an "educated guess" because it was made after considering as much data as was available—and suffering as little face time as possible.

Unfortunately it was the unkempt, dirty factory—the one where they hadn't any time to spruce up—that had been the real profit center. So after the wrong factory was shut down, management realized, "I guess Jenkins in accounting was right after all. Didn't we fire him last month?"

Whenever a productive factory was shut down like this, it was met with crowds of angry workers and union reps who couldn't understand why they were being fired—especially when they had been so busy. They demanded to see the proof, but since management had simply made an educated guess, there wasn't any proof.

But with applied math, through a detailed computer model, companies can track rising shipping costs, inventory storage, and currency fluctuations in real time and can stay up to date, ending any need for "educated guesses." This gives board members and union reps hard proof that a decision to close up shop was the correct one, and not arbitrary.

Norske Skog, a $4 billion Norwegian newsprint manufacturer (the second largest in the world) built a detailed computer model of their global operations in order to identify—right down to individual machines—where they were losing money. In an industry that is shrinking, they are profitable because they acted quickly and utilized the available technology to make them more efficient.

Just because technology can track productivity doesn't mean you can watch from a safe vantage point. Leadership needs a serious presence not only for driving deadlines, but also to catch the new discoveries that technology will provide in the form of real-time feedback.

For the first time in human history, management can track employee *and* machine output together! This used to be science fiction, but today it is reality. Leadership needs to set the tone of fairness in this new data model–managed world so that employees don't feel as though Big Brother is making every decision from an office "upstairs."

Morale and motivation become more important line items as we move deeper into the twenty-first century.

Do As I Do, Not As I Say

In our age, setting the tone means leading by example. If you don't, you lose respect—and your talent base.

Even the military understands this. For thousands of years, whether among the samurai or the Roman centurions, the military worked pretty much the same all over the world: Break down new recruits both mentally and physically, then build them back up into soldiers. Fear and intimidation were the cornerstones of this process. After all, battle conditions would be far worse than any drill. The real purpose of this millennia-old hazing program was to weed out those who weren't military material early and prepare those who were for real combat. Soldiers who were well trained as a unit could overcome fear on the battlefield better than those who were not. And they obeyed their commanding officers, sometimes with blind loyalty.

This system worked fine up until a few years ago, when the US Army noticed that the rate of new recruits dropping out of basic training had climbed to 10 percent. The problem? Millennials do not respond well to the intimidation tactics and command methods of most drill sergeants. In the military, just as in corporate settings, the strict hierarchy of the organizational chart is being rejected.

A close Gen Y friend, Gabe, recently returned from two tours of duty in Iraq. His stories of basic training are surprising. It turns out that the US Army training centers decided to stop the hemorrhaging of new recruits by implementing methods that Gen Y understands: leading by example.

When I pressed Gabe to tell me more about his experiences, from boot camp to actual battle, he described how well his drill sergeants worked with him and prepared him for battle. He also told about actual combat situations where his commanding officer went and flushed out insurgents with him. Without the officer, Gabe feels, he would not have survived. We were most surprised when Gabe said, "My drill sergeant did everything I did. Side by side."

Drill sergeants are now more mentors than disassociated commanders barking orders from the safety of high ground. Being expected to run the same obstacle courses as their newbies has made the drill sergeants better as well. Louis Gossett Jr. and Richard Gere from *An Officer and a Gentleman* is out, Kevin Costner and Ashton Kutcher from *The Guardian* is in. In other words, recruits are motivated by a sense of "If my leader can do it, so can I."

To some, this may sound like coddling, but the recruits are staying and quitters have dropped significantly. Since many graduates of basic training will be sent off to Iraq, Afghanistan, or Pakistan within six months, we'll see very quickly if this new learning method is effective in real battle situations.

This reminds me of my parents saying, "Do as I say, not as I do." In today's world, the opposite has become true: "Do as I do, not as I say."

Dying on the Vine

As Baby Boomers, we were never prepared for the shift to a global marketplace. Many of us are unsure where we are going as a country, so we hold on to the old ways of thinking and working. We were raised on a steady diet of John Wayne movies, "America is always the hero" history books, and a solipsistic approach to world politics. The result is an entire generation suffering from what behavioral coach Tim Davis calls "adult resistance learning." Our culture is literally trained to resist change.

Many Boomers are "waiting for the jobs to return." This is something we can no longer afford to do, because certain sectors have moved more than 70 percent of their economic model onto the Internet. Add to that the fact that the very idea of what a job is has changed. Companies understand it is better to have a freelance, seasonal workforce than to be paying so much in salaries, benefits, and sick pay. Consultants pay their own health care, taxes, and retirement. Responsibility is shifting to the individual. It is the return of the artisan economy.

During a conversation I had with him in 2009, Brad Peterson of Strategic Asset Management (SAMI), a global consulting firm, said it very succinctly: "Outsourcing is [very] old news to the rest of the world. Countries like Germany figured out how to work with India, China, and Brazil more than fifteen years ago." In plain English, the United States is very behind.

Time for Boomers to up their game.

As entire sectors shrink and traditional jobs move overseas, many of us will have to change careers and adjust the ideal of what future employment will be. Despite the 2009 auto company bailouts, many workers in that industry stand to lose their pensions and retirement benefits, just as former Enron employees did. As an example, GM's pension obligations are so huge that if the company sold all its assets and its entire inventory of cars, it would still be able to meet only a small percentage of them. This is a disaster waiting to happen.

In the midst of all this, I trust that great leaders will find a way to move forward. First on their list is to think out of the box, by listening to Generation Y. With a completely different set of skills, Gen Yers were raised to have entrepreneurial skills and a voracious appetite for technology. They are already trained for globalization. Boomers, sad to say, never were—but even Boomers can move forward by letting go of their opinions, listening, and seeking retraining.

Everywhere, corporations are looking for the cheapest way to get things done and using technology to automate as much as they possibly can. It is not a good or a bad thing. It is the bloody transition from the Industrial Age to the Information Age. Horse and buggy manufacturers didn't completely disappear one hundred years ago; the sector just shrank as automobiles replaced them.

The funny part is that for quite some time, automobiles looked like carriages without a horse attached, right down to the spoke wheels; hence the nickname "horseless carriage." But as car designers turned their backs on the past, they were freed up to reimagine what an automobile actually should look like. Form began to follow function.

So, how will your business start to change as we turn our backs on the past and start cutting a path into the future? What devices will change? What processes? We are still a long way off from flying cars and personal jet packs, but be assured that as technology disrupts multiple markets, some sectors will shrink or disappear while still others will replace them and grow.

Leaders are still needed, but their role is changing. Sitting in an ivory tower, preparing a great speech, will give way to a hands-on, more democratic approach to managing, an approach that includes helping to bridge the gap between generations while keeping an eye on the bigger picture. As a leader, getting down and dirty and working side by side with your best and brightest will put you in direct contact with change. Work on making the business better at what it does.

You can always go back up to thirty-five thousand feet for a better strategic view, and that's the point. People on the front lines can't see all the pieces you see, and the smart ones know this regardless of their generation. They want a boss who can see the work they do, listen to their input, and implement those suggestions. After all, you may not need to know how your enterprise software works or about the bugs the new version has, but people on the front lines need to know. They just need a boss who listens when they tell you what needs to happen to make it all work better and more efficiently.

People trust managers who understand that everyone in an organization is valid. Listen, learn, implement, and guide. That's a leader's job.

Know Thyself

The hardest lesson I had to learn in business is that I couldn't expect integrity and ethics from people who have none whatsoever. In today's world, where everything is transparent, your personal brand is a representation of the company you represent. Name any business leader and chances are, you know their company. Your customers do not see you as separate from your brand. They see your employees as a representative of that brand as well. This is why the values you embody internally will be reflected to the outside world in the products you create and the services you provide.

I am constantly on the lookout for corporate brands that are disconnected from what they represent out here in the real world. Inside the ivory tower, your company may appear to be a utopia of great ideas, but outside the whitewashed walls, the people buying your products have an entrenched perception that may not be in line with your vision of Camelot. Their perception may or may not be the truth, but it is what they *believe* the truth to be that is at stake here. And by the way, once someone has an opinion about your brand, it is very hard to change it—actually, it is next to impossible.

Over the years, while Netflix was gaining ground in a world that was embracing e-commerce, Blockbuster lost their leadership position, remaining stagnant as their shrinking customer base moved to the convenience and home delivery that technology brings. Simply put, their customers' habits changed; browsing a video store on a Saturday night is no longer necessary. Blockbuster lost their leadership position.

When a company sits still with a "wait and see" attitude, they leave themselves vulnerable to the competition. Instead of leading the market, Blockbuster reacted to stay alive.

For a while I thought they were down for the count, but Blockbuster has finally upped their game by offering Blockbuster On Demand through a new V Cast Video application debuting in conjunction with Motorola's Droid X smartphone. And new Droid users are in for a treat as well: the new mobile device (I can't really call it a phone as that is just one thing it does) features a 4.3-inch high-resolution screen alongside a dual-flash, 8-megapixel camera, HD camcorder, and dual high-speed connectivity for downloads to stream and share personal HD content. It's a perfect portable platform for movies.

Although Blockbuster's On Demand service has been available at home for years, offering it to mobile phone users is a stroke of genius, and a nice chess move I might add. Blockbuster just might stay relevant in the twenty-first century after all.

To be seen in a new light may require more than just retooling your business; it may require a complete identity change. This is why NYNEX, which stood for New York New England Exchange, changed their name to Verizon, to spread out past those states' borders. It's hard to sell products in California when you are named after East Coast states, especially one that has a reputation for being a little rough around the edges. Hey, fuggedabouit!

Another name change I like came about from listening to a customer base. In the seventies, the words "federal" and "express" together conjured up images of stability and speed, but in an age where companies with names like Google are making headlines, the old criteria is out the window. Federal Express did something smart. They realized everybody was calling them FedEx and instead of fighting it, changed accordingly. As they relaunched their new brand with a suite of new services, they relaunched their identity as well, with a new series of logos for each division. It was brilliant business.

Amway Global is also changing negative public opinion by transitioning to their new identity: The company is putting its best foot forward by sponsoring soccer events, listening to the marketplace, and meeting potential sales reps right where the negative opinion exists.

Sometimes a competitor will force you to change your business model or your products. For example, Domino's Pizza decided to start listening to customers back in 2008, especially after losing significant market share to newcomer Papa John's. Hearing customer feedback that their pizza tasted like cardboard didn't sit well, but it was the truth—straight from the marketplace. They listened and changed their recipe. The change was so deep and profound that they showed their efforts in a series of national commercials. As a result of two years of testing and product research, the sauce, cheese, and crust were reconfigured in hopes of convincing consumers to give Domino's another shot. Domino's revenue is up 32 percent, which tells me that the change was a significant success.

If only all companies would listen to their marketplace and change accordingly.

Laser Beam Focus

The key to success is to figure out what your company represents to the consumer, and be exactly that to them. Stand for one thing and one thing only. Cluttering up your brand with new products and offerings that are not aligned with what you are known for is a recipe for disaster.

Remember Starbucks Restaurants? Probably not. The restaurant idea bombed miserably because no one saw, nor will they ever see, Starbucks as a full-service restaurant. Starbucks is an Italian-style coffee shop, period.

How about Microsoft Xbox? It has been losing money since Day One. No one sees Microsoft as a gaming company, and they never will. As a matter of fact, the teens immersed in Xbox games aren't even aware that Microsoft makes the darn things. I do know that Microsoft will never abandon the Xbox because they are looking more long term and have a bigger agenda, but they are throwing money at it until that marketplace actually manifests. Microsoft has the money to burn, but unfortunately, most companies don't have that kind of war chest or time.

When companies pursue avenues outside their brand's perception or expertise, they are asking for trouble. If you are seen as the expert for a particular product, you can't simply start making stuff in a completely different category and expect to be a profitable leader, especially when someone else already dominates the market. By staying focused on what you do best and only on that, you can assure leadership. If you decide to go off on a tangent, understand that you will be wasting money.

If you do decide to enter a new market, create a new brand separate from your core.

Would you be surprised to find out that Kraft also makes batteries? Duracell is their leading brand, but Kraft is also smart enough to know how to keep their brands separate and laser beam focused. They also know that competing with Grey Poupon would be a waste of time and money. Kraft's mustard is not a highbrow brand, and they know it. I like professional speaker Jane Atkinson's advice: Pick a lane and stick to it. So don't switch lanes and pretend you are something you are not.

Do you know what your company's brand or products stand for in the marketplace? If you don't, it may be time to ask honest questions. Make sure the company putting the survey together doesn't pander to you by asking questions whose answers will make you look like a saint. After the survey comes back, if you don't like what you hear, then maybe it's time to make some radical changes.

**Ask for the raw truth.
Without it, you can't do any damage control.**

Who, Who Are You?

Now let's talk now about your core values—yes, *your* values. In a world that changes as rapidly as ours, the way you express your passions and values must keep pace yet remain true to who you are.

One of the things I love to do most is run leadership retreats. In my experience it is best to strip down the past, the stories, and the "woulda, coulda, shouldas" residing in every executive's head. Those stories don't matter. They are like fairy tales, to be archived in the corporation's lexicon of achievements. Because today's consumers want to know *what you have done for them lately.*

As their markets shrank and were redefined, The Sharper Image, Fortunoff, Spiegel, and many other companies couldn't figure out how to reinvent themselves in a way that would keep potential consumers from tossing their catalogs into the garbage. These companies failed to adapt quickly enough to a changing market because they kept clinging to the past. Internally, they assumed they were leading the market no matter what happened. Boomers grew up on the brands and considered them solid and trustworthy. What these companies failed to understand, however, was that no such relationship existed with the Internet consumer. The companies failed to understand that in cyberspace they would have to start fresh and create a new story.

Many of these companies started out as leaders almost a century ago. They were innovative and unique, and they created entirely new marketplaces. But they forgot to keep reinventing themselves. Over time, they became companies looking for a market instead of maintaining their leadership position. L.L. Bean and Spiegel have had to reinvent their brands for the Information Age by increasing visibility online or through their storefronts.

By starting fresh and letting go of expectations, assumptions, and past glories, leaders can stop doing things they feel they have to do and start doing things they want to do. It is extraordinary to see leaders reignite the flame that made them join the company in the first place. Passion is what makes underdogs into champions.

The Internet is a chance to start a new story, to convey your intensity, passion, and trustworthiness. Just as you must keep reinventing your brands to stay in touch with consumers, you must adapt who you are internally in order to lead your ever-evolving organization. External change may come from external forces, but ultimately it is the internal driving force of your organization that is reflected in what you create.

If you want to be in the hearts and minds of your customers, then you have to have the company inside your heart and mind as well. Ever chat with someone who is enthusiastic about what they do? They are contagious to be around.

**Imagine turning your employees
into advocates for your vision.**

Take a look at Kashi. Here's a company where the people throughout the entire organization are passionate about their products because the employees at Kashi are exactly like their customers—natural food lovers who are healthy and fit and have active, outdoorsy lifestyles. Their passion for healthy choice is contagious. When was the last time one of your employees seemed passionate about working at your company?

Knowing who you are will keep you from wasting time pursuing markets that are not in your company's best interests—a mistake Atari should have recognized before they tried to compete with IBM. When you know what your company is all about, you stop making silly mistakes.

Know thyself. It will save you time and energy.

The Age of the Transient Brand

In 1992, as assistant producer for a large, New York–based production company in charge of large-scale corporate sales meetings, it was my job to oversee just about every single aspect of the operation, both in New York and on-site. At one particular show at the Marriott Marquis in Atlanta, Georgia, for the pharmaceutical giant Merck (Merck, Sharp & Dohme at the time), I had snuck down to the ballroom to check everything out; it was the night before an 8:00 AM meeting. After chatting with the police officer assigned to our ballroom, I excused myself to slip backstage.

Although I had done this many times, standing backstage always gave me a sense of wonder and awe. Hoisted up onto steel scaffolds fifteen feet off the ground were nine towers, with a total of thirty-six Kodak slide projectors configured to create movie-like animation and special effects. The rear-projection video projector looked like a futuristic military cannon. It had taken sixteen technicians more than four days to assemble the steel, wood, carpeting, lights, and projection equipment. There were more than 216 lights over the main stage, three massive main screens, and remote control winches to pull two additional movable screens into position. The sixty-foot stage was huge, to say the least. It was all part of making the CEO of Merck look like a rock star.

As I looked around at all the latest multimedia equipment surrounding me, I thought to myself, *I can't believe I am working with the latest and greatest in cutting-edge technology.* It just couldn't get any better, right?

**But in fact, the glitz actually interfered with my
ability to see over the horizon and into the future.**

Our entire business relied entirely on Kodak products: slide film projectors, Kodalith film in 35 mm and large-sheet format, and of course, Kodak's 35 mm and 70 mm slide film and two-and-a-quarter chrome camera film, along with equipment and chemistry for processing. I literally used hundreds of thousands of feet of their slide film per year. It was the industry standard, the brand trusted above all other brands.

Even though I was still relying on Kodak, I had already bought and begun using my first Mac computer. To my delight I had found I could get two days' worth of work finished within three hours. No longer did I have to send artwork out to be assembled by a printer, nor did I need to use a typesetter or an airbrush artist. All I had to do was learn to use the software. A revolution was happening, and I was part of it.

Yet no one in my industry—and that includes me—realized that this same revolution was going to take over every aspect of the corporate theater and events business. Within five years, every piece of Kodak equipment I was standing next to on that stage would be replaced with sleek, RGB-computerized rear projectors. Even the conventional computer systems we were already using for speeches would be replaced by a laptop and PowerPoint software. It seemed as if it happened overnight; slide film, mounts, and slide projectors were no longer needed.

**Within a five-year period, the multibillion-dollar
corporate events industry stopped using Kodak
products and embraced laptops.**

And laptops didn't just eliminate older technologies; they eliminated jobs, too. Special effects slide photography that had once required highly skilled professionals became a simple task that the computer-savvy designer could handle easily in Photoshop. In the corporate theater business alone,

one Mac IIci replaced three departments and nine people. "Technological efficiency" became the watchword of the new Information Age, and Kodak lost billions of dollars.

Either Leading a Revolution or Losing It

I realize now how foolish I had been to think that the technology that I was using in 1992 would stay the same. What made me scratch my head at first was how things changed so quickly and how easily people accepted the change. Now I understand that as a Liquid Leader, you have to put your company out in front of changes in technology. You have to set an example for a new generation of workers. You have to continuously evolve your brand to lead the market, or you will get left behind.

With the advent of digitization, Kodak's brand took a beating in the commercial over-the-counter retail markets. Their $5 billion camera and film market was decimated by digital cameras, cell phone cameras, and at-home desktop photo printing. Yet Kodak just seemed to sit there. Even a joint venture with Nikon didn't seem to help. What destroyed their dominance as a consumer brand were three inventions in particular: laptop computers, the Internet, and digital photography.

The funny thing is, Kodak *invented* the digital camera, but for some unknown reason chose not to lead the revolution. They lost their leadership position to camera companies willing to push all things digital and invent infrastructure and products to support the new tech. Casio, Nikon, Canon, and upstart Olympus began to take a chunk out of Kodak's market, leaving the yellow-and-red giant sadly in last place. Here was Eastman Kodak, the innovator that almost single-handedly invented the entire photography industry—and as we approached the twenty-first century, I began to wonder if they would make it.

It took time, but digital photography began to outpace film and became the apparent leader in the future of photography. High-end companies like Hasselblad didn't require you to buy a new camera; instead, they designed interchangeable sensors that worked with their current two-and-a-quarter film-based cameras. Brilliant.

And even when Kodak reentered the digital camera market, they were seen as a dinosaur. Despite being a trusted American brand, they were no longer leading; they were following. Kodak was last to enter a market they should have pioneered. Inertia had set the pace, when instead their battle cry should have been "Hurry up and follow our lead."

Today's brands can't afford to make that sort of mistake. They must watch closely at how technology is changing their business, and take action. If not, many will be left behind—eventually going out of business. Look at Polaroid, for example. What do they stand for? Who knows? I don't have a clue. The Polaroid brand has become meaningless in the twenty-first century and needs an overhaul—fast. So far, they've abandoned their proprietary film technology in 2008 to focus on their sunglasses and LCD technology, along with a line of digital cameras. Recently, Polaroid chose Lady Gaga as their creative director and new face of Polaroid. After years of controversy, Chapter 11 bankruptcy, and ping-pong ownership, this may be the comeback Polaroid needs.

This is the era of unstable, transient brands. Those that don't evolve, adapt, or do something will die out.

Like the dinosaurs, we see evidence of one company after another, in a last-ditch effort to save their skin, filing for bankruptcy protection. Hopefully part of their restructuring is about flexibility and innovation, both as an organization and as part of the role of a Liquid Leader.

As the twenty-first century heats up, you are going to notice things that make your old way of thinking obsolete. Take virtualized servers: No longer is it cost-effective to keep the company servers on the premises or pay a staff to maintain them. Why employ an IT department when a simple phone call can add as many servers as necessary for a monthly fee? Now you can hire a company whose sole mission is to protect your data. That company will provide this service over the Internet with several server farms scattered around the world, with redundant backups throughout the system, all for a monthly fee.

And that's just for starters. Add the advantages of a remote workforce, the ability to pound out a letter from your cell phone, and easy access to videoconferencing over your desktop, and you can see that the old concept of a fat corporation with big, glass-and-steel high-rise headquarters is quickly becoming a dying model. Look at any Internet brand and you get the picture. Yes, these brands have nice fancy headquarters, but they keep overhead down by using technology to take advantage of their network, warehoused inventory, and infrastructure.

Stop Following, Start Leading

All this sounds scary to a linear thinker. How can my company's data be strewn all over the world? How could it be more cost-effective and efficient to hand it all over to a digital security server farm? Why can't it stay right here in my office? How did outsourcing my MIS department become more profitable and safe than having it here internally? How can a company with one headquarters office and no storefronts be a multibillion-dollar business leader?

The best thing you can do is learn the advantages of any new system. Listen to the experts, get on board with the changes, and ask as many questions as possible that are outside the box, such as "What else can I virtualize?" and "What technology might be out there to upgrade my production?"

Letting go of traditional thinking will help you embrace each new software upgrade and new business model change. It will also help you adapt your organization with mercurial efficiency when you discover new business models. And it will give you the ability to adapt to your changing workforce as a leader who exemplifies new ways of doing business.

When was the last time that you saw an IBM typewriter or computer? You mostly see IBM servers and network towers—B2B stuff—if you are lucky enough to stroll into the back of your IT department. What you cannot see is IBM's other services and products. The virtual world is just one of the new ventures they are headed into. It is clear that companies like IBM are not bogged down in old traditional thinking. They are reaching out, learning, and redefining new markets and strategies. And once they understand the lay of the land, they take action.

IBM keeps their brand innovations in our minds by serving us strategically placed TV spots—ads that make us go "Wow! That's sounds kinda cool." Meanwhile, Microsoft is developing interactive and smart flat screens, Google is using Bloom Energy's Bloom Box to power their data centers, and BMW is developing a hydrogen car. A revolution is taking place.

Let's look again at Kodak, for their story has a surprise twist. It took ten years, but using their knowledge of the science of imaging and printing, Kodak has found a new niche: They have repositioned themselves as a provider of high-end security products. Although they still make film and film products, two-thirds of Kodak's $10 billion annual revenue is now from digital products, half of which didn't even exist five years ago. It is a very profitable business from a happy accident. Turns out, Kodak will be with us in the twenty-first century after all.

But Kodak is lucky as well as smart. They had a vertical business model and a century of established trust. It kept them alive during a period when they would have otherwise stumbled. Does your organization have one hundred years of established trust and a brand name known worldwide? If not, you cannot afford to live off your past until you figure it out, as Kodak did. You need to keep reinventing yourself with a sense of urgency.

Kodak is an accidental innovator, but their brand still is perceived by Gen Y as an "old" brand. But with their new line of desktop printers and Flip handheld HD video cameras that allow a user to make instant videos ready to upload to YouTube, Kodak has a chance of reinventing their story for a new consumer—and assuring they will be around for another hundred years.

Longtime established brands may not realize it yet, but if they aren't in people's faces, consistently updating their brand and evolving it, over a very short period of time they might find that two-thirds of the population does not know who they are.

Timberland, for example, was a hot brand during the nineties. Thanks to Tupac, Dr. Dre, and every hip-hop trendsetter out there, Timberland's products appeared in rap videos and were embraced by hip-hop as *the* must-have footwear. Headed by CEO Jeff Swartz, Timberland grew eightfold—valued at $1.6 billion at their height. But recently the bling wore off and hip-hop moved on, leaving Timberland behind. The company lost $150 million in revenue seemingly overnight—never expecting their market to change so quickly.

Relying on one source of revenue is dangerous.

Today Timberland is attempting to find a market by refocusing their brand on the rugged image they were known for in the past, running a series of funny, claymation-inspired viral videos in which the Timberland PRO does amazing feats of strength utilizing the steel toe of the boot. It may be too little too late, but at least they are taking some sort of action by appealing to a younger audience that finds these types of ads humorous. Whether it drives sales remains to be seen.

Today's CEO must start looking for other markets when times are good, because target markets are fickle and will be looking for the next big thing before you know it. Assuming your market will never change is corporate suicide. Searching for new markets and new strategies while you are immersed in profits is the heart of survival. Look at personalities like Madonna, John McEnroe, and Steve Guttenberg, who disappeared from public life for so long that they lost the interest of their target markets. While all three have had minor comebacks, their brand images will never return to their glory days. With today's finicky customers, if you're out of sight, you're out of mind.

To stay relevant and up to date, stay ahead of what your customers need. Otherwise you'll wind up becoming a company looking for a market.

Again, the customer is always asking, "What have you done for me lately?"

Tales of how the company was founded and how they became a market leader back in the day may have worked well as a motivational tool during the nineties, but that story is more than ten years old. If your CEO keeps repeating it at the annual training meeting, your company may be suffering from stagnation. Remember, returning to the glory days is impossible.

Clinging to the old status quo will be dangerous as our economy gets pounded. It's time to get bold and courageous, time to create new markets, time to create a new work ethic, time to reinvent your company and its brand.

It truly is survival of the fittest.

Back to the Future

Imagine what business categories you could create if you let go of the way things should be and started thinking about what *could* be. Ask yourself, "What world of possibilities might I create today? Over the next five years? Over my lifetime?" Many of the best companies have already repositioned themselves. They haven't turned their backs on their core businesses by any means, but they have used their networks, platforms, and knowledge to develop additional profit centers in hopes of grabbing market share now and in the future.

Getting in on the ground floor is smart. Cisco, for example, is involved in videoconferencing—they already have the networking and hub knowledge in place to be a dominant player. Microsoft is into gaming with the Xbox, which might seem weird—a loss of shareholders' equity—until you realize that every household will someday have one mainframe computer in the home, managing everything from environment to entertainment, and that by entering the home with an Xbox, Microsoft is assured that they will be at least in the top five choices. They'll be in the running with Sony PlayStation 3, Apple TV, and Nintendo Wii. And of course Apple has taken its own leap, by controlling more than just music content through iTunes.

Who else is jumping in and taking advantage of their already existing networks, even though at first glance it might look completely off base from their core market? Try Wal-Mart; they've become the leader in electronic medical records, which seems to make no sense at all because Wal-Mart is a retail store. But Wal-Mart also offers eye doctor services, a pharmacy, health care supplies, etc. And since they have everyone's information, why not take advantage of that fact and start a database and compete with

Siemens? Wal-Mart has the data to manage, along with patients and doctors, so why not simply manage it all? Smart.

When a major business shift seems to be taking place, isn't it best to look at your already existing markets and networks to figure out what you can do with them?

One Hundred Years to Overnight Success

When American Express launched its money-order business in 1882, American Express Travelers Cheques became the ubiquitous symbol of frontier banking for places where the only banking was several days' ride by stagecoach, train, or horseback. The product quickly became a hit in Europe, where no such financial product existed. It made banking so much easier when customers could travel from country to country without having to figure out the exchange rates and convert currencies. Not bad for a joint venture between Wells Fargo and John Butterfield that was supposed to last only ten years.

Almost a hundred years later, despite being the first consumer credit card, Carte Blanche was knocked out of the lead position in that market the moment American Express introduced its American Express Card. How? Because Amex took advantage of the worldwide banking network they had already established over a one-hundred-year period. Carte Blanche had no such network.

In other words, instant credibility, instant access, and instant worldwide exposure made the American Express Card the number one card in the world literally overnight. Their already existing banking infrastructure and brand recognition (the Roman centurion and blue logo) helped make them *the* early dominant player in a global economy.

The lesson? Brands once known for a particular core business model may need to shift that core business to survive, or like the ones mentioned above, may need to take advantage of an already existing network in order to make an early leap forward.

Ask yourself, "What new industry can we invent from our already existing suite of products and networks?"

What business models or categories can help you move quickly into the twenty-first century? Do you have a new category of business that can make your company the leader in its own arena? Can this new category take advantage of your already existing network? What do you need to change in yourself as a leader in order to see and embrace the newly emerging profit centers? Getting rid of entrenched opinions is a start.

Great brands with great leaders at the helm adapt to the changing business climate, whatever those changes may bring. Maybe those brands won't be known by their core business anymore, but they will survive.

Just take a look at companies that have had to reinvent themselves over and over again As mentioned earlier, Sumitomo, a four-hundred-year-old company, started out as bookshop in Kyoto around 1615. To this day Sumitomo management is guided by the "Founder's Precepts" written by founder Masatomo Sumitomo, a Buddhist priest, in the seventeenth century during the last era of the samurai.

Or consider India-based Tata, soon to be one hundred fifty years old. Or how about Stora Kopparberg (now Stora Enso), founded in the thirteenth century? How many times do you think these companies had to reinvent their business model to stay alive, or abandon their core competency because their market was shrinking into oblivion?

Each one of these companies faced modernization time and time again; whether it meant electricity, air travel, fax machines, overnight shipping, or the Internet, they adapted. Now, how will you make the leap?

Letting go of the limited thinking of the past and opening wide to the distinct possibility of an unlimited future filled with anything can help you create the next big thing in business. By keeping your brand image fresh and alive and awake to the changing market, you assure your survival over the long haul. It doesn't matter how you get there, as long as you take action.

"Success" is an action word, and leaders must take action to remain successful.

6TH LAW

A Liquid Leader Takes Responsibility

A smooth sea never made a skilled mariner.

—English proverb

Psst! It's on Your Shoulders for a Reason

don't believe someone can write a singular primer for what leadership is. There are just too many variables. But I can give you a blueprint of what leadership is not. The news is filled with plenty of examples of leaders without a sense of integrity, honor, and responsibility.

Fortunately there are also plenty of examples of those willing to go the extra mile and stand for values that rival those of the greatest mystics. These are uncompromising leaders who will listen to the most critical customer or employee for the kernel of truth and who will reshape an entire organization if that is what is called for.

I look back to the greatest influences in my own leadership style: several of my school teachers, scoutmasters, and college professors. The vice president who took me under his wing more than twenty-five years ago and showed me the way. And even the occasional celebrity who just struck up a conversation with me. Each embodied integrity. There was no compromise in their work or their life, and their word was their bond. If they said they were going to do something, they did it.

Across the globe, people these days are disappointed with the leadership around them, and not just politically but also in the marketplace. The tolerance level of the average citizen and the average consumer has reached the boiling point. Enough is enough. It's time for a new guidebook for leadership with new standards.

Today's technologies can be used in ways that the average citizen is yet unaware of. Privacy issues, taxation, freedom, prosperity, and sovereignty are in question as the new frontier of technology has given us the ability to monitor our every move. Do you ever wonder how much of your personal information marketers have? How would the dollar be affected if the economy went entirely digital? Identity theft, tracking software, digital banking, and enforced commerce are very real problems already affecting us all.

It is the mission of a Liquid Leader to be open to new trends and leaps in technology, but at the same time you need to stay awake. Our responsibility to these trends ends when people's freedom is removed. It is not our job to shy away from them or fear them, but it *is* our job to stay diligent. Great things are possible if we keep our values and our honor intact, and if we stay true to the integrity that has made people in the United States believe that nothing is impossible. These core values are what we need to spread around the world.

As Alexander Hamilton put it, "Those who stand for nothing fall for anything."

Romancing the Conversation

When I was a preteen in the seventies, I thought building forts was about the coolest thing ever. My friends Frank and Dieter and Dieter's brother, Pete, would scout out an appropriate location with maximum privacy and minimum vulnerability—you know, in case we got attacked by our sworn enemies. We would spend days building the fort and then weeks refining it. Eventually we decided to upgrade to a tree house, a nine-by-twelve platform, four stories off the ground in a mature maple tree in Dieter's backyard.

Dieter decided that we would use his father's power tools to build our tree house the right way. First we bolted the frame to the trunk with doubled up two-by-fours; then we used a jigsaw and trimmed it to shape. A skewed trapdoor and a coat of paint put the final touches on our project.

We would ride our bicycles to the local Turkey Hill market and get Coke slushies, then return and disappear into the leafy canopy of the treetops. We were careful to save every drop of the slushies on the journey home, to maximize our fun up in the tree house. It was our way of telling the world to go to hell.

The tree house became our sanctuary. In our world we could swear, look at dirty magazines, chew bubble gum cigarettes, or just talk. It was our own hand-built private domain, where no adults could enter. We could speak as sixth-graders in our own language with our own rules. It was great fun. It was private and free. And one thing was for sure:

There were no marketers lurking over our shoulders,
no creepy guys in suits appearing out of nowhere,
trying to analyze our buying patterns or influence our
soft drink choices.

The sanctuaries of childhood are something we all try to manifest as we get older: country club memberships, drinks with colleagues and friends, girls' nights out, bowling leagues, trips to the beauty salon, converting the garage to a den (aka "man cave"). It is actually the very human need to hang with people we know and do what humans do best—talk to one another.

Taking the Tree House Online

Today, the technological revolution has given us a happy accident: the gathering of human beings into like-minded networks for social interaction. Once again people have banded together in perceived safe environments to chat, swear, tell jokes, and just be human. Just as in our childhood, we have created fragmented sanctuaries, only now these sanctuaries are online.

Whether for business or pleasure, human beings like to gather together with people who have the same interests and experiences. Mountain climbers don't want to listen to spelunkers; they want to hang out with other mountain climbers. Women who suffer from breast cancer want the company of others who understand what they are going through. Without the shared experience, there is no understanding, compassion, or trust.

Author Seth Godin calls these gatherings of like-minded individuals "tribes." Behavioral economists follow these tribes and try to track and predict their activity, especially their buying patterns and purchasing potential. But a strange thing is happening: It's not working. In the new cyber sanctuaries, old-style branding initiatives look fake and incredibly intrusive.

People are tired of giving up their personal information just to get access to a site or to get a simple product discount. They're tired of filling out a warranty card for things like down jackets. Just give me the discount without having to fill out stuff! People are tired of being sold pharmaceuticals for some syndrome that didn't exist a decade ago. They're tired of being told how important they are, while being kept on hold for fifteen minutes. They're tired of logging onto a corporate website and not finding the basic information—like a 1-800 number, a street address, or the name of a real person to contact—on the home-page. People are tired of paying a premium for identity theft protection when it should be built into the system. They are tired of being placated with a FAQ page that doesn't answer their question. They are tired of legitimate companies placing spyware on their computers to get them to buy more software—software they already own. They are tired of buying a color printer for a decent price, only to discover that it eats a steady stream of ink cartridges. In short, people are tired by lazy organizations that don't take responsibility for their actions and that use the Internet as an excuse to create distance when it is perfect for getting closer.

Corporations that are afraid to create a one-to-one relationship with their customers are using their websites to create distance. On the other hand, companies that thrive on customer service are using technology to do the smart, responsible thing: develop exactly those kinds of one-to-one relationships that other companies fear. By using a combination of 1-800 numbers, websites, contests, and viral videos, these customer-centric companies are developing unique ways for people to interact with their brands. They listen to what a customer wants rather than tell them what they want. They are not afraid to take responsibility for who they are and what they sell.

Serious discussion about our problems is easy to avoid. But the great leaders engage in hard discussions every day, because the rewards are the greatest. After all, customers are not statistics, demographics, or pie charts—they are people! Companies that understand this gain customer loyalty.

Riding the Wave of Radical Disruption

During the Industrial Revolution, profession after profession shifted completely or, in many cases, was completely wiped out due to new ways of working and the technological influences of new inventions. Case in point: With the invention of photography, an artist's responsibility shifted. Before photography, an artist's "job" was part historian, part archivist—an illustrator of our day-to-day existence, sketching history in stunning, realistic portrayals as it was happening. But as the camera took over their jobs, artists began to paint in a new way, and thus Impressionism was born. The change didn't kill portrait painting or archival quality sketches. It only opened up what being an artist meant. Seurat, Gauguin, Matisse, Caisson, Van Gogh, Modigliani, and Toulouse-Lautrec opened the doors for the likes of Picasso, Dali, and Pollack. I am sure the transition was scary, but it was necessary.

It wasn't just artists and craftsmen who felt the impact of the technological explosions of the Industrial Revolution. Horse-and-buggy companies such as Studebaker transitioned nicely into automobile manufacturers, while those that resisted watched their market shrink, eventually driving them out of business. The new era was forcing changes regardless of who was on board.

A similar shakeup is happening today as we transition from the Industrial Age to the Information Age. Just as electricity in the home and office changed not only how we worked, but also when and where we worked—marking the beginning of the Industrial Revolution and the introduction of high-rise buildings and elevators into our working lives—the technology of the Information Revolution will do the same. Digital pictures of people working in cubicles will be *soooo* twentieth century.

Just look at the business sectors impacted by technology over the past ten years: Offset printing evolved into digital; now, uploading business cards to an automated website is the norm. The computer allowed a single user to be a one-person designer, photo retoucher, Web designer, and illustration studio, all in one. In the banking industry, networked ATMs and online banking have eliminated the need for tellers in brick-and-mortar offices, giving customers greater control. Access to data in realtime has evolved into day trading, and beyond that, into upgraded online financial research for both financial institutions and individuals.

Some business models will be eliminated, while some will transition into something completely different and others will become hybrids of their former selves. Everything is becoming virtualized, and this shift is causing radical disruptions. And to survive all this will require the disruption of our entrenched business thinking as well.

Each and every piece of new technology should be questioned as to how it will affect people's lives. Will it create a new sector? Consumers are making these changes, because they are demanding more from their lives. To stay relevant in the customer's mind, leadership will need to remain diligent, able to anticipate a need before a customer is aware the need exists. Companies that seem to have the ability to maintain a market lead have the entrepreneurial spirit and methodologies of a start-up, no matter how large the company gets. They are the companies that seem to stay ahead of the radical changes that identify transition from one era to another.

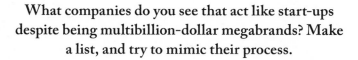

What companies do you see that act like start-ups despite being multibillion-dollar megabrands? Make a list, and try to mimic their process.

Listening to new ideas and looking for market trends, technological influences, new platforms, and recent implementations will keep your company alive during the coming shake-up. The consistent habit of looking for a need and discovering new markets before others do is the greatest survival tool I can pass on to you.

As Richard Maybury points out in one of his newsletters, "Economics is not a math course, it's not the study of charts, graphs, and equations. It's the study of living, breathing, thinking, feeling humans." Pay attention to people, both internally for ideas and externally for your customers' feedback. The ideas are out there; you just have to pay attention and think like an entrepreneur.

One to One (and on a Scooter)

The Internet was supposed to create one-to-one relationships, but most companies are using it as an opportunity to get rid of their entire customer service department in favor of a website.

The great part about being online is that if you are willing to drop your ego, the truth is there in the online conversation. Just listen to or read what customers are saying. Their chat is not controlled by some marketing survey designed to make everyone in the boardroom happy. It is raw, unpolished, angry, and truthful, and it is anything but fake. It's real feedback in real time, and it's free. Hello?! This kind of market feedback once cost millions and took months to accumulate.

But there is a caveat: As soon as a corporation decides not to just participate in an online community, but also attempts to dominate it, that community will reject the corporation's presence and move somewhere else. This is why corporations pushing for online regulation just don't get it. The truth is right in front of you, and attempting to control it isn't going to get you the real story. When corporate marketing attempts to control conversations, the world it creates is skewed and unnatural. But the real conversation continues at the core, leaving marketing on the fringes.

Look, for example, at the media channels that have been regulated and have shut out regular people; magazine publishing, television, and radio have created one-way conversations and made sure anything that doesn't fit into the conversation gets weeded out. How does this affect us? Think about it: Which presidential candidate gets the most airtime? How much "medical knowledge" have people obtained from commercials? Whether you shut down the Internet or not, the negative conversation will still be there.

Vespa was smart enough to know how to get people to change their paradigm, and it wasn't through control or traditional advertising. The scooter company opted instead to get male and female models and celebrities to ride up to key locations—nightclub entrances, sporting events, local gathering places—on top-of-the line Vespas. When celebs showed up riding the scooters, Vespas instantaneously became a transportation must-have. Viral conversation, not millions of dollars in advertising, sold Vespas.

I call this word-of-mouth advertising "viral momentum," and the conversation starts from within the group. As a leader, you have to romance this conversation.

Today many of us can't even imagine a world without marketing and PR, but it's time to start. The world shaped by regular human beings isn't easy to deal with responsibly, but at least it is closer to the truth. After all, I don't need OxiClean to make my life better, yet public relations experts and marketers are trying to convince me that I do. The Internet is one of the few places I can go to get away from brands shouting their message at me.

The Death of
Customer Service

In the good old days of retail, when you went to a store to buy groceries, you handed your list to a clerk, who would in turn run around and get your groceries for you. Customer service was the hallmark of such legendary brands as the Texaco Service Station, Cadillac, and Macy's.

All that began to change in 1916 when Clarence Saunders opened his first Piggly Wiggly and asked shoppers to get their own damn stuff and bring it to the register by themselves. It was radical thinking back then. Since those early days, retailers have been trying hard to get paying customers to do more and more work while using technology to skim their staff.

Stand-up comedian Johnny Watson proclaims, "I've used the self-checkout aisle so much, I got employee of the month last week. They gave me my own parking space, a plaque with my name on it. In a few more years, I just might make district manager." Funny, yes, but the truth is, this is fast becoming the norm. In order to cut costs, more and more companies are replacing people with technology. The era of 100 percent do-it-yourself service has begun.

The New York City subway system in recent years eliminated tokens and token-booth operators in favor of MetroCards and vending machines. Riders now use a magnetic card to enter the subway system, and they can add monetary value to their card with either cash or a credit card at a MetroCard vending machine. If you need to figure out how the system works, token-booth clerks have been reclassified as "station managers," just to answer questions and keep the system running smoothly during peak hours. Certain high-volume stations still maintain a booth clerk to handle actual money transactions, but this is becoming increasingly rare. Clearly the NYC transportation authority doesn't really want to engage their riders when it comes to money transactions. As subway prices rise, the slow death of customer service is becoming apparent. "Pay your fare, take the train, and don't bother us" is the message they are conveying.

Consider the last time you checked out of a hotel, or rang up your own stuff at Wal-Mart, or bought a movie ticket in the lobby instead of from a cashier. More and more companies are asking customers to do things that were once the company's responsibility.

Self-service is great because of the money it saves, but it can cause problems, too. When you find a mistake on your bank statement, just see how easy it is to get a hold of a human being.

But it's not all bad. Every time I go to my local Stop & Shop, it has become easier and easier to check out by myself. And I like it. I want to go at my own pace, and I usually really don't feel like talking to anyone when I'm trying to get out of the store. In Japan one can find vending machines on the street, providing everything from bottles of Suntory whisky to Hugo Boss suits. It is exciting that technology can deliver in such a way. But it's not for everyone.

In Real Relationships, We Listen

Customer service is unnecessary in certain industries, especially those where automation can create an even more satisfying experience. In those industries, technology *is* customer service. Yet other companies are jumping on the automation bandwagon without thinking it through or considering whether the technology makes sense for them and their type of business. They are cutting customer service without replacing or upgrading it, and losing customers as a result.

Despite the fact that technology has given companies the ability to create one-to-one relationships—and to improve their products and services through real feedback—most use technology as a barrier to keep customers at bay with a "take it or leave it" attitude.

Companies that understand how technology can be used to create a new era of customer service *will rule* the future! (Add a Dr. Evil laugh here.)

The truth is that the old customer service paradigm is being expanded to include a relationship-driven marketplace. No longer can someone simply introduce a product, sit it on the shelf, and launch it with a marketing ploy. Today's consumer listens to the thought influencers first, mainly their own network, and then makes a decision. If the viral conversation about your product is negative, don't try to fix the conversation; take responsibility and fix your product. Then learn how to effectively tell others about it. It is about creating an Information Age relationship. And as in all real relationships, friends listen to one another.

Microsoft is still trying to manage the inertia created by the negative chatter about Vista. The truth is, Vista had way too many hypersecurity protocols that the average person just did not need. With all its bells and whistles, Vista slowed down workflow.

Instead of immediately going back to the drawing board, which would have earned them respect, Microsoft ran a series of failed ad campaigns in which real people told their stories about how great Vista was. To confuse consumers more, Bill Gates was in a few of these ads with Jerry Seinfeld, attempting to convince one PC user at a time how great their products are by living with them a few days. Great—two of the richest guys in the world are going to live with a middle-class family for a couple of days in the family's wood-paneled basement. It may have been funny to Bill and Jerry, but it was sad and desperate to the rest of us. Vista just didn't come up to par with an Apple operating system. The nerds were trying to be hip and cool, yet failed miserably.

A Guitar Hero Becomes a Training Video

While changing planes in Chicago on the way to a professional gig, Canadian singer Dave Carroll noticed two baggage handlers tossing instruments around out on the tarmac. He didn't put two and two together until he got his badly damaged $3,500 Taylor acoustic guitar back at baggage claim. Carroll tried for more than a year to get the carrier, United Airlines, to pay for the $1,200 repair, with no luck. To deal with his frustration he made a video, *United Breaks Guitars*, and posted it on YouTube.

Once the video went up, it became an instant hit, receiving more than 3.5 million views. And here is where United did things right. Instead of forcing Carroll to take the video down, the company contacted him and made amends, by giving $3,000 to the charity of his choice.

Ironically United said the reason they didn't pay Carroll initially is because he didn't report the damage within twenty-four hours. Now United uses the video to train service reps on how to do a better job, take responsibility, and know when to bend the rules.

United understands the online conversation: Reputations can be managed organically. A negative image can be corrected and even used as a funny example of what not to do, to ensure that it never happens again.

Boomers are familiar with customer service. We grew up with it and we expect it, maybe more than we should. But Generation Y doesn't really know what customer service is, and they don't know they are entitled to it. In the Internet-driven economy, the New Economic Order, consumers just want to get in and get out. Customer service is what will set your e-brand apart.

Online consumers talk—a lot. If your stuff sucks, word gets around. If your stuff is great, word gets around as well. Creating viral videos won't fix the problem. Gaining back a customer takes a huge effort and lots of money. Seduction marketing is replacing real customer service. It's the follow-up that matters now, the continuation of the online relationship.

Try a little romance if you want to keep your brand alive. Talk to the marketplace, and spend time with the people who actually use your products. Give them incentive to come back. Invite them to private get-togethers in the real world. Make them feel special.

The Internet is great for measuring a marketing campaign, If you are off target with your brand, you will know within seconds that something is wrong when conversion doesn't take place the way you anticipated.

Another great thing about the Internet is that when you make quality products or even correct a problem immediately, your customers become advocates overnight. Your goal is to get the people using your stuff, to start recommending it: great products first, great customer service second.

Once that's done, the online conversation will take care of itself.

It's About Convenience

As consumers today, we simply don't have time to stand in line to buy things. And why should we, when technology gives us the ability to reach out into our world and order whatever we want as long as we pay shipping and handling? It's a small price to pay for convenience, but a preference for convenience doesn't mean it's okay to treat customers like dirt.

Our workaday world has collided with our leisure and personal worlds as work, buddy interaction, and entertainment converge and together became the guiding principle of our lives. Boundaries have disappeared: People play at work, and work while at the gym. The borders that kept us sane and kept the business world separate from our real lives have been erased. Every single moment is crammed full of something to do.

The dot-com boom changed the business landscape forever. It was screaming loud and clear that there was a new way to do business. Pay close attention to the survivors of the recent economic downturn—they will be revising once again the way we work and buy.

All this is about customer service, about knowing what the customer really wants, and how they want it, so you can deliver the goods. For example, Sears has created a better customer service paradigm by offering real-time price checks in order to stay competitive and ahead of their competitors.

To come up with similar or better ideas, just watch the online conversation for trends—trends that have always been there.

Some companies will continue to manage from high up in an ivory tower because, depending on the type of business they are in, it may be the only way to run things. And that's fine; those businesses may not need to come down and meet their customer head-on. But most businesses will have to leave the ivory tower and listen.

Busy, Busy, Busy, but Are We Getting Any Work Done?

Those not in the technology sectors may not understand what is happening. An Internet-savvy, technology-driven workforce is on the cutting edge of the change. Business meetings are shifting to online worlds, companies are using technology to automate their manufacturing, and commerce is transferring to a digital environment. The workaday world is speeding up, and those who embrace the speed will transition into new markets and adapt new ideas and methodologies. Those who resist will be stuck on the sidelines. Many will not know why their jobs have been eliminated.

Advances in our digital devices like laptops, cell phones, PDAs, digital video recorders for our home cable box, and home computers, along with networking technologies like global satellites, fiber optics, desktop videoconferencing, and high-speed Internet connections, have dramatically changed our relationship with time management. No longer are we chained to running home to the family computer to check our email account. Today anyone can get their emails delivered to their cell phone— as well as browse the Internet and download music without being attached to a central location. We can even videophone on our cell phones or laptops. This data portability has us feeling as if we are always connected, twenty-four hours a day, seven days a week.

We are now convenience-centric. If a conference call works better while you are on the way to the airport in a taxi, so be it. Our traditional linear approach to time is now becoming obsolete. But many of us approach multitasking in the wrong way, by text messaging during a movie, or emailing someone at 2:00 AM. We think we are being productive when in fact, we are not. We are busy, but we must learn to be smart about it!

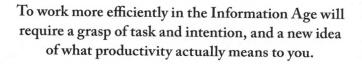

> To work more efficiently in the Information Age will
> require a grasp of task and intention, and a new idea
> of what productivity actually means to you.

Each of us has a different relationship with technology and the benefits it brings. Some of us love the convenience of a GPS gadget for navigation, while others hate the intrusive, Big Brother–type devices that GPS supports. Some love to pay bills from their online bank account, while others mistrust any online transactions. Some see airport scanners as a necessary evil for catching the bad guys, while others see the system as encroaching on individual freedoms, creating a panopticon at best.

Most people, however, are reacting to technology rather than commanding it to do our bidding. We are overlapping things that should be managed better, like fielding phone calls when family dinner is under way. If someone can't let you alone about business for a half an hour, you might want to loosen up your schedule. Either have Pop-Tarts for dinner or shut the phone off for half an hour. It's your choice in the new time management paradigm.

Don't Manage Your Time—Manage Yourself

What should really be at the forefront of this conversation is how to use the convenience of technology to make our time management fluid and obedient to our twenty-first-century needs and expectations. Borderless time management is how parallel thinkers approach their time, and it's how you should, too.

One way for you to take responsibility as a leader is to prevent work from encroaching on your personal time. Instead, manage your work better. If you are scheduled to take a phone call from the chairman of your board on Saturday at 10:00 AM, then do it. But be very clear and diligent about how much time you will spend on that phone call, and be sure to keep everyone on agenda. There is nothing more rude than encroaching on someone's personal time and wasting it with witty anecdotes. We teach people how to treat us, and by upping your game a notch, you will force others to follow your lead.

If you must text message someone while at a movie theater, wait until the credits roll, or get up and go into the hallway. Remember, you can't do two in-depth tasks at once. Pick one at a time, and focus on that one task in the moment. By the way, in case you didn't get the memo, it is still a major faux pas to answer your phone in a theater, even if you are Brad Pitt.

I'm not talking about being stubborn. I'm not suggesting you take on an "I am at home so don't call me" attitude. I'm talking about leveraging and managing technology at the same time. Twenty-first-century time management is about creating flexible boundaries. Using the technology as a platform for making our lives easier is what it's about. The iPhone is probably the best example of what I am talking about. Most Boomers, and I am sad to say I was one of them, couldn't understand why anyone would listen to music on a cell phone, or watch a movie on such a small screen for that matter. What I was missing was a simple point: The phone is not a phone anymore. It's become a device that allows us to connect to our personal network and have access to the things we want in the moment.

Visiting a strange city and looking for a restaurant that serves Thai food? How about directions to a comedy club in Manhattan? Or getting access to email while walking down the street? Rescheduling a business meeting without making in a phone call? Attaching a photograph of your car stuck in traffic and texting it to your wife to let her know you'll be late? It's about the ability to access information and make life more convenient. It's not about passing the time with useless, time-consuming games and devices.

Cool, huh? George Jetson didn't see this one coming. We can watch our favorite TV shows when we decide to, instead of being forced to sit down on a Tuesday at 9:00 PM when we have more important things to do.

Manage your workload, email, and phone calls better. Use the latest apps to make life easier by switching to email and texting instead of making phone calls. Give contact info to those who really need it, including emergency numbers for when they absolutely have to reach you. Managing your phone time will be a huge burden off your shoulders.

Here is a good barometer to help you figure out whether you are managing your time well: Do you get a negative feeling when the phone rings? Do you jump out of your skin? Do you feel compelled to answer every call? If any of these are your reality, remember this: You do not have to answer every single phone call. Once you've freed yourself up, it becomes paramount to field only those calls of greatest importance. Change the ringer on your phone. Maybe every member of the board of directors gets a special ring tone that allows you to know without even looking at your phone which call has greater importance. Your administrative assistant gets one ring, while your wife and children have another. Try not to be Pavlovian about it either; we have a tendency as human beings to give a sharp, shrill ring to things of greater importance. Do yourself a favor so you don't jump out of your skin—tone it down. Choosing a pleasant ring tone for calls from your wife and the members of your board of directors will help keep you calmer.

In today's environment, you must combine responsibility for your organization with responsibility for your personal life. By sharing in your technological needs and new time-management lifestyle, you get your spouse and family to support a bigger vision. Also, work closely with management to define the boundaries of work and personal time. You may find that everything is negotiable, and with remote-access software and open-source databases, working from home has become a way for corporations to manage office costs. What will be hardest to accept is that fact that each part of your life will need to be managed—leisure, family, and work time each will need to be given boundaries and assigned intentions. Simple hanging-out time may be extinct altogether; still, managing it all better, rather than following the crowd, will free you up so you have choices. More choices mean greater freedom.

Instead of reacting to technology, use it as a time management tool.

Just look at how many applications come with the iPhone that can make your life easier to manage (as of this writing, over 100,000 apps and that number is growing). Text messaging has evolved into "sexting" and can be romantic, but it's no substitute for real experience in terms of actually having a face-to-face conversation. Our cities are filled with handholding couples, chatting loudly on their own separate phone calls and glancing at each other occasionally. That glance lets me know the relationship is new. Couples who have been together a while don't even acknowledge each other as they walk hand in hand. Ahhh, modern romance.

But to keep your sanity, pick one day when you will be completely out of touch with technology, then let everybody in your network know this. My wife and I have an agreement: Sunday is our day together—no cell phones, no Internet and email, and no work. I know this isn't for everyone, but if you are in a long-term relationship and don't want to wake up thirty years from now sitting next to a total stranger you call your wife or husband, I suggest you both pick a day to shut it all off.

I for one use technology for what it was built for—to make communications more convenient and to make it do my bidding. FYI, you can download this book for your iPhone, iPad, or Kindle.

Doing Your Homework for Sanity

Technology, if managed properly, will give you more free time. Schedule your emails, text messages, and general work to when you want to do it rather than when you feel like you should do it. Some businessmen choose to work on their commute home on the commuter railroad. They set up their laptops in front of them and crunch numbers. With wireless connectivity, you can upload tomorrow's numbers before you pull into the station. The rest of the evening could then be free to spend with your family.

Is it really necessary to respond to every email that pings your desktop throughout the day? Try to manage how you respond to emails. Spend the first ten minutes of each morning prioritizing them, determining what's junk, who can wait, and who needs a response as a priority. Give your staff some credit, and let them manage the smaller stuff. Only the big things that need your immediate attention should come across your desk.

Ask yourself a few questions: How many emails do you respond to in one day? Do you waste time writing long-winded speeches to the group? Is that necessary? Do you feel you must CC every single person in your department to simply answer "yes" to a coworker's question? There's tracking every aspect of a project, and then there's annoying. Ask yourself if you are the latter. Many an obsessive emailer is actually someone who has crossed the line from covering their you-know-what to going overboard.

Twenty-five years ago, how much work did you finish, considering interoffice communications of the time? And today, what percentage of emails do you read and respond to instead of actually doing your job? Our "business" is why it is hard for America to compete. We are emailing, chatting, and IMing one another to death. Managing your phone and email will make you more productive.

Start looking into the nooks and crannies of your life, and ask yourself where it is possible to leverage your time. What needs to be changed here to get my work finished? If during a vacation you spend one hour each morning at your beach house preparing that proposal, not only will you have more free time for your family, but it will also seem as if the document wrote itself.

If you are having trouble with this concept, think back to when you were in high school and college. If you were like most teens, you tried to maximize the fun experiences against the homework experiences. If you had a study hall, you did your homework. If you were on the bus to a track meet, you brought your homework. Each moment that could be leveraged to finish your homework was maximized so you could have more free time for play. Socializing and personal time took priority, while homework was regulated to moments of availability. You knew you had to get your homework finished, so you carved out tiny slots of time where you integrated some work time into your fun time. This made your teenage life manageable and kept you sane. Remember?

Establishing Twenty-First-Century Boundaries

Many boomers still feel that without hard, backbreaking work, they aren't really earning their paycheck. This is Industrial Age thinking, smacking headlong into the Information Age and coming up short. If you want to get ahead in today's work world, work smarter, not harder. This is why there are twentysomething billionaires and broke Boomers who are unable to retire. One generation was taught a work ethic, and the other was taught to be brilliant. They simply think differently.

So, how can Boomers change? Try looking at the way you approach everything from here on out. Technology can help you get your work done faster, easier, and less expensively.

Eventually, machines will begin to talk to one another and human interaction will be a small part of the Internet, freeing us up to do the best we can while skipping the minutiae. Yes, it frees us up to do more, but if we aren't careful, we may become both busier and less effective. In other words, as we speed up to meet the demands of the twenty-first century, we need to also let go of the unnecessary stuff along the way. We need to eliminate time-consuming events that interfere with our personal aerodynamics.

Why do you think Cisco bought Flip Video? Or put millions into launching its Unified Videoconferencing? Or the Intercompany Media

Engine (IME) suite of products and support? Because Cisco understands that as bandwidth increases, it becomes easier for meetings to be virtualized—produced by anyone, anywhere over a simple network. In the near future, meetings will not be events one flies to; they will be held entirely in cyberspace, with video screens representing each attending member from locations around the world. Since Cisco specializes in the pipes and the hubs that make the Internet work seamlessly, it becomes a no-brainer that they would eventually provide the videoconferencing devices to make events easier to produce—and to bring down the cost, I might add.

This will shrink meeting budgets at production companies. They will have to repurpose their core competency from meeting services such as staging, lighting, speaker support, graphic design, and event management to added-value activities such as training, broadcasting and video production.

Eventually those screens that Cisco provides today will become digital holograms or avatars representing the individual. Flying to an actual meeting will seem antiquated.

And that's just how Cisco is changing business-to-business communications. On the consumer side, with the purchase of Flip Video, Cisco will be a dominant player in visual networking where people can share personal videos and images over a social network. Multiple technologies will be creating a sort of cyberbilocation. And this is just one of their products.

Boomers Need to Tweet Too

If Cisco and IBM are paving the way for the future, what are *you* doing to prepare? You will need to eliminate what is wasting your time and maximize what is enhancing your way of life. Every moment starts to take on new meaning when approached this way. Discipline is the cornerstone of time management, and you now have the tools to manage yourself better. The resources are at your disposal.

And that leads me to discuss how you can leverage your network. In case you haven't heard, socially driven microblogging sites are changing the face of business. Twitter is a social networking site that allows you to broadcast short bits of text—no more than 140 characters long—and share them with your network of followers. Just like blogging, Twitter lets you write mini messages—aka microblogging—that other people can read. You can do this all day, and many amateurs do just that. It may seem like a big waste of time, but when you look at what it could become once the next generation of Twitter-like sites evolves, you will be astounded.

I use Twitter to get my news when I get home in the middle of the night. Many stories that the mainstream news isn't covering are covered on Twitter. Case in point: When terrorist bombs exploded inside the Oberoi Hotel in Mumbai and deaths began to mount, Twitter users on BlackBerrys inside the hotel broke the story—live.

Tweets (slang for each Twitter post) came from inside the hotel while the tweeters stayed one step ahead of the terrorists, chronicling the blow-by-blow details of their exodus to safer ground. More importantly, the electronic dialogue from the people inside helped police understand just what was happening, before the terrorists even made their demands. *Forbes* magazine called it "Twitter's moment."

This form of amateur journalism is called "citizen journalism," a hyper-localized form of the man or woman on the street just reporting on their blog, Web page, or social network what is happening in their immediate area. In the era of free information, it is driving mainstream news and newspapers out of business.

For centuries, when something newsworthy happened, a reporter would show up soon afterward to report it. Hyper-reporting, however, happens even as the news is taking place. For the big news stations, this is impossible; they can't be everywhere all the time.

In contrast, sites like Twitter are showing us how targeted information over a network can be, because citizen journalists don't filter what they say. They respect the fact that people are smart enough to choose what news is relevant to them. Unlike most major news companies that choose the news for us and blast it at us—mostly based on viewership and advertising revenue—citizen journalism taps into the core of a network.

It is not newspapers that need to survive; it is journalism that needs to survive.

Readers on Twitter can choose to receive updates by phone, Web, RSS, or instant messaging. The brevity, combined with the spectrum of delivery systems, makes Twitter a powerful way to reach your people.

You probably are still not convinced. What if I told you I watched a serious IT manager use Twitter to find an obscure piece of free software to solve a serious problem on a corporate server? What if I told you his network responded to his query within five minutes?

Twitter is about tapping into your group's knowledge base and taking the responsibility for expanding your network. Choose wisely, and you have an intense army of intelligent problem solvers. What if I pointed out that Twitter can be accessed and used from any device that has a browser— a laptop, a cell phone, a BlackBerry device, or an Internet terminal? Even your car can receive tweets. Now you have access to an entire network no matter where you are.

Where Facebook and MySpace have redefined a person's Web presence, similar to a publishing model, Twitter is a broadcast medium allowing users to send out their thoughts and to receive responses. Businesses are starting to use Twitter to reach potential and existing customers. Whole Foods uses Twitter to let users know about specials. Bestselling author and venture capitalist Guy Kawasaki uses it to promote his blog and books. Larry King uses it to promote guests and promote one-to-one responses from his audience. Best Buy uses Twitter as a Q&A forum for potential and existing customers.

It is not like email. It is an open forum of your best and brightest, and it is redefining customer service.

Asking the Right Questions of Technology

Like I said, Twitter is just the beginning. The next level to evolve will increase the speed of business, especially if your IT department builds a proprietary microblogging network to reach employees, speed up communications, and reach out to shareholders. What if your CEO could microblog to an investor relations site that is password protected? When you start to see microblogging's potential as a communication network tool, it changes the silliness you may be seeing today. Accenture developed the Facebook-style Performance Multiplier for that exact reason: to speed up their internal performance evaluations while helping managers keep track of goals and compliance.

By eliminating the things that waste our time, we can spend more time actually working, or spending time with our family, or taking that vacation we've always wanted. We just need to retrain ourselves. Take a quick look at your life and objectively eliminate the things that are no longer necessary. Think of small things that will benefit you just as much. Can you order your groceries online instead of waiting in a long line? How can you apply this same methodology to ordering your company's supplies? How about streamlining the ordering of raw materials with an up-to-date price monitor and ordering engine? Instead of a series of meetings and face-to-face time with your staff, why not send out proprietary video podcasts from the CEO, directly downloadable to everyone's iPod? Asking these types of questions will get you to start refocusing your energy rather than scattering it. After all, technology is a tool for you to use, not something you should be enslaved by.

This speed will require a new type of interpersonal management geared more toward an individual's skill sets and tasks rather than where they are located. And since our workdays are no longer linear, this new personal style of work will change the way we approach time management.

Ironically, time management is not about managing time but about managing ourselves.

Managing your time better will help you be free to enjoy this life a little more. Retraining ourselves as to what is possible will be the first stage in efficiency. We must learn to put our adult resistance learning aside and just take it all in.

The second stage is to retrain our minds into looking at the impossible and believing it is achievable. That will take a little more effort. Try getting into a racecar if you want to experience the impossible. Or look into the spiritual program *A Course in Miracles* to see what I mean. If we haven't been exposed to it, we may never know there is an amazing universe of phenomena out there.

As I have pointed out, time management is not about managing time; it is about managing ourselves. A Liquid Leader starts by taking the responsibility for making their life more efficient and establishing the boundaries to do so.

7TH LAW

A Liquid Leader Leaves a Lasting Legacy

Given enough time, any man can master the physical.
With enough knowledge, any man may become wise.
It is the true warrior who can master both and surpass the result.
—Chih-hi, founder, Mount Tien T'ai Buddhist monastery in ancient China

What Will You Be Remembered For?

The Industrial Age business story of the dynamic corporate hero who rides into town to create big profits and save the company seems to be a fairy tale at best. As soon as the heroic leader resigns, the company stock usually takes a nosedive and the executive committee starts to see the holes in the hero's methodologies. Yet everyone is left wondering how the leader could have fooled so many for so long. Not all executive stories are like this, but there are enough high-profile ones to make the public leery of anyone in the business world. But for some strange reason, the same executive committee starts looking for another hero to save the company.

This dysfunctional model misses a serious point: If the heroic leader was so great, why didn't they build a company that runs on its own, without a leader? These old-style leadership models are set up to make the hero *look* like the guru (even though the staff did all the work)—a guru we can't live without—while at the same time making sure no one knows how he did what he did. It appears to be a slick Las Vegas magic show when in fact, it's nothing more than a parlor trick designed to make Wall Street happy.

Functional leadership, on the other hand, makes sure there are dynamic systems in place, champions the message and the methodologies, and aligns everyone to the mission of the company. These organizations have leaders who develop a lasting legacy and leave behind a strong, self-reliant company, long after the CEO has left the building. These environments are more democratic, and the leaders who build them rely on their people and trust their decisions.

A Prize to the Swift

A good friend of mine, Doug, is a race car driver and one of the few African Americans active in this sport on a professional level. During his off time, he often races illegally—kind of like those races in *The Fast and the Furious* but through New York City during rush hour. Because of his strategies, he usually wins.

One unseasonably warm October day, Doug asked me if I wanted to check out his new racecar. Being a NASCAR fan, I naturally said, "Yep." It didn't look like much—just a jet-black, European edition Ford Contour with a racing spoiler across the back trunk. But the European edition of this car is built to race on the Autobahn and has about as much in common with its American counterpart as a German shepherd has with a Chihuahua.

I was ready to start our journey, thinking Doug might get us up to eighty-five max. After all, it was around six o'clock in the evening, and Manhattan and the surrounding boroughs are well known for their traffic jams.

Doug took off at breakneck speed, and my head shot back in the seat. When I looked at the speedometer, I was shocked to see the needle fluctuating between eighty and 120 miles per hour. Doug weaved in and out of traffic as we headed east, with the efficiency of a seasoned pro. To me, it was all a blur. I squinted my eyes to avoid the light from the sunrays reflecting off the mirrors and chrome.

Some of Doug's moves were ninety-degree laterals, yet somehow he squeezed between cars to get across three lanes of traffic. To say his driving scared the daylights out of me is an understatement.

Minutes later, on the Cross Island Parkway, we encountered a small car that wanted to race us. Naturally, Doug engaged him and blew past him. I gripped the hand rest, giving new meaning to the term "white-knuckled ride." I like driving fast as much as the next guy, but imagine sitting in the cockpit of an F-16 with the windows wide open. Despite the fact that I train in Shaolin Kempo Jiu Jitsu three times a week, I have to admit that I don't have the most masculine of screams.

In fewer than ten minutes we had gone from Seventy-eighth Street and Broadway in Manhattan to Elmhurst, Long Island. I know most of you are thinking this is incredibly reckless and dangerous behavior. I agree. But the point of this driving experience with Doug would last a lifetime. What I took away was a profound sense that just because I think something is impossible, that doesn't necessarily mean it is. If you had told me that I could go from the Upper West Side of Manhattan to the beginning of Long Island during rush hour traffic in about ten minutes, I would have said you were nuts. These days, I refuse to get in the car with Doug unless he promises to drive slowly, and he has kept his word so far.

But I recall that something strange had taken place as our speed broke ninety: The other cars seemed to be standing still. At this speed, it was easy to see the openings between them, something that was not apparent at fifty-five miles per hour and actually made it easier to maneuver in between. Now I know why NASCAR and Indy Formula One drivers are capable of certain moves; they are moves that are impossible at slower speeds. To quote John Chambers, CEO of Cisco, "Without exception, all of my biggest mistakes occurred because I moved too slowly."[4]

I apply the lessons I learned from my racing experience with Doug to my coaching business every day. I ask, "What does *impossible* look like to you?" and "What would you do if you knew you could achieve the impossible?" and "What would you do if you had all the money you ever needed?"

I don't recommend a high-speed joyride, but you can speed up in your business world and it will quickly seem normal. Trust me, you'll eventually stop screaming. I did.

What does life look like at 120 miles an hour? Is it faster, or does time appear to stand still? Try it! You'll like it.

---

4 Reprinted from the March 29-30 issue of Bloomberg *BusinessWeek* by special permission, copyright ©2009 by Bloomberg L.P.

The Disruptive Power of the Entrepreneurial Start-up

While speaking to a large corporate audience in what would prove to be his last keynote address, the legendary football coach Vince Lombardi gave his audience a major piece of wisdom. "I'm going to share with you the key to success in any business," he said, and then paused.

The room fell into a deep silence as the audience leaned forward. The pause continued a while longer, building the excitement.

"The secret, in a word, is 'heartpower,'" Lombardi continued. "Capture the heart, and you've captured the person. Get people to fall in love with your company."

Look around you at the companies that you love to follow and the leaders who run them: Meg Whitman, former CEO of eBay. Steve Jobs of Apple. Reed Hastings of Netflix. The late Anita Roddick of The Body Shop. These leaders, among so many, stand out—and so do their companies—because their passion for excellence is contagious. But a greater observation is necessary. They didn't just get there because they showed up and started talking. They built a solid company based on a passionate decision to upset the status quo, because they didn't *like* the status quo. Using the products they created to change the way we do things took perseverance, stubbornness, and passion, through the good times and the bad.

Great leaders do just that. They create a contagious, passionate vision with everything they touch. Many of the leaders I mentioned above can get angry, excited, and fired up because they care about their people and the products they send out into the world—and almost all of them never graduated from or even attended business school.

Simply put, they integrate the people who work for them as like-minded human beings with all the same passions and drive as anyone else, an integral part of the company's goals. These leaders never treat their employees like subordinates.

> These leaders have made a lifetime commitment to becoming better by keeping their eye on the trends and raising their standards, and it shows in every inch of their organizations. They capture the heart *and* the imagination.

The biggest danger for a company nowadays is when they stagnate, refusing to evolve. I believe this comes from a myth, the belief that one big idea is enough to live on happily ever after. In today's environment, consistently great ideas must be cranked out and brought to the forefront as quickly as possible. In order to leave a legacy, leaders must act and think like entrepreneurs.

Medium and large companies that run like entrepreneurial start-ups often create relatively small team-to-team and peer-to-peer environments. Hierarchies appear fuzzy to an outsider because these environments are flexible, creative, and free of rules and regulations. Even the CEO is available to every member of the staff. Plain and simple, these medium and large companies operate like *small* companies.

Internal Darwinism

In entrepreneurially run organizations, each team member is an active participant in the company's success. Participants become contributors in this type of paradigm, solving problems themselves, free to make decisions that in larger organizations might take weeks for approval from higher-ups. These organizations operate on cyclical time, not linear time. Each member takes responsibility for when and how the work gets done. People begin to rely more on inspirational moments than on a clock.

People in these types of organizations are contagious to be around, as they begin to eat, sleep, and drink what they are working on. This is when team members begin to develop an almost cultlike following, becoming evangelists for the brand and working at midnight just as easily as they might work at 10:00 AM.

This is the power of running your organization like an entrepreneurial start-up. People become fully engaged in these environments, refusing to leave. In many of these organizations, the bulk of employees have been with the company since its inception. No matter how big your company may get, keep everyone in the organization in touch with the passion of the company's vision.

Every great leader I have coached maintains these uncompromising qualities. Their leadership styles are uniquely based on their personality and the values they truly believe in. They are contagious to be around and have a vision so clear and intoxicating, they are capable of drawing in a new hire, making each and every one feel as if they are part of a contributing force. These qualities also calm new hires, especially when someone has to work with a famous leader.

Inside these entrepreneurially run companies, it boils down to one thing and one thing only: trust. Ensuring that every manager, executive, and team leader is heads and shoulders above the rest requires time and effort. You must raise internal standards but give up control. By raising your people's standards and professionalism, you can step back and trust that the work is getting done to exacting standards.

Start destroying the bottlenecks of communication and approval. Trust is the key to a lasting legacy.

Technology will entice more and more people around the world to become entrepreneurs, and entrepreneurs always create disruption as they destroy entrenched business models in favor of a more efficient and more profitable business model. It is business Darwinism.

As John Doerr of Kleiner Perkins venture capital firm—who invested in Netscape, Amazon, Google, and Bloom Energy when they were just starting—stated on *60 Minutes* with Lesley Stall, "That's my job, to find entrepreneurs who are going to change the world—and then help them."

So, I ask you now as a leader, here in the death throes of Industrial Age thinking, what kind of company are you going to invent? Where do you want to go? What possibilities are out there awaiting you? The ideas are endless.

Acting Local, Thinking Global

Of the planet's 6.8 billion people, 4 billion live in conditions that are not much better than they were in the year 1500. Many of the children in these underdeveloped countries go barefoot throughout their entire childhood. Simply running, playing, or walking to the doctor all become high-risk activities when done without shoes. This exposure can cause cuts and bruises that have trouble healing, and when exposed to contaminated soil and parasites—a common problem in these countries—the majority of these barefoot children run the risk of amputation and even death.

But one entrepreneur had the chance to change this. In 2006 while visiting Argentina, American traveler Blake Mycoskie came to the sad realization that most children he befriended in the South American country had no shoes on their feet. What was more astonishing was that none of these children had *ever* owned a pair of shoes.

And because they had trouble walking to certain places, they could not attend school, where shoes are a prerequisite along with a school uniform. Without school, they would grow up to become uneducated adults, incapable of joining a global workforce.

Blake decided to do something about this disparity by founding TOMS Shoes on a single idea: For every pair of shoes purchased, TOMS will give a pair of new shoes to a child in need. And thus the One for One program was born. As their company motto states, "Using the purchasing power of individuals to benefit the greater good is what we're all about."

Since 2006, TOMS Shoes has been instrumental in giving more than six hundred thousand pairs of shoes to children in underdeveloped and developing countries. The consumer who buys a pair of TOMS Shoes does so with the full awareness that they are helping a child in an underdeveloped village get a chance at an education, as well as lowering the mortality rate.

TOMS is one of the best examples of a twenty-first-century entrepreneur. Capable of helping the planet while making commerce fun and socially responsible, most young entrepreneurs are discovering it's not that hard. Instead of sponsoring some 6K run for the local Yuppies, why not use your profits to help those who actually need our help?

The company's nonprofit organization Friends of TOMS also coordinates Shoe Drops around the world in order to drop off their shoes in remote areas and at the same time give employees and volunteers the experience of giving TOMS shoes firsthand. In March 2010, during a Shoe Drop in the northwest region called Shyira Diocese, Rwanda, TOMS, in partnership with Kris Allen (2009's American Idol winner) and Arkansas-based organization Bridge2Rwanda, distributed one thousand pairs of shoes to children in remote villages. This was TOMS' first personal visit to Rwanda, though they had been giving shoes there through another giving partner, World Vision, for some time. Kris sang and played guitar with the kids, inspiring them to laugh, smile, and dance. Now, another thirty-two thousand pairs have been distributed by Bridge2Rwanda volunteers and local Rwandan organizations to kids in these same communities.

Doug Piwinski, TOMS' newest family member, who spent his very first days working for TOMS on the Rwanda Shoe Drop, said it best: "What I realized while in Rwanda is that all the beautiful and amazing people I met there were connected by something bigger than any one person—the One for One movement. That's such a powerful feeling, and I can't wait to do more."

So why not place this kind of commitment at the beginning of your mission statement?

Changing the World, One Laptop at a Time

Establishing what your organization stands for is an essential part of today's leadership. People want to buy products from companies that are socially responsible. Greed is out; lending a helping hand is in.

Nicholas Negroponte, founder and chairman emeritus of MIT's Media Lab, started to see this same disparity among the world's children. In 2001, while visiting a school he founded in an impoverished village in Cambodia, Negroponte watched, entranced, as the school's students hopped on the Internet using cheap laptops he had bought on eBay, just to check on Brazilian soccer teams.

The children's reaction was intuitive and immediate. And so was Negroponte's: "What if you could provide a laptop to every kid on the planet who lived in such conditions?" And thus One Laptop per Child was born with a bold mission: to get a computer into the hands of every child in the world, no matter how remote or destitute they may be.

Could it be done? The key was to create a laptop that is affordable yet capable of operating in countries where there is no modern electrical grid system—or at least none that is reliable—and no Internet connectivity. A laptop becomes a self-contained, portable classroom in a box.

Negroponte's nonprofit developed several versions of the laptop over the years: the Children's Machine, 2B1, and, most recently, the XO-1, manufactured by Quanta Computer. All this is a true homage to ingenuity and the natural evolution of what is possible when smart people want to save the world.

The first design was introduced in November 2005, at the World Summit on the Information Society, held in Tunis. Negroponte unveiled a $100 laptop computer, the first Children's Machine. Designed for students in the developing world, it had either a hand-cranked generator or solar power, depending on which model you chose. It had wireless Internet connectivity, too. More surprising was that the green-and-white laptop was capable of withstanding extreme heat, sand, and water, even with its modest price tag. This was not an easy task, considering that at the time the most expensive computers had neither this kind of durability nor built-in connectivity.

Today, most XO-1 models come with a built-in, hand-cranked generator, making the unit self-powered in a world where the majority of children have no source of electricity in their homes. These rugged computers have a small 7.5-inch screen capable of being viewed in extreme sunlight (because many of these countries have "classrooms" outside), and a graphical user interface called Sugar that is intended to help young children collaborate. The XO-1 includes a video camera, a microphone, and a hybrid stylus/touchpad; uses flash memory instead of a hard drive; and runs Linux for an operating system. The long-range Wi-Fi mesh networking protocol allows many XO-1s to share Internet access, so as long as at least one of them can see and connect to a router or other access point.

Recently, Negroponte traveled to Colombia to deliver laptops inside territory once controlled by guerrillas. Surprisingly, the effort is backed by Colombia's Defense Department, which sees One Laptop per Child as an investment in a region that desperately needs to join the twenty-first century after forty years of bombings and kidnappings. To take a third world country and connect its children to the rest of the world will provide long-term change.

But One Laptop per Child hasn't affected only poor countries—it's also affected the entire computer-manufacturing world. By making available a cheap computer with such radically powerful and flexible capabilities, Negroponte's idea has pushed manufacturers to rethink the standard for an off-the-shelf computer. If all this durability and connectivity can be found in a $100 laptop, why should we pay $3,000 for something less durable? Just for a bigger screen?

Negroponte has raised the bar on our expectations and forced manufacturers to give us more for our money. He has left a legacy all over the world.

Greater Reach, Higher Goals

Just look at the other companies out there that are committed to being better to their workforce and to the world. Ben & Jerry's is committed to wholesome ingredients, better business practices, and a respect for the Earth and the environment. Seventh Generation spreads the word about how toxic our world is and sells nontoxic household products, including organic tampons, biodegradable laundry detergents, and chlorine-free diapers.

It is time for us to become greater, to make a pledge to ourselves and to our children to become better leaders and hold others to a higher standard.

Our reach today is farther than anything possible ten years go. A civil war in Indonesia affects prices in America. After all, when 70 percent of the world's goods are being shipped by freighter through Indonesian ports, a local war will affect prices nine thousand miles away.

The point is, our reach is greater than ever before. Every age is defined by how it handles knowledge and education, and so today we need leadership that understands that we are only as strong as our weakest link.

Shedding the old ways of thinking is incredibly necessary for a company's survival in the Information Age. To build a company that can survive long into the future will require constant diligence. This diligence comes from great leadership. And great companies never stray from their mission and foundation. They stand for something bigger at the core of their mission statement, while embracing the disruptive change from era to era. They do this because they understand that disruption has been a part of normal business cycles throughout history.

These companies create a lasting legacy for innovation by embracing a three-pronged foundation:

- Committing to integrity and sound management
- Not pursuing easy gains
- Maintaining an air of entrepreneurship

I cannot take credit for this model. It is from the oldest company in the world, the four-hundred-year-old Sumitomo Corporation.

Bullying, pushing, and screaming do not make for confident leadership. As a matter of fact, any leader who acts like that is really operating from the opposite ideology, from a core of fear. Your job is partly that of a shepherd, confident in the direction ahead and yet ready to change direction for better pastures.

From the Stone Age to the Internet Age, we are not much different mentally and physically than our ancestors of one hundred thousand years ago. But each age changed our ancestors' expectations. Although we had the capabilities to handle it all, progress slowed down when information was centralized and controlled. Temple priests and priestesses, kings and Pharaohs all kept writing, communication, and knowledge a secret. In other civilizations where knowledge flowed freely, we can see much different results. Greek society, the Roman republic, and the Ottoman empire are examples of information flowing freely under a very crude common law and of the freedom and individual prosperity that such law brings.

Information changes everything. Scribes used to control the information and history of an era. But once the printing press became a ubiquitous part of an early publishing industry, the printed information flying from its ink-soaked presses was instrumental in educating Europe and bringing about the Age of Enlightenment. The distribution of pamphlets forged the unrest that brought about the Revolutionary War, and knowledge is what made a single student stand against the tanks in Tiananmen Square, China.

Most of us have been taught that human progress has taken place slowly and is getting better and better. This is not true. Almost all human progress on this planet has taken place suddenly and explosively in the past 235 years.

The Next Hundred Years

So where does that leave us today? What will our age be known for? Will we be defined by our skyscrapers and by government buildings that look like temples to the gods—masonry and glass and steel structures, incapable of lasting more than a few hundred years?

Despite all the predictions that the Internet will bring about a new golden era of equality and prosperity, will we return to a form of global feudalism driven by subtly enforced commerce but within a very real panopticon? Will our rights be determined by how much money we make? What will be used to judge us in the annals of history?

We need to demand that our world governments and the world's corporations operate under a higher standard, a human standard. When corporations have greater rights than the population, we have a problem.

Leadership has a chance to lead into a new era of trust and prosperity, unencumbered by the past, standing on a new age of integrity. How we handle the next hundred years starts with each and every one of us and the legacies we choose to leave behind. We now have a chance to spread a global age of true enlightenment, filled with education, training, and instant information sharing.

Bruno Bettelheim pointed out in *The Uses of Enchantment* that when we grow up without the valuable and sometimes harsh lessons woven into such raw fairy tales as the Brothers Grimm, we never really learn the deep importance of our life lessons. By only hearing stories with happy endings we become adults who are sadly unprepared for real life, because we only seek out happy endings and solutions. It also breeds a culture that knows nothing about shame or the concepts of right and wrong.

I propose that we journey forward to find our own stories in these dark times of economic uncertainty and look for long-term solutions rather than lose ourselves in quick fixes. The bold and adventurous inherit a better world by creating a higher standard for the world they choose to create. Words like "integrity," "respect," "honor," "value," and "leadership" can no longer be taken lightly. We must venerate them in our actions and expect others to do the same.

I ask you as a leader to make that journey with me. One small step for the human race, one giant leap for humankind, as leadership enters a new century.

The Yellow Brick Road

With a really great team of smart people, intense and continuous brainstorming sessions, and some serious visionary goal setting, any strategy becomes possible. But make no mistake about it: I am not some wide-eyed, crystal-chanting, granola-eating, Birkenstock-wearing New Ager. I am a Cusp Baby Boomer raised on the original *Speed Racer* cartoons, KC & The Sunshine Band, Watergate, Sunday nights with *Mutual of Omaha's Wild Kingdom* with Marlin Perkins, and *The Wonderful World of Disney*, with the Vietnam War overshadowing it all.

The impossible is possible to me because I saw the first man standing on the moon—broadcast live. It taught me that great leaps require discipline, a steady set of goals, and a solid belief that no matter what, we are going to get there. In today's climate, I throw away the notion that "seeing is believing" in favor of "believe it and you will achieve it."

One-of-a-kind ideas require offbeat people who understand the bigger picture. When people believe they are changing the world, and when they are given the tools to do so, chances are that they *will* create a better world for us all. They just need the chance to be creative in their own field, whether it's physics, mathematics, psychology, spirituality, filmmaking, or what have you.

These are people like Dean Kamen, the inventor of the Segway Personal Transporter. At sixteen, while working at New York's Hayden Planetarium, Kamen secretly installed his own home-built audiovisual controllers. Working there at night gave him the freedom to test and perfect his inventions. He soon turned these homemade devices into a viable home business. Since Dean was only sixteen at the time, it was paramount to keep his age a secret to customers. So his mother did all the invoicing and answering the phone while his younger brother brought his friends over after school to solder components. That was in 1967, and it was just the beginning of Dean Kamen's career.

New Ideas, New Lives

While Dean attended college in the seventies, his older brother, then a medical student, complained that there was no reliable way to give steady doses of drugs to his tiny patients, babies with leukemia. So Dean, while still running his audiovisual controller business full-time, invented the first portable infusion pump, capable of administering micro-amounts of drugs to infant patients who had previously required round-the-clock hospitalization or multiple visits per week. Once he adapted the pump to administer a steady dose of insulin to diabetes patients, Dean's Auto-Syringe was able to give patients a quality of life and freedom they never had before.

In 1993, Dean's company DEKA Research and Development unveiled an almost-silent, twenty-two-pound portable kidney dialysis machine, freeing kidney patients from enduring grueling four-hour visits to hospitals and dialysis clinics three times a week. At a time when similar devices were as big as dishwashers, Kamen revolutionized patients' lives. The simplified dialysis machine, the size of a briefcase case, allowed patients to travel.

Another of Kamen's ideas came while watching a man in a wheelchair try desperately to negotiate a curb. Could a wheel chair be built that could hop curbs with ease, while still maintaining its balance? Eight years of development and $50 million later, in 1999, the iBot Transporter, a six-wheeled robotic "mobility system," became a reality. The iBot can climb stairs, traverse rocky terrain, and even stand and raise its user to eye-level with a person who is standing.

Using the technology developed for the iBot, Kamen next invented the Segway PT, an electric, two-wheeled, self-balancing, human-transport device controlled by the user by simply shifting their body weight.

Today, Kamen's DEKA is treading into science fiction territory with the highly versatile and rugged Luke prosthetic arm (named so because of

Luke Skywalker getting one in *The Empire Strikes Back*). Already in clinical trials, the project is being funded by the Defense Advanced Research Projects Agency and tested on veterans who have lost limbs in battle. The arm is currently controlled by an array of pressure-sensitive sensors located in the user's shoe. But what makes this prosthetic way ahead of the pack is its micro-sensitivity. Now a user can easily pick up an egg or a plastic bottle of water. In the past, these objects were easily crushed by even the most advanced prosthetic arms. This is the big leap that patients with missing limbs have been waiting for—control over delicate tasks such as shaving, cooking, or just drinking out of a bottle. Luke can give a user more freedom and control over tasks that are potentially scary and even dangerous with older technology.

Dean believes that technology and ingenuity can solve social problems as well, one of these being the need for fresh, clean, drinkable water. That's why he invented the Slingshot, a water purifier that prompts vapor distillation by zapping tainted H_2O with a UV laser, making once contaminated water safe for drinking. In a time when pollution is rampant, there is limited access to electricity, and contaminated water from human feces is a leading cause of cholera in many third world countries, the Slingshot could help millions of impoverished people all over the globe—virtually overnight.

The Slingshot gets its power from another of Kamen's inventions, the Stirling engine. Funded by several million dollars of Kamen's own cash, the engine is based on a concept first dreamed of in the 1890s and eventually made practical for the *Gemini*, *Apollo*, and *Space Shuttle* missions: fuel cells. The Stirling engine is capable of running on any fuel, making it practical even in countries without access to petroleum products. It can provide electricity to entire villages, giving emerging economies access to electricity and eventually the types of devices we take for granted here in the United States, including telephones, computers, and the Internet. And the Stirling engine generates no pollution whatsoever. This could change every single industry in the world that requires some sort of engine, while eliminating the pollution that is emitted from our current combustion engines—all within our lifetime.

Kamen and his team are working hard to make the engine affordable and portable for anyone. So instead of implementing cutbacks and carbon taxes, why not implement the Stirling engine worldwide? Global carbon emissions could be cut by 75 percent in our lifetime simply by using a Stirling engine in every automobile in the world.

> The future of our planet is in the hands of smart engineers (like Dean Kamen), who are able to ignore profits and governments in order to solve problems that bring us into the twenty-second century. As Kamen has said, the only difference between science and science fiction is time.

Although Dean Kamen holds more than 440 patents and would be considered a genius in any age, the most amazing thing about him is that he never went to college for physics or industrial design—he is self-taught. His degrees are honorary. It doesn't take long to realize that Dean is a genius of a different ilk, unburdened by ego and with the foresight to surround himself with an entire company of smart people. He is a leader who understands it isn't all about him. This is a true Liquid Leader.

How Many Einsteins Can Fit on the Head of a Pin?

One person in one lifetime has a certain amount of output that is finite and measurable. But a smart person understands that the way to change our world is to increase that pool of ideas and output by a thousandfold—for example, by giving young future geniuses a platform for their ideas, so they can see firsthand how engineering can be applied to solve an array of problems.

That's why Kamen founded the FIRST foundation (For Inspiration and Recognition of Science and Technology) in 1989, to give young high school students a chance to see just how engineering can change our world, and perhaps to inspire them to choose careers in engineering or technology. With access to actual engineers, FIRST participants can take their ideas off the page and into the real world. They can learn through personal experience that engineering isn't just about building bridges; it is about solving problems through multiple disciplines. And FIRST promotes a philosophy of teamwork and collaboration among these young engineers, encouraging all competing teams to remain friendly and even help each other out in the heat of competition.

Conventional wisdom is not something that drives Dean Kamen's imagination. His inventions are based on solving compassionate problems with engineering and his own personal mantra—he invents things that *ought* to exist here and now.

Pay attention to that. Sometimes it is obvious things that just ought to exist, period. Sometimes it is the most obvious things we resist most. Remember, the engineers at NASA thought windows were a stupid idea on the first space capsules. If those first astronauts hadn't insisted on a couple of windows, they wouldn't have made it back to Earth (it's kind of hard to steer without windows to see your target).

Smart ideas always come from creative people individually, but when you fill an entire room with brilliant, creative people, there is nothing they can't solve. In truth, this kind of legacy is what every Liquid Leader strives for.

Good-bye, Cubicle Life

Anyone graduating from college or high school since 2000 has been trained to be an entrepreneur. Millennials reshape their jobs and their worlds to fit their lives rather than adapt their lives to fit to the work-place demands. This entrepreneurial mind-set is an innate part of this generation—not just in the United States but globally.

Fifty years from now stories about working in cubicles, copper wiring, and the idea of separate countries will be ones your children will regale their grandchildren with. In a hypercompetitive world that is going through so much change, where does that leave those who are just medio-cre? And what will happen to youth in the future as more is expected from them no matter how young they may be?

Forget nuclear fusion and science fairs. We may see teenagers in the not-so-distant future starting companies while still in junior high school, just to prove their business model ideology is sustainable. Those who get venture capital groups interested get a B. Those who get a private equity firm interested get an A+.

It's all about which road you want to go down. Either way, leadership is evolving into something completely different. What you hold in your hands today may be obsolete tomorrow. Change is the only thing we can rely on. After all, it is the only constant in our world.

And with that said, I look forward to being a correspondent on the front lines for a new age of leadership.

Does Thinking It Make It Happen?

Things are changing dramatically for all of us. As I said before, society as a whole is changing. The Information Age is inspiring a new age of enlightenment, but this time it will be global.

Hard sciences such as chemistry, mathematics, and physics have worked for millennia as systematic models because they work each and every time. As we learn more and advance in these disciplines, we add on to each model another layer that supports and continues to get the same results. Each works because the model that makes it work is sound. It is why Stonehenge, the pyramids, and the Great Wall of China still stand today. Their engineering principles are sound.

Soft sciences such as archeology and history, on the other hand, use nearly the same analytical and quantitative processes as hard sciences, but they also allow input from other disciplines to improve the outcome. An example comes from archeology: When engineering is applied to the study of Stone Age archeology, we learn that ancient builders used complex mathematics to construct sites like Avery or Stonehenge.

Meanwhile, much as quantum physics is changing how we view our physical world, the metaphysical theories of noetics are gaining ground and changing everything we ever held as "reality." Noetic science is the study of the measurable effect that human thought has on our physical world. According to noetics, thoughts have mass and therefore have an impact on our physical worlds.

This isn't some New Age magic trick. Findings at the Princeton Engineering Anomalies Research (PEAR) lab and the Institute of Noetic Sciences (ION) have proven that human thought, especially within a group and properly focused, has the ability to affect and change the physical mass of things.

Whether we are aware of it or not, our thoughts—both positive negative—interact with our physical world and change it, right down to the subatomic level. Noetic experiments have shown categorically that projected thoughts and emotions impact the molecular structure of water. In conjunction with the Internet, noetics studies how a single thought or idea, called a meme, can spread. When the conversation about this idea builds up enough momentum, how long until the conversation actually becomes a real thing, manifesting in the outside world? Can our socialized cyberworld discussions actually manifest into physical reality? According to studies at Princeton and ION, the answer is yes.

Eastern philosophies may have had it right all along, that our thoughts are things. We are the cause, not the effect in our world. So personal success expert Napoleon Hill seems to have had it right too.

Believing Is Seeing

If this is true, and I believe it is, noetics is a huge leap forward in human thinking and action. It means we hold within our current state of consciousness the seed to creating the kind of world we choose—as long as we focus positively on a singular vision that is charged enough to be contagious.

Now that you know this may be true, what kind of leader do you want to be? Great leadership starts with you. It is not some mystical ideal that others hold close to their heart. When you carry yourself with integrity and discipline, others feel it, resonate with it, and are inspired by your presence.

Add to that a singular vision bigger than yourself, and you can change the world. Look around the company you run. Take a good look at the people who make your products every day. They are waiting to be inspired, to be sent on a mission of greatness.

This is why having a singular vision as a leader is so important. If everyone is aligned to a vision within the organization, then that company can move mountains—especially if two thousand, five thousand, or even one hundred thousand people are in alignment. Nothing can stop a company with this kind of management. This is enlightened leadership.

Walking between the skyscrapers of New York City recently, I reflected once again on the great divide between Boomers and Gen Y. Is it possible that the divide is only in our minds? Technically I see myself as a visitor in this world, not trapped by marketing experts in any demographic. I am a lifelong entrepreneur of the Information Age, always looking for opportunities and new business models.

Walking along that day, I stared as I passed a middle-aged man reading the *New York Times* on a Kindle. We chatted for a moment about the new electronic devices making life easier, and then I continued my walk. I could have sworn I heard, echoing in my mind and across the concrete jungle, the classic Bob Dylan song lyric: "Oh, the times, they are a-changin'."

Acknowledgments

This book is dedicated to all the executives, entrepreneurs, bloggers, small and large business owners, managers, employees, and consultants navigating today's uncharted storm of leadership. Those who put in the time and effort to become better leaders know what I am talking about. The next five years will be a bumpy ride economically. But as I always say, it is easy to be a leader when the economy is doing well and money is abundant—it takes a different set of skills when economic forces change like the wind. Great leaders are those who can navigate during the good times as well as the tough times.

When I started writing *Liquid Leadership* it became apparent that although I can tell a story and have quite a treasure trove of experiences, it's easy for the sheer volume of information to become overwhelming. I began to understand the saying "It takes a village." To write the book you now hold in your hands required a team effort, and I could not have achieved this goal without the following people, to all of whom I am very thankful.

First I have to thank my former colleagues at K2 Design. Without those years as a start-up, hypergrowth, private placement, and eventually as an IPO, I wouldn't have any street cred. I received a million-dollar business education in that seven-year period. So a special thank-you goes out to David Centner, Douglas Cleek, and Matt De Ganon. It was one hell of a ride, wasn't it? To every colleague, employee, board member, and business advisor at K2 Design, I thank you for teaching me so much.

I would also like to extend a big thank-you to everyone at Greenleaf Book Group who made this dream a reality. To Clint Greenleaf, whom I met at the National Speakers Association, and to Tanya Hall, Bryan Carroll, Katelynn Knutson, Randy Burgess, Bill Crawford, Sheila Parr, Kim Lance, Lari Bishop, and Kristen Sears: You have been such great champions of the vision that is *Liquid Leadership*. Thank you for all the hard work you put into such a great product.

A funny thing happened when I turned forty-five years old. I found myself standing in a karate dojo that summer, taking on some serious training and learning the mixed martial art of Shaolin Kempo Karate and Jiu Jitsu under the guidance of Master Charles Raimond, fifth-degree black belt. This is the same style of mixed martial arts you would see on *The Ultimate Fighter*. So when I tell you it is intense . . . well, you get the picture. A special thank-you is in order for Master Raimond and all my training partners at Villari's Martial Arts in West Islip, Long Island, New York: Ken, Gene, Ryan, Nick D., Kevin and Justo, Randy, Monty, Nick P., Kevin R., James, Lori, Bryan, Peter, Michael, Tom, David, Master Snoble, and, of course, my nephew Sebastian. I could not have dreamed of a better crew of individuals with whom to learn, train, and grow. You have earned my trust and respect.

To Jane Atkinson, Michael J. De Luca, Jr., Dave "the Shef" Sheffield, Coach Charles "Chic" Hess, Brad Peterson, and Vince Poscente, thank you all for being my mentors, coaches, advisors, and bottomless resources. Your guidance and support have helped immensely. All of you have been champions of my vision. If you ever need my help, do not hesitate to ask, for I will not hesitate to be there for you. And thanks again, Vince, for introducing me to the great folks at Greenleaf.

To Kent Gustavson, thank you for your hard work, creative advice, and input. If there is one person who comes to mind as someone with the creative spark, it is you.

Thank you goes out to those individuals who gave me their time to be interviewed for *Liquid Leadership*: Glenn and Marie Andrew; Ken Braun; Leah Burdick; Richard Carey; Jordan English Gross; Coach Charles "Chic" Hess, EdD; Michael J. De Luca, Jr.; Dan Kusnetzky; Joanne LaRiccia; Sumya Ojakli; Brad Peterson; Jason Stephens; and Bill Sobel.

To my alma matter, Lebanon Senior High School, thank you for the Distinguished Alumnus Award 2009–2010. I will live up to it every single day. A thank-you also goes out to Marianne T. Bartley, EdD, super-intendent of schools; Principal Tom Jordan; and Lebanon School Board president John Shott. And to the students of Lebanon High, thank you for your support.

I actually started this journey thirty-five years ago, so thank you to Miss Passman, my junior high English teacher, who encouraged me to write.

Thank you to Bob Lawton. I cannot thank you enough for your wisdom, insight, and good humor. Thank you for helping me wake up.

To Harold Klemp—through your guidance, patience, and mentorship, I now know that mastership is possible.

A very special thank-you to my sister-in-law, Marlene Edmond. Thank you for the sanctuary in which to write *Liquid Leadership*. Our political debates have enlightened me to envision a larger picture. Thank you.

To my mother, E. Diane Reed, who died before this book was finished. You showed me true strength by rejecting chemo and accepting that it was time to go *home*, your mission accomplished.

To my father, Dr. Michael W. Szollose, who showed me what discipline can really accomplish when properly applied. I was a kid who was all over the place, attempting to do everything all at once. Your guidance showed me to slow down my thoughts and embrace the flow of logic, one task at a time. From you I learned discipline, which comes from the word "disciple," and who is a disciple? Someone who follows a master teacher out of love. Discipline, therefore, is when we follow ourselves.

To my grandfather, Charles "Hottie" Bowers, who taught me to never give up, always keep my sense of humor, and no matter how many lemons life dishes out, make lemonade. After a landscaper planted dying evergreen trees at my grandfather's restaurant, it became apparent that the landscaper would neither fess up to nor correct his mistake. It wasn't worth suing over, so my grandfather spray-painted those trees green and lit them with green spotlights. For twenty years no one ever knew that the trees adorning the front of his restaurant were dead and brown. So, to my grandfather, thank you; Pap, you taught me how to "march to the beat of a different drummer," and I will always do so.

To my stepbrother, Rick Shockey—our debates always make me stop to ponder, and I appreciate your presence in my life, more than you may ever know. Our long talks over steaks at Ruth's Chris have been inspiring.

To my nephew, Sebastian Edmond—thank you for showing me every day what it means to be a black belt. Gen Y, video games, computers, and technology in general have changed our world in so many ways. You have shown me how it has been for the best.

I had two best friends from my lazy days of growing up in a small town. We did everything together—grew up together, were in Boy Scouts, spit off bridges, went fishing, collected a few coins for a soda or two, and built a tree house. We attended the same community churches, grade school, junior high, and high school . . . eventually separating for college. Astoundingly we are still best friends to this day.

To have those best friends, Dieter Hauer and Frank Workman, as my friends after forty years has been an amazing journey of friendship, brotherhood, patience, and sometimes just plain silliness that comes from people who have known one another for so long. We've been best men at one another's weddings; we've been present at family events and funerals; and we hang out whenever we're "home." I feel incredibly blessed to have such friendship in my life. Wherever I have been and whatever I have done in life, they have shared in that journey and supported me, no matter how silly the situation. I thank you both for teaching me what friendship really means.

To Christine and Tedd Jenkins, thank you for the golden opportunities you have entrusted to me. From leadership training workshops to speaking engagements, it has been an honor to work with you. Thank you for providing me with a podium to pass on to others different ways to enhance their leadership skills. A special thank-you as well goes out to Penny M. Panoulias, Shabri Foy, and Sue Keck. I have learned so much from your knowledge and patience. Thank you.

To Joanne LaRiccia of *JoJo's DreamCart* on PBS—thank you for the quality you bring to all our projects. Without your hard work and diligence, I am not sure where my ideas would be.

Words do not do justice to the contributions of my wife, Norma Edmond, but I will try. They say every successful man has a woman behind him. I disagree. Every successful person has a spouse with whom they stand side by side. They are the ones who put up with the good and bad times yet still find enough love in their heart to support the dream, and to give encouragement in those moments when we all want to give up. Norma has been involved in creating this dream as much as I have in writing and creating it. Without her, there would be no *Liquid Leadership*. I know it sounds like a cliché, but I didn't know what love was until I met my wife. Her support, constant challenging of my ideas, and loving gaze and contagious smile have kept me better than if I had been left to my own initiatives. I thank God every day that you are a huge part of my life and the world we share together.

Each and every one of us has a mission to fulfill. This book is the beginning of my mission, a launching pad to share what I've learned so far while standing on this orb we call Earth.

Whether through our business or our personal life, we all have something to share and learn. Everyone's experiences and expertise—whether a technique, a story of initiation, or a memory of crossing the finish line despite insurmountable odds—can make each of us a better leader. So I have to thank you, the reader, in advance. Although we have yet to meet, I look forward to hearing about your leadership experiences in a bold new business world.

About the Author

Brad Szollose is a recognized thought leader, author, entrepreneur, business coach, and speaker, specializing in transitioning leaders from Industrial Age methodologies to the management strategies and emerging markets of the Information Age.

He is no stranger to the boardroom: During the dot-com era of the early nineties, Brad cofounded K2 Design, Inc., raising more than $7 million in private placement and becoming an IPO. K2 became the first dot-com agency to go public, with sixty employees and valued at more than $26 million. During Brad's tenure at K2, the company experienced 425 percent growth and received the Arthur Andersen New York Enterprise Award for Best Practices for Fostering Innovation.

Brad served on the K2 board of directors from 1996 to 2001 and on various private boards since. Today, Brad travels the globe speaking to corporations, executives, and entrepreneurs on Information Age leadership strategies, Gen Y management, and new business models for a global village.